Praise for *Heavy Hitter Sales Linguistics*

"Understanding sales linguistics will help you map out all aspects of interacting with customers—how to get the first meeting, what to say to differentiate yourself, and strategies to close the deal."

Scott Raskin, CEO, Mindjet

"Steve Martin provides practical everyday advice on how to take professional selling to the next level."

Monty Carter, President, TELUS Enterprise Solutions

"I see it every day. Salespeople come up with a product pitch and drop it on anyone who will pick up the phone. Spray and pray. This book outlines the correct approach to selling. It's about making a personal connection by truly understanding prospects' needs and speaking their language."

Michael Nelson, Vice President of Sales, ON24

"If your activity levels are high but your closing rates are low, it's time to change your thinking! By mastering the concepts in this book, you will learn to speak in a language your customer understands. Learn the art of harmonious communication and watch your sales and income soar!"

Mike Viola, Executive Vice President of Sales, Oasis Outsourcing, Inc.

"Another Steve Martin book that I couldn't put down. A truly different book that translates linguistics to the real world and will give you an edge."

Joe Vitalone, Vice President of Sales, Americas, LifeSize Communications, division of Logitech

"When it comes to sales, there are a lot of resources that teach selling. Only Steve Martin teaches SELLING and developing salespeople beyond the customary sales skills!"

Frank Maylett, Executive Vice President of Sales, inContact

"Salespeople reflexively fixate on demonstrations and presentations. Their companies also reinforce this behavior. *Heavy Hitter Sales Linguistics* focuses on building winning relationships by structuring interactions based upon individual linguistic profiles. It includes entirely new sales concepts based upon the latest neuroscience, which make the book not only interesting to read but highly valuable to even the most experienced salesperson."

Peter Riccio, Vice President of Mid-Market Sales, Taleo

"*Heavy Hitter Sales Linguistics* captures Steve Martin's master-level knowledge of sales linguistics and makes these techniques available to everyone. This book can help any salesperson who is interested in understanding and affecting their customers' subconscious buying decisions."

Mark Sarojak, Director of Global Sales and Marketing, BAE Systems - Geospatial eXploitation Products

"Clarifying the complex issue of communication and showing the means to improve salesmanship to the highest level, *Heavy Hitter Sales Linguistics* is as simple as it is fascinating to read."

Peter W. Fellinger, Senior Manager Business Development, Lufthansa Airlines

Heavy Hitter Sales Linguistics

Other Books by Steve W. Martin

Heavy Hitter Sales Psychology
Heavy Hitter Sales Wisdom
The Real Story of Informix Software and Phil White
Heavy Hitter Selling

Heavy Hitter Sales Linguistics

101 Advanced Sales Call Strategies for Senior Salespeople

Steve W. Martin

TILIS Publishers

TILIS Publishers
24881 Alicia Parkway, #E293
Laguna Hills, CA 92653

www.tilispublishers.com

Ordering Information
Orders by U.S. trade bookstores and wholesalers. Please contact Cardinal Publishers Group: Tel: (800) 296-0481; Fax: (317) 879-0872, www.cardinalpub.com.

Cataloging-in-Publication data
Steve W. Martin, 1960-
    Heavy hitter sales psychology : how to penetrate the c-level executive suite and convince company leaders to buy / Steve W. Martin.
    p. cm.
    Includes index
    ISBN 9780979796142
1. Selling--Psychological aspects. 2. Marketing--Psychological aspects. 3. Business communication. 4. Success in business. I. Title

HF5438.25 .M37366 2009
659.10688 20Cdc22   2011938086

Printed in the United States of America

First Edition

16 15   6

Cover design: Kuo Design
Interior design and composition: Marin Bookworks
Editing: PeopleSpeak

Contents

Introduction to Sales Linguistics: The Seven Principles of Customer Communication

Without language, you really wouldn't exist. You wouldn't be able to share your ideas, display your personality, and express yourself to the world. You couldn't communicate your needs and desires to others, or the never-ending dialogue within your mind would stop. The words we speak truly define who we are. However, since we are talking all the time, we underestimate the complexity of communication and take the process for granted.

The conversations salespeople have with customers are quite complex. They consist of verbal and nonverbal messages that are sent consciously and subconsciously. Successful customer communications are the foundation of all sales, and Heavy Hitters (truly great salespeople) naturally speak in the language of their customers. The question is, What do they say?

Language is studied in many well-established fields. Sociolinguistics is the study of language use in society and social networks. Psycholinguistics is the study of how the mind acquires, uses, and represents language. Neurolinguistics is the study of how brain structures process language. Today, an exciting new area of study called "sales linguistics" applies aspects from these fields to the conversations salespeople have with customers. The goal of sales linguistics is to understand how salespeople and their prospective customers use and interpret language during the decision-making process. The seven principles of sales linguistics are these: every customer speaks in his or her own unique language, salespeople build rapport through harmonious communication, the customer will always lie, persuasion requires a personal connection, sales intuition is language based, sales calls should be classified linguistically, and the final decision made by the customer is based upon human nature, not logic.

Customers Speak Unique Languages

Each person on this planet speaks his or her own unique language. All the mundane and traumatic experiences of your life have determined the language you use. Just as no one else has had your exact life experiences, no one else speaks your precise language. Therefore, the language two people use to describe the same situation may be very different. Unfortunately, most companies arm their salespeople with a "one size fits all" company sales pitch.

The first premise of sales linguistics is that every customer speaks in his or her own language. It is based upon understanding the customer's interpretation of your message and its associated psychological impact. For example, reading the word "snake" might cause you to visualize a rattlesnake, a python, or a cobra. While these are all specific interpretations of the word, they all may naturally evoke fear and negative emotions. Conversely, if you raised a pet snake as a child, you probably have a positive mental association. Since the personal meanings of words can vary greatly, you may even have thought of an unscrupulous businessperson when you first read the word "snake."

Rapport Is Harmonious Communication

Unfortunately, when most salespeople meet with prospective customers, they talk in only their own language about their product's features, functions and benefits. When Heavy Hitter salespeople meet with customers, they talk their about their problems, plans, and personal aspirations. They speak their customers' language in order to build rapport.

Rapport is a special relationship between two individuals based upon harmonious communication. However, human communication occurs in several different forms and on several different levels. An immense amount of information is conveyed verbally, phonetically, physically, consciously, and subconsciously. Heavy Hitters naturally adapt their mental wiring and language to mirror the customers'.

Whether Inadvertently or on Purpose, the Customer Will Always Lie

Salespeople expect deception from competitors. However, the most damaging deceptions actually come from customers. Salespeople are on a mission to learn the ultimate truth, "Will I win the deal?" And they want to find the truth about winning an account as early as possible.

Customers will lie to you for a variety of reasons: to protect themselves, to make you feel better about yourself, and to help your competitors. As a result, customers will say things they don't mean and mean things they don't say. When you ask at the end of your sales presentation, "Does everyone believe we are the best solution?" even though everyone nods, the audience may include objectors who will try to sabotage your deal later on.

Persuasion Requires a Personal Connection

Salespeople are paid to persuade. But what makes them persuasive? Is it their command of the facts and their ability to recite a litany of reasons why customers should buy? In reality, the most product-knowledgeable salesperson is not necessarily the most persuasive one because it takes more than logic and reason to change buyers' opinions. A personal connection must be established.

Persuasion is the process of projecting your entire set of beliefs and convictions onto another human being. It's not about getting others to acknowledge your arguments or agree with your business case; it's about making them internalize your message because they believe that it is in their best interests. Ultimately, persuasion is the ability to tap into someone's emotions and reach the deeper subconscious decision maker within that person.

Sales Intuition Is Language Based

The mind does not treat all information equally. Some information is ignored, some information is misinterpreted, and some information is generalized based upon past experiences. Unfortunately, many salespeople edit information to support their preexisting beliefs. Salespeople with "happy ears" tend to believe what they are told by the customer. Others view the world through rose-colored glasses and will always interpret information emanating from the customer in a favorable light. Such ambiguities and delusions are disastrous.

Conversely, Heavy Hitter salespeople accurately interpret information using their sales intuition. They are continually cataloging their successes and failures based upon all the different types of verbal and nonverbal languages the customer is communicating. They store patterns of individual and group meeting behavior. Through their sales intuition, they are able to integrate their spoken words with the sales situation based upon their experiences with similar types of people and past sales cycles.

Sales Calls Need to Be Segmented Linguistically

Sales call segmentation is a method of categorizing customer interactions based upon the psychological motives behind the customer's use of language. Customers participating in sales calls are classified into four different decision-making roles depending upon how they process information, how they behave as part of a selection team, their political power, and their personal disposition toward their company.

The segmentation strategy provides a predictive framework to anticipate customer behavior. Since the salesperson has a deeper insight about customer behavior based upon past interactions, he is able to create more compelling presentations and conduct more persuasive sales calls. This strategy also serves as a communication methodology to educate and prepare the colleagues who will attend the sales call with the salesperson.

The Final Decision Maker Is Human Nature, Not Logic

We typically equate persuasion solely with satisfying the analytical mind. However, we are not as objective and analytical as we think, and even the most well-thought-out decision is ultimately determined by emotional and subconscious influences.

Selling requires capturing the hearts and minds of customers based upon a strategy that takes into account the emotions of the decision maker as well as the logical reasons to buy. Customers aren't completely logical decision makers in the real world. The decision-making process is a blend of human nature and logical rationalization. At the foundation of all sales is a relationship between people. The interaction between these people, the intangible part of the sales process, is ultimately responsible for the decision being made. Logic and reason play secondary roles.

Customers' inertia, the drive to "do nothing," far outweighs the logical reasons you espouse for buying your product. You can recite a litany of reasons and a laundry list of benefits, and customers still won't buy your product. You need to package these ideas in a format that leaves an impression and creates a call to action that customers understand and that persuades them both mentally and emotionally to proceed. This requires you to establish "dominance" during sales calls and gain the willing obedience of customers. From the perspective of sales linguistics, *dominance* is when the customer listens to your opinions and advice, internalizes your recommendations and agrees with them, and then follows your course of action.

Heavy Hitter salespeople are accomplished communicators who know what to say and, equally important, how to say it. Through their mastery of language, they are able to convey and decipher deep underlying messages that less-successful salespeople miss. While using the same language as most salespeople, they have developed an uncanny ability to influence nonbelievers to trust them and persuade complete strangers to follow their advice. Through sales linguistics, you can learn how they turn skeptics into believers and persuade prospective customers to buy.

This book is for senior salespeople, those who have been in the field for five, ten, and fifteen-plus years. However, most salespeople don't like to read. You see, your brain was built to talk. It was not designed to read. While speaking comes automatically and is a natural part of the brain's development, reading is a skill that must be learned. It requires three different areas of your brain to work together in close coordination. Therefore, *Heavy Hitter Sales Linguistics* is formatted into short chapters of just a few pages. Each chapter ends with a call to action or tip to implement the subject discussed. You can read the book sequentially or only the chapters that interest you.

Write in this book and highlight passages you find interesting. Make notes in the margins about tactics you plan to try. Bend the corners of pages that are important to you. Most importantly, complete the exercises. The exercises will help you internalize the concepts so that you can use them on your next sales call.

You already know how to sell. The ultimate goal of *Heavy Hitter Sales Linguistics* is to help experienced salespeople expand their influence within their local office, region, sales organization, and company. This requires not only winning more business but also having a methodology to explain to others how and why you win.

1. Communication and the Mind

Upon your birth, your brain was a tiny, malleable computer. Even though all the circuitry was in place, the software had yet to be installed, so its functions were extremely limited. As you experienced the world, your senses began gathering more information and turning on all the software switches inside your mind.

During the first five years of your life, 90 percent of your brain's growth and development occurred.[1] Your mind evolved as it interacted with the world around you and recorded strange and exciting new experiences. You learned to speak by mimicking the people around you, and by the time you were five years old, your vocabulary was about twenty-five hundred words.[2] Today, your mind knows the meaning of about fifty thousand different words.[3]

Your brain has an incredible capacity to sort, prioritize, and process. As you read this book, your lungs are breathing and your heart is pumping blood to all parts of your body without your having to think about it. Meanwhile, you are consciously moving your eyes to the next word to be read and saying that word to yourself. When you reach the bottom of the page, your hand and arm will automatically execute a complex series of muscle movements in response to commands from the brain to turn the page.

Your brain has three major parts: the cerebrum, cerebellum, and brainstem. From a sales perspective, we are most interested in what is happening within the cerebrum. The cerebrum controls our voluntary functions, such as body sensations, learning, emotions, and language.

Most of the recent advances in understanding the inner workings of the mind have come from brain scans and neuroimaging techniques such as PET (positron emission tomography) and FMRI (functional magnetic resonance imaging), which make it possible to observe human brains at work. These images reveal changes in activity of the various brain regions depending on physiological activities. For example, while a person is seeing, hearing, smelling, tasting, or touching something, certain areas of the brain light up on the scan.

While neuroscientists have named the parts of the brain and know their overall functions, the three-pound pale gray organ still remains a mystery. No one truly knows how the mind works. Somewhere deep inside you is you. You are surrounded by your conscious, or "controllable," and subconscious, or "uncontrollable," minds, which in turn are surrounded by your internal dialogue. Your internal dialogue is the never-ending conversation you have with yourself. It's repeating the words of this sentence to you now. It is very dominating. It's always on, always engaged, and always talking to you. It drives the language you speak to prospective customers during sales calls as well as your actions. Your customer's internal dialogue is equally active.

The conscious mind, subconscious mind, and internal dialogue affect your external communication: the words you speak and your voluntary (planned) and involuntary (unplanned and inadvertent) body movements. Figure 1.1 represents the interaction between external communication and the mind.

It's helpful to think of this diagram when meeting with customers. Usually, the subconscious mind is busy managing all the systems of the body (nervous, muscular, respiratory, digestive, and circulatory) without much effort, and it is working independently of the conscious mind most of the time. However, during a sales call, the spoken words and actions of the participants can have an immense effect on the subconscious mind, resulting in changes to the body. These involuntary body movements provide important customer feedback when analyzed in conjunction with the customers' verbal conversation. It is extremely important to monitor all of the sales call participants for these bodily changes. Are they tense or relaxed? Are they breathing faster or slower?

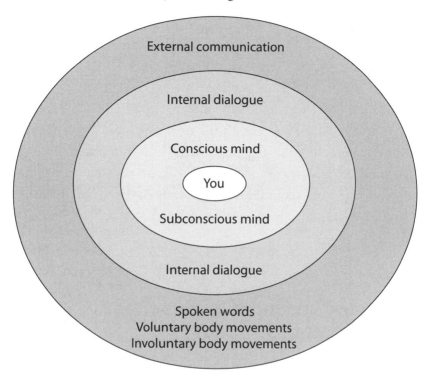

Figure 1.1 External communication and the mind

The subconscious mind retains information that the conscious mind doesn't. Storing everything in your conscious mind simply isn't efficient. Remember the last time you misplaced an important item (your keys, wallet, or glasses)? At first, you employed a conscious strategy to find it. You may have thought about where you had recently been and gone back to those locations. If you didn't find the item, hours, days, or weeks may have gone by. Then suddenly, without specifically thinking about it, you knew exactly where it was. Your subconscious mind found it.

In the same way, when your prospective customers say, "Let me sleep on it" or "I will get back to you," they are actually saying, "Let me see if my subconscious mind has any objections since it has some additional information that I don't have right now."

Sales Call Strategy: During the sales call, your words and actions have an immense effect on the conscious and subconscious minds of the prospective customer. One of your top priorities is to recognize and correctly interpret all the different types of verbal and nonverbal information the customer is communicating to you. The most important part of a sales call is not your product pitch. Instead, it is the customer's reaction to what you say. In other words, always think about people first and products second during sales calls.

2. Understanding Customer Benefactions

The grand strategy behind a successful sales call is based upon selling to human nature. Customers purchase products that increase their happiness, esteem, power, or wealth. They rationalize these psychological decisions with logic and facts. For example, a vice president of a manufacturing company may explain that he wants to buy a new conveyor system because it will save a million dollars a year when, in reality, he is making the purchase to show the CEO that he is a prudent, fiscally conservative businessman. The desire to impress the CEO (the benefit) drives the conveyor system purchase (the action). The term "benefaction" refers to the psychological benefits that determine a person's actions.

Four core psychological drives determine selection behavior. These four benefactions are well-being, pain avoidance, self-preservation, and self-gratification. Physical well-being, the will to survive, is one of our strongest desires. It weighs heavily in the minds of both customers and competitors. Making customers feel their jobs are safe in your hands is a top priority during sales calls. Ideally, you would like them to believe (whether it is true or not) that the competitive solutions are actually threats to their livelihood. Customers are equally concerned with maintaining their mental and emotional well-being.

When something is hurting you badly, the desire to eliminate the source of pain can be all-consuming. Pain is one of the best purchase motivators because customers are forced to act quickly and decisively to eliminate it.

Companies experience different kinds of pain all the time. Nuisances can create dull aching pains in every department, such as a temperamental copy machine. Throbbing pains may reappear occasionally, like Internet service providers that go down momentarily every few months. And stabbing pains require immediate attention, for example, when the order-entry system is down and products can't be shipped and sales cannot be made. Companies can live with dull aches and cope with throbbing pains as necessary. But the stabbing pains receive immediate attention and dictate budgeting.

Self-preservation, the third core psychological drive, is the desire to be recognized for our unique talents while still belonging to a group. Customers and salespeople alike naturally seek the approval of others. Customers purchase items that they believe will enhance their stature and protect their group position. They not only want to be respected by their peers but also want to become group leaders. Naturally, salespeople want to be pack leaders too.

Self-gratification is our desire to put our own needs before everyone else's. Customers will go to great lengths to purchase something that makes them feel better about themselves and superior to others. Egos drive the business world.

Unfortunately, most salespeople are taught to sell solutions solely based upon customer pain. In fact, well-being, ego, and self-preservation are the real motivators behind most sales. The list below reveals the true reasons why customers buy your product. Consider these customer statements:

- I have big career ambitions.
- I want to be more powerful.
- I'm risk averse.
- I want my team to be happy.
- I'm naturally skeptical of vendors.
- I like to be part of a group.
- I want the security of a marketable skill.
- I want that promotion.
- I want to keep my job.
- I like new challenges.
- I want to please others.
- I want to be important.
- I like you!

It's not solely your product's performance, ease of use, or efficiency that customers are in love with. It's you. Therefore, your priorities should be to earn customers' love and trust by understanding their personal needs, desires, and fantasies. You must know if they are just trying to hold onto a job, prop up their importance, or bring about a long-awaited promotion. Once you understand these desires, you become part of the customers' political landscape, aligned with the decision-making process.

Sales Call Strategy: The conscious mind is obsessed with achieving four benefactions: physical and mental well-being, pain avoidance, self-preservation, and self-gratification. People buy products they believe will help them fulfill deep-seated psychological needs: satisfying the ego, being accepted as part of a group, avoiding pain, and ensuring survival.

You want customers to view you as the only person who can address their personal needs, solve their painful business problems, and help them achieve their career hopes and life's desires. You want them to sincerely believe that you are the only salesperson who is truly acting in their best interests.

3. Establishing Mutual Trust

All sales calls start with a handshake. The handshake started as a way of validating that a person wasn't carrying any weapons. It is a ritual that occurs very quickly at the beginning of a meeting. Unfortunately for salespeople, mutual trust is not achieved as quickly. It is earned over time and not freely granted. Depending on the product you are selling, it may take many meetings over many months to gain a customer's trust. Once achieved, it can be lost in just a few seconds if the information you have given is proven false.

At the heart of every successful sales call are mutual trust between both parties, the competence of the participants, the identification of personal benefactions, and rapport. The pyramid of meeting success in figure 3.1 illustrates this concept.

The middle level of the pyramid is competence. The first aspect of competence is the personal fit between people. Since the sales team members are a direct reflection of their company's competence and culture, the customer wonders if this team will capably manage their long-term relationship. Are they technically competent? Do they understand my problem? Are they pleasant to be around? The sales team, on the other hand, determines if

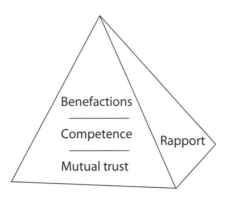

Figure 3.1 The pyramid of meeting success

the customer's selection team has the wherewithal to make the decision, authority to purchase the product, and ability to implement it.

The other aspect of competence is the fit between the product and the customer. How well does the product solve the customer's technical problem? Will it operate as promised? What features of the product is the customer unsure of? How good is the product's technical support? What is the product's future release schedule? The questions regarding personal and product fit must be answered satisfactorily.

At the top of the pyramid are benefactions. Entering into a meeting, each party knows what the overriding goal of the sales team is. It's to sell the product. What's the customer's goal? More specifically, what are the benefactions each participant has for achieving this goal? What are they trying to accomplish psychologically, personally, and politically? Decisions are influenced by politics. Politics are based upon self-interests. Every sales call provides you the opportunity to understand and influence these self-interests.

At the foundation of all sales is a relationship between people. Heavy Hitters have an innate talent to build these relationships by creating rapport, which is defined as "harmonious communication." Their presence has an appeal that makes a customer feel at ease. The customer enjoys their company. They build personal alliances based upon understanding individual wants and needs. The customer trusts them.

Sales Call Strategy: The sales call involves the process of building a relationship by turning a stranger into a friend and a skeptic into a believer. The first step in the process is to establish mutual trust in which both parties are assured of the competence of each other. Through investigative conversation, you must understand the customer's benefactions and how well your product fits the customer's needs. Finally, developing rapport by connecting with the customer is your top priority in every conversation with the customer. The sale won't happen without rapport.

Immediately following each sales call, rate the level of rapport you established from one to five, with five being the highest. Ask others who attended the call with you to do the same. Compare your ratings against previous sales calls and whether or not you lost or won each deal. You'll soon recognize that rapport and revenue are directly related.

4. Using Customer Fantasies

People connect with others very quickly, and first impressions can have a long-term impact. Customers tend to make snap judgments early in the sales process based upon whom they like and respect. By demonstrating your competence, you expose your competitors' incompetence.

Knowing the details of how your product works and being able to answer customers' questions about your company are obviously vital parts of sales. However, the real questions to answer honestly are, Compared to the salespeople I am competing with, how well do I know my solution? and Is my industry expertise an advantage, or is my weakness a disadvantage? If you don't know the answer to either of these questions, your fear of being outpositioned and blocked from the account by your competitors may come true.

Those who are feared are hated. You want customers to realize that your competitors are riskier than you, uncaring, deceitful, and unable to fulfill the customers' fantasies. However, you need to understand what fantasies are. Most people think that fantasies have to be really big, like "One day I will be on the cover of *Time* magazine." In fact, fantasies can be very small. Some people think of fantasies only in a sexual context, when in reality most fantasies are quite mundane.

Fantasies are just unfulfilled wishes. For example, you might wish to finish this book quickly. Until it's fulfilled, this wish is one of your many fantasies. You also might want to make $500,000 next year. That's a bigger, longer-term fantasy.

Customer fantasies can be big or small, specific or general. For example, the CEO might wish to leave work on time today in order to be home for an important family dinner. The vice president of North American sales might want to become the vice president of worldwide sales. The CFO might want to become the president and chairman of the board someday. Each of these fantasies has a different scope and duration.

When you have built relationships, demonstrated competence, and proved that you can fulfill fantasies, you will naturally dovetail with the internal politics of the decision-making process. Most importantly, using the strategy of selling to the human nature of customers forces your competitors to use a strategy based solely upon the products they sell. Because your strategy is stronger, you put your competitors in a position of weakness. Never forget, your sales call strategy is to dehumanize the enemy by differentiating yourself personally, as figure 4.1 below shows.

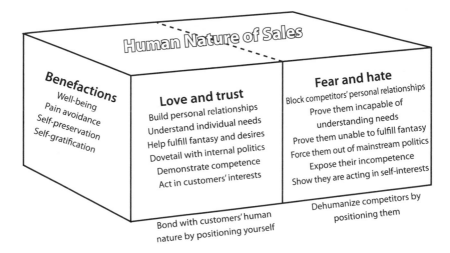

Figure 4.1 Human nature of sales calls

All salespeople want their customers to like them. But it requires a linguistic strategy to establish the personal connection to become a trusted advisor who is loved by the customer (see chapters 34–36). Proving you are more trustworthy than the competition is based upon truthful communication (see chapter 33), and the customer will fear your competitors when you speak their unique languages (see chapters 36–39) and your rivals can't.

Regardless of the complexity of your product or the sophistication of your customers, the final decision maker is always human nature. To validate this statement, all you have to do is think back to the deals you have lost when your product and price were best. You came in second place because you had third-rate relationships.

Sales Call Strategy: Before a sales call starts, silently remind yourself that one of your objectives is to determine the fantasies of all the participants. Try to theorize what their short- and long-term fantasies are. Go ahead and make a deep psychological diagnosis about what is driving each person's fantasy. A person who wants a promotion to vice president to gain more power is quite different from someone who is seeking the promotion for personal validation or a bigger paycheck.

Customers have many different types of fantasies, and quite often they need help from vendors to fulfill them. Therefore, ignoring customers' fantasies is a big mistake. You must tap into them before your competitors do. However, customers will not usually broadcast their fantasies. It's up to you to figure them out and convince the customers that only through your solution can their fantasies be realized. Now think about your last sales call and write down the fantasy of each participant.

5. All Buyers Are Liars

A salesperson told me about an e-mail from a prospective customer that left him devastated. The customer questioned the validity of the salesperson's product, his company's capability, and his professionalism. The e-mail cited a laundry list of reasons why he and his company were inferior. Obviously, the customer wouldn't be buying his product.

The most distressing part of the e-mail questioned the salesperson's acumen. It detailed how his presentation to the selection team had been ill received and went on to describe how the team's requests for information weren't responded to for days and even weeks. To make matters worse, the customer sent copies of this e-mail to the seniormost executives at his own company and numerous people within the salesperson's company. The e-mail closed by saying, "I hope you will take this feedback constructively and look for ways to better meet the needs of your customers." However, the e-mail had a major problem. None of it was true.

Why did this happen? Stress causes decision makers to act very differently than normal. It essentially forces them to lie. Therefore, a fundamental premise of all sales calls is that whether inadvertently or on purpose, customers will always lie. This applies to lower-level evaluators, midlevel managers, and C-level executives.

Now this may seem like a harsh statement; therefore, it requires further explanation. First, we need to define the different types of lies customers tell because some are more destructive than others. Of course, customers tell fibs and falsehoods that contradict the truth. Other times, they'll simply withhold important information from you, which in itself is a lie because they haven't told you the entire truth. Worst is when they are giving a competing salesperson proprietary, privileged information that they are not sharing with you.

Lying often occurs subtly, for example, when customers overemphasize the importance of a certain feature or present an irrelevant step in the decision-making process as a red herring to throw you off the scent of the truth. Sometimes, customers will strictly adhere to their selection-process guidelines, never giving any more information to you than they say they're allowed to give. Usually, each of these types of lies is intended to hide their personal bias toward another competitor.

In the case of the hapless salesperson who received the damaging e-mail, the lie was sent to keep the salesperson out of the account. The decision maker had wanted another solution from the start of the sales cycle and sent the e-mail to prevent the salesperson from further pursuing the account. It was a blatant attempt to ruin the salesperson's credibility and reputation so he couldn't talk with any of the C-level executives in the organization.

However, sometimes customers lie out of benevolence—they will lie to protect a salesperson's feelings. Most people don't enjoy hurting or humiliating others. In addition, you were taught at the earliest age "If you don't have something nice to say, don't say anything at all." It's also human nature to avoid confrontation. So when a sales call ends and the salesperson asks, "Will we win the business?" most customers will give an optimistic answer. They don't want to let down or embarrass the salesperson, so they'll tell a lie for momentary relief. However, the truth will be revealed later—usually when the customer avoids the salesperson's follow-up calls.

Sales Call Strategy: Prospective customers will like some salespeople and dislike others. To protect themselves, they will instinctively try to keep any conversations with the disliked salespeople at a nonpersonal business level. They'll rebuff the attempts of the disliked salespeople to befriend them. Meanwhile, they will reveal much more about themselves to their favorite salesperson. One of the most important questions to ask yourself about the prospect you are meeting with during the sales call is, Are you lying to me? If the answer is yes, you must find out why.

6. Utilizing the Human Communication Model

A sales call is a scheduled communication event. Salespeople create long-term relationships between companies based upon the process of communication between the people who work for these companies. This process is very complex. However, since we are communicating all the time, we may underestimate the complexity of communication and take the process for granted. We tend to ignore the subtleties and, for the most part, become preoccupied with our side of a conversation.

It's important to recognize that people communicate in layers. These layers are very flexible and can be combined in many different ways. Layers can be entirely eliminated or they can be fused together to form entirely new meanings. The layers of the human communication model are shown in figure 6.1.

Content	The actual words spoken
Phonetic	The enunciation of the words you are speaking
Purpose	The reason or point you are communicating
Word catalog	The system used to interpret and present those words
Internal dialogue	The never-ending dialogue inside your mind
Physical	The impact the words you are receiving or sending have on your body

Figure 6.1 The human communication model

The human communication process is also very efficient. We have the flexibility to send the same message structure with distinctly different meanings. Take the following example:

- Mary, could you please send the report.
- Mary, could you *please* send the report.
- MARY, COULD YOU PLEASE SEND THE REPORT.

All these sentences use the same words but result in very different interpretations. When Mary reads the first sentence, she will feel a low sense of urgency and receive no indication of any unhappiness that the report has not been sent. The other sentences imply a different sense of urgency and even discontent that the report hasn't been sent.

The human communication model layers are like piano keys. Different sounds, or meanings, are created by pressing particular keys together in patterns or repetitions. Piano keys may be depressed forcefully or softly, just as communication may be explicit or subtle. The combination of keys may result in a soothing melody or just noise. Each of the layers is explored in detail in chapters 7 through 12.

Sales Call Strategy: Let's say you went on ten new customer calls last week and met with groups ranging from one to four people, for a total of thirty people. What percentage of the people did you connect with? In other words, how many did you feel truly liked you, believed in your message, and wanted to see you again? Most likely, the percentage was lower than 50 percent. One of the reasons is that the human communication model is unique to each of the people you met. The point is, if you say the same thing in the same way on every sales call, you're making a mistake because each person communicates differently.

You have a competitive advantage when you use the human communication model to understand how the customer communicates. It provides the framework to help you adapt your communication style and language to each individual in order to create greater rapport than the competition and differentiate yourself.

7. Being Aware of the Physical Layer

Everyone is well aware of the physical layer of the human communication model (fig. 6.1). You were introduced to this layer when you were a baby. When you were two days old, you were able to distinguish a happy face from a sad face. Soon thereafter, you naturally understood that a smile, hug, or kiss is to be interpreted as something very good.

The physical layer is also known as "body language." Unfortunately, this term has been sensationalized over the years in books on everything from dating to cosmetic surgery. However, since it is the more widely recognized term, I use it interchangeably with the "physical layer." Body language can be very subtle or more powerful than the actual words being spoken. Body language is unique in that it is a three-dimensional language. Heavy Hitters are masters at reading body language and using their own bodies to communicate. When considered in conjunction with the other layers of the human communication model, the physical layer plays an important role.

When people are discussing issues they are passionate about, their hearts pump more blood and their skin flushes. The volume of their voices may rise and their speech quicken. Conversely, people who are bored or apathetic will fidget or become lethargic. People who are worried may feel sick to their stomachs, and their bodies will broadcast this. Consequently, you should stay astutely aware of the physical communication of the body. Here are four key reasons why you should understand the physical layer:

- The key to developing long-term successful relationships is rapport. Just as you develop rapport by using the customer's spoken language, you also develop rapport at the physical layer. In other words, you want rapport with the customer's body as well as mind.
- During sales calls, you are continuously searching for feedback on the prospect's receptivity to your solution, and the physical layer provides important nonverbal reactions to your statements. It provides another visible checkpoint that can be used

to ensure everyone participating in the meeting understands and agrees with you and your sales pitch.

- You want to be able to "perceptively persuade." Perceptive persuasion involves leading the customer to buy your product. The physical layer provides another channel by which you can communicate with customers and influence them to buy. Here's another way to explain this: the words you say and the words other people say to you affect your entire body. As a result, the body is continuously influencing your mental state.

- It could be argued that what's important isn't what customers say during the sales call; it's what they don't say. A survey conducted by UCLA made some startling statements about persuasion. When respondents were asked to judge various speakers' performances, 7 percent said the words they used were most important, 38 percent said it was the quality of their voices, and 55 percent said it was their nonverbal communication.[1] These results suggest that more meaning is derived from the nonverbal communication than from the actual words being said.

Heavy Hitters want to communicate with a customer's physical layer in order to develop rapport. They are aware of a customer's body language and analyze it to ensure they are communicating effectively. They also try to understand any communication from the customer's subconscious that may be revealed physically. These unintentional messages will help them determine their chance of closing the deal.

Sales Call Strategy: Most salespeople recognize the obvious information presented to them by a customer during a sales call, such as written technical requirements and formal decision milestones. However, customers will say things they don't mean and mean things they don't say. Your ability to correctly recognize and interpret misleading, subtle information will enable you to create the correct account strategy. Search for false or contradictory information from the physical layer that signals the true intentions of the customer.

8. Monitoring the Internal Dialogue Layer

Every waking hour, a stream of communication is going on inside your mind. You are always talking to yourself. This conversation is an unedited, honest discussion that represents your deepest feelings. This is the second layer of the human communication model (fig. 6.1)—the internal dialogue layer or simply the "internal dialogue."

Usually these internal conversations remain internal. Occasionally, they'll slip out. We are all familiar with the term "Freudian slip." A Freudian slip happens when you say one thing but mean another. Freudian slips often occur because you are having two simultaneous dialogues—the words you are speaking externally to others (content layer language) and the internal dialogue within your mind. Sometimes you accidentally substitute a word from your internal dialogue into your external dialogue. In other cases, you get confused between the two. For example, you may create a new word that is a combination of the first syllable of your content word and the last syllable of your internal dialogue word. In either case, these slips can be very embarrassing.

Usually, the words being spoken externally are a subset of the internal dialogue. In between is an editing process to filter the precise statement. This is particularly true on sales calls. Customers will heavily edit their honest thoughts, as represented by figure 8.1.

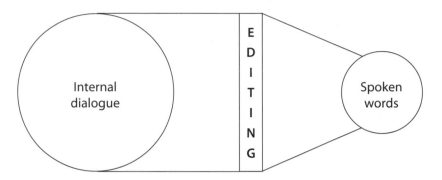

Figure 8.1 Spoken words as a subset of the internal dialogue

When people are being totally honest, they repeat their internal voice word for word without editing. People also abandon the editing process during times of great emotions: when they're very sad, extremely mad, or ecstatic or experiencing any other intense feelings. When people are consumed with their emotions, they don't have the wherewithal to plan what they are going to say. The words are spoken in the same instant that they are created within the mind.

During the sales call, your internal dialogue is at its loudest. It is constantly communicating, telling you what to say next and how to respond to questions. It also monitors the rapport being established with participants. You can't turn off your internal dialogue. It's always there, always working consciously. It's also being affected by your subconscious memories of past experiences (see chapters 9 and 14).

Sales Call Strategy: When you make a sales call, you are not talking to people. You are actually talking to their internal dialogues. Understanding this will help you conduct successful sales calls because your main concern is a customer's state of mind. Remember that the words customers actually say represent only a fraction of their true feelings.

9. Matching the Word Catalog Layer

The tool set you use during sales calls is language. The words you speak are a collection of symbols ordered to express your reality. The words you speak truly define who you are.

We mistakenly assume other people speak in our language, but they really don't. We incorrectly believe that their words are based upon the same symbolizations as ours. In reality, words are linguistic labels for very complex personal experiences. For example, words like "childhood," "marriage," and "success" can evoke very complicated feelings and memories. The word catalog layer of the human communication model (fig. 6.1) is responsible for the interpretation and meaningful association of words.

Words are not the flat, black-and-white letters depicted in the dictionary. They are three-dimensional objects that contain feelings, sounds, and pictures when they are said or read. Even the shortest words can trigger small dramas within the mind because words are tightly intertwined with memories.

All of the experiences of your life have determined the language you use—the surroundings where you grew up, the language used by your loved ones, where you went to school, your friends, your career, the amount of money at your disposal, and even your spirituality. Just as no one else on this planet has had these experiences, no one else speaks your precise language. Therefore, the language two people use to describe the same situation may be very different.

You and the customer have accumulated unique sets of memories. The conversations you have together are quite complex because the languages you both use come from different worlds. Ultimately, conversations are streams of information that are transmitted and received in completely different formats.

Sales Call Strategy: Unfortunately, when many salespeople meet with prospective customers, they talk in only their own language and only about themselves. The subject of the conversation is me, me, me: my company, my product's benefits, and my product's features and functions. Because the meeting is so important and they're nervous, many salespeople understandably fall back on reciting their canned marketing pitch. When you meet with customers, talk about them, them, them: their problems, their values, and their plans and desires. Most importantly, speak the customers' language by adapting your language to match their word catalog. We'll review word catalogs and the exercises you can use to determine the customer's word catalog wiring in detail in chapters 17 through 20.

10. Recognizing the Purpose Layer

Words are assembled to communicate an idea or experience. Every sentence of every conversation between salespeople and customers is purpose driven. One way to think of this is that customers have an ulterior motive for everything they say. Of course, you and I have been communicating with selfish interests all of our lives.

For example, before my children were old enough to talk, they would cry to let the world know of their unhappiness. As parents, my wife and I would then proceed down our mental checklist of what they might be crying about. Through the process of elimination, we determined whether they were hungry, wet, or cold or just needed to be held.

As my children were learning how to talk, their language capability was limited to labeling. They would see a dog and say, "Doggie." My wife and I would excitedly confirm, "Yes, doggie!" Soon thereafter, they learned they could use words to get things they wanted. They were able to grasp that if they said, "Cookie?" with a certain enunciation, they would frequently receive a cookie. They were able to communicate with a self-centered purpose.

Salespeople and customers are just as self-centered in their communications. Each is constantly trying to extract information from the other. Salespeople will collect this information to create their account strategy, the long-term plan to win a deal. They are trying to uncover technical, political, and personal information in order to assess their current position and continually refine their strategy. To implement the strategy, they will determine a tactical plan and the daily tasks that are required.

Meanwhile, customers are trying to obtain information about the salesperson's company, products, and customers. Their main goal is information assessment. Whether formally or informally, they have developed and prioritized their needs. They need information in order to measure the fit of the salesperson's solution.

Three types of information are presented by customers during sales calls: obvious, interpretative, and calculated. Obvious information is a validated fact or a tangible object that can be seen and touched. An example of obvious information is a prospect's business card, which shows the person's title and contact information. Interpretative information requires the observer to make a personal judgment to determine its meaning. For example, someone might refer to a color as "tan" while another person may call it "light brown" or "beige."

Calculated information is based upon the combination of obvious and interpretative information. For example, when a customer spends an hour more than allotted to meet with you (obvious information) and after the call you felt it went well (interpretative information), you would calculate that the odds of winning the business are very high. Whereas obvious information is concrete and definite, the meaning of calculated and interpretative information is more subtle and subjective to personal judgment.

Sales Call Strategy: During a sales call, try to pay attention to why something is said and how it is said, rather than what is actually said. In essence, you want to understand the story behind the story and theorize what is truly on the customer's mind. Therefore, you need to study the purpose, content, and structure of the language the customer uses. Try to discern obvious information from interpretative and calculated information. Don't let your personal biases and opinions influence an honest assessment of the success of the sales call.

11. Altering Meaning with the Phonetic Layer

The phonetic layer of the human communication model (fig. 6.1) is the enunciation of the actual words strung together in the form of a sentence. This layer can alter the meaning of the sentence to convey a completely new or sometimes opposite meaning. For example, let's say I tell my wife, "Your hair looks great," but my voice trails off at the end of the sentence. She would immediately be concerned that her hair does not look good. This incongruence would then cause her to ask what I actually meant. Congruence can be thought of as "truth in communication." If I say to her, "Your hair looks great!" and emphasize the word "great," my sentence is aligned (congruent) with the content of the words.

If the customer says to you, "We'll find some time to schedule a product evaluation" in a sullen tone with a lack of enthusiasm, you know you probably won't be invited back. Conversely, if the sentence is said with excitement and conviction, the customer is far more serious about moving forward.

Phonetics can be consciously applied to spoken words to create greater impact or to clarify the meaning. Telling a customer, "Yeah, we have the feature too" is different from exclaiming to a customer, "Yes! We have that feature!" The last statement exudes confidence and excitement and is said with a different purpose. This is known as "marking."

Marking words calls the listener's internal dialogue to pay attention. Marking has two purposes: it alerts the listener's conscious mind to highlight a specific thought, and it tells the subconscious mind to remember what might otherwise have been ignored. Words can be marked by varying their pronunciation with inflection, volume, pitch, speed, or accent.

The most common way to mark is to increase the volume. However, decreasing volume, even whispering, is just as effective in business meetings. In addition, words and phrases can be used to mark other words. If I say, "Listen up!" "Here comes the important part," or "If you're wondering what's next," your awareness and anticipation are heightened.

You can even use all aspects of body language, including hand gestures, facial expressions, posture, and movements, to mark words. You can point at the audience, raise your hands above your head, shrug your shoulders, move to the right or left, or make other body movements to distinguish certain ideas. Regardless of how you mark words, the listener's internal dialogue hears them and processes the information in the conscious mind immediately.

Meanwhile, the subconscious mind recognizes the specific words that were marked.

Sales Call Strategy: The manner in which customers pronounce words provides vitally important information about their honesty and intent. Truthful communication occurs when all layers of the human communication model are in agreement—for example, when spoken words match the way in which they are said. Incongruence is misleading communication where layers of the human communication model contradict each other—for example, when the customer's enunciation contradicts the words being said.

During a sales call, you can highlight your important thoughts by "marking" your words with different enunciations. The volume and tone of your voice can be used as cues to capture the attention of the customer's internal dialogue. Try this on your next sales call. Slow down your tempo of speech by half when you are covering the most important reasons why the customer should do business with you and watch the customer's reaction. Does he lean slightly forward toward you? Touch the face with a hand? Appear more introspective? If so, you have successfully marked and subconsciously distinguished these thoughts.

12. Speaking Content Layer Languages

Who taught you how to become persuasive? You probably learned much of what you know by trial and error. Or you might have known a naturally persuasive coworker, friend, or colleague and tried to emulate your mentor's methods, honing your skills through informal interactions.

You may have taken debate, public speaking, and communications classes while in school. However, they most likely focused on hard skills such as the memorization and presentation of structured arguments. Anyone can recite facts, and two people can say the exact same words with entirely different results. Mastering the soft skills—understanding how to build rapport with skeptics, how people process and interpret information, and how to dovetail your ideas into a person's personal desires—is what ultimately makes someone influential.

The content language layer (the actual words being spoken) is what most people think of and listen to when they are having a discussion. However, you can actually speak four different content layer languages that will ultimately determine your persuasiveness with customers.

- *Intersecting activity language.* Interests, hobbies, and personal pursuits by which the customer displays his personality, beliefs, and values. We will examine the intersecting activity language in chapter 36.
- *Technical specification language.* The androgynous, nonpersonal, and technical communication that is based upon the nomenclature and technical terms of the customer's industry. We will analyze the technical specification language in chapter 37.
- *Business operations language.* The language that is specific to the daily running of the customer's business and how it relates to the person's role in the organization. We will study the business operations language in chapter 38.
- *Confidential language.* The most powerful trust-based language by which the customer explains his personal needs, desires, and plans along with the strategy by which to fulfill them. You can learn about the confidential language in chapter 40.

Although we will discuss each of these languages in detail, it's important to mention the different types of dialects now. When most people think of the word "language," the first association that comes to mind is English, French, Spanish, Japanese, and so on. However, these are only local dialects by which words are delivered. Accordingly, the fundamental principles and concepts of sales linguistics are applicable to any dialect of language regardless of its origination.

Sales Call Strategy: Persuasion is not solely the recital of logical arguments or factual information to a listener. Instead, it is the process of projecting your entire set of beliefs and convictions onto another human being. It's not about getting others to acknowledge your arguments or agree with your business case; it's about making them internalize your message because they believe that's the only way to create real change. In order to accomplish this goal during sales calls, you should understand and be able to fluently speak the four different content layer languages with your customers.

13. Conscious and Subconscious Communication

With or without conscious effort, you most likely have mastered each of the layers of the human communication model. However, the *interaction* between the layers is of particular interest to salespeople. When people speak, the layers are totally interactive. Any layer can communicate with any other layer as shown in figure 13.1. The layers can also be combined to form complex statements that can convey additional or different meanings to content-layer words.

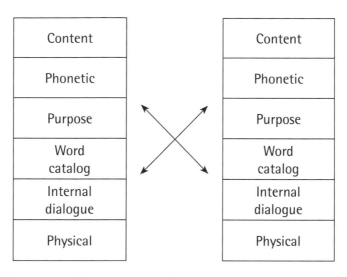

Figure 13.1 Human communication

Here's an illustration of how the various layers can be combined, using the example from chapter 6 of asking Mary for a report. Suppose I see Mary coming to my desk to give me the report. Following are some of the ways I could respond to her:

- *Physical.* I could give her a big smile and a high-five. She would obviously interpret this to mean I was pleased. My communication is congruent because my facial expression and hand slapping are communicating the same message.
- *Content plus phonetic plus physical.* I could say "Thanks" in my normal tone of voice but present a very forced, fake smile. My communication is incongruent. Mary would have to do some internal assessment as to what I was trying to communicate.
- *Physical plus content plus phonetic.* Holding my arms over my head, I could say at the top of my voice, "I see I *finally* have my report!" This congruent communication would definitely get the point across about my unhappiness the report was late.

The content layer, the actual words being spoken aloud, represents only a fraction of the total communication spectrum that is being presented during any conversation. Additional layers can be added on top of each other to convey even greater meaning. The layers can be used selectively to abbreviate our thoughts and speed up communication while still preserving the original message. For example, we shrug our shoulders instead of saying, "I don't know." The layers can be aligned to create holistic, congruent communication. Your sales intuition naturally interprets congruent messages as being honest and true. However, if the layers are at odds with each other, or incongruent, you know further investigation is required.

Each of the communication layers can also communicate both consciously and subconsciously between themselves. For example, when a person lies, the subconscious mind will affect the phonetic and physical layers of communication. The pitch, tone, and volume of the voice may change along with the person's posture, demeanor, and skin tone.

The ability to effectively send and receive information from each layer of the human communication model is a critical component of sales intuition. While it is easy to recognize the communication being sent consciously via spoken words, the subconscious information being sent is just as expressive, but it's much harder to recognize and interpret. It is important to realize that the subconscious and conscious are communicating at all times, internally within the self and externally to others as illustrated in figure 13.2.

Finally, to further complicate the process, human communication is always occurring in several different forms and on several different levels. An immense amount of information is being conveyed, phonetically, verbally, physically, consciously, and subconsciously. The dark continent of the human communication model is the subconscious mind. It has the ability to permeate each layer. As it seeps through, it sends out signals about a speaker's honest intent.

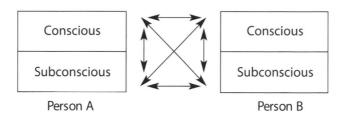

Figure 13.2 Conscious and subconscious communication

Sales Call Strategy: Whether the customer is speaking or listening to you, you need to evaluate each layer of the human communication model and determine its message and meaning. You should develop the ability to listen and sense all of the information a customer is projecting, regardless of whether it is being delivered consciously or subconsciously. Another term for this ability is "sales intuition."

Many struggling salespeople fixate on the content layer and the words from customers' conscious minds. They miss the critical information that would enable them to predict if they will win or lose the deal. Pay attention to all the layers of human communication because every sales call is an opportunity to add information and experiences to your sales intuition. Heavy Hitters use their intuition to create and execute the sales call strategy that gives them the highest likelihood of winning. Based upon their intuition, they will determine what they should say next, decide how to respond to a question, and select a course of action.

14. How to Recognize Visual, Auditory, and Kinesthetic Wiring

Your word catalog is more than the dictionary inside your mind that determines a word's meaning. It is also the methodology by which you ascertain correct interpretations of a message and associate complex psychological meanings.

You have developed a lifetime of experiences that are unique. These experiences, both good and bad, have shaped your perception of the world. Through your senses, you are constantly adding to your cumulative knowledge of how your world functions. As you accumulate new experiences, they are edited and influenced by your history. As a result, it is accurate to say every person functions in his or her own unique world. Your world is your own personal reality. You use your "word catalogs" to catalog your experiences and describe your world to others, as shown in figure 14.1.

Reality	Sensors	Influences	My reality
As it is	Sight, sound, touch, taste, smell	Family, money, work, friends, schooling, spirituality	Experiences cataloged

Figure 14.1 Cataloging reality

Through language, we represent our thoughts and experiences. We use words to represent the sensory experiences of sight, sound, touch, taste and smell. The map we use to describe and interpret an experience is based upon one of three word catalogs—visual, auditory, and kinesthetic. "Visual" refers to pictures and imagery, "auditory" to sounds, and "kinesthetic" refers to touch, taste, smell, and internal feelings.

Most people use one word catalog more frequently than the others. This word catalog has become their default, or "primary," mode of communication. You can identify someone's primary word catalog by listening to the adjectives, adverbs, and nouns they use in conversation.

People whose primary word catalog is based on sight will describe their experiences in visual terms. They are likely to say, "I see what you mean," "Looks good to me," or "Show me what to do." People with a primary word catalog based on sound will say, "Sounds great," "Talk to you later," or "Tell me what to do." People with a primary word catalog based on feeling might say, "I've got it handled," "We'll touch base later," or "I don't grasp what you mean." You'll find more information on determining your own and your customer's word catalog in chapters 16 and 17.

An additional level of psychological meaning also derives from the word catalog. The word catalog attaches a psychological interpretation to words. Let's think about fire for a moment. We easily recognize the difference between the flames from a burner on a stove and a raging fire consuming a high-rise building. Although they are both fires, they each create different mental and emotional interpretations. When we think of a stovetop fire, we might picture warming a can of soup or creating a culinary feast for friends. When we think about a terrifying high-rise fire, the impact on our emotional state is quite different. Your word catalog not only created the mind's-eye picture of both fires but also pulled forward the psychological meaning associated with each usage.

Sales Call Strategy: You have had a completely unique set of experiences in your life. And you have kept a record of your past existence by cataloging pictures, sounds, and feelings. As you make your way through your daily life, you are interacting with the outside world by repeatedly sending and receiving messages based upon your word catalog. Never forget, each customer's background is very different from yours so each speaks a unique language.

Great benefits in communication and persuasion are gained if you understand your customers' primary word catalog and adjust your communication to fit their worlds. Recognizing this concept is extremely important for senior salespeople to recognize. The customers you are successful selling to are probably wired like you. Your goal is to be able to successfully sell to customers of all types. Therefore, you must be able to recognize different communication types and adapt your communication style to match them.

15. How People Receive and Transmit Information

If you are right-handed, you have a dominant left side of the brain. If you are left-handed, you have a dominant right side of the brain. Your brain is wired a certain way because two hemispheres make up the cerebrum. The right side controls the left side of the body. The left side controls the right side of the body. This cross-management occurs because the nerves connecting to the body cross the spinal cord. You were born with this wiring and you cannot easily change it. Similarly, you are wired a certain way to transmit and receive information.

In conjunction with your genetic wiring, your mind developed strategies to interpret the wide varieties of information you had to contend with. To remember what you had seen, you had to think in pictures to imagine or replay what you saw. To remember what was said, you had to recall sounds. You would repeat to yourself what you heard. To remember what you were doing, you had to form an association between your body and feelings.

Three channels of information continually bombard your brain with information: visual, auditory, and kinesthetic. You can't turn off your senses. You can't slow down your vision, turn off your sense of touch, or silence your hearing. Your mind has had to adopt a strategy to assess and prioritize incoming information. While you were born with a tendency to prefer one stream of information over another, during your childhood you adopted the channel-processing strategy your mind uses today. Figure 15.1 below represents how people receive and transmit different streams of information.

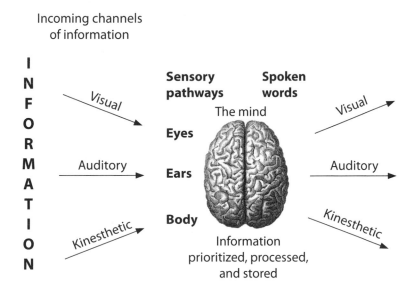

Figure 15.1 How people receive and transmit information

You've used your strategy for decades now. It is ingrained in your mind. The majority of the words you use in daily conversation actually reflect your strategy. You favor certain channels of information and vary the use of words according to these channels. In addition, the language you use is intimately connected with who you are.

Some people have a more dominant ear (the one you use when you talk on the telephone), a dominant leg, and even a dominant eye. To determine your dominant eye, take a sheet of paper and cut a hole about one and a half inches wide in the middle. Hold the paper out in front of you at arm's length and use both eyes to stare through the hole at an object that is at least twenty feet away. Now close one eye at a time. The object will remain in the middle of the hole when your dominant eye is open and will be covered by the paper when your weaker eye is open.

Similarly, people have a dominant, primary word catalog. A word catalog is the mind's method of gathering information, accumulating knowledge, and recording experiences based upon the visual, auditory, or kinesthetic senses. Your word catalog is also responsible for the association of psychological meanings to words. Your dominant word catalog might be visual, auditory, or kinesthetic. You also have a weaker, secondary catalog and, finally, a recessive catalog.

People process information with their word catalogs using pictures, feelings, or words, according to the strength of each catalog. Because spoken language is the system we use to communicate our experiences, people describe their experiences and convey their thoughts in terms that match their word catalog wiring.

However, people do not use one word catalog exclusively. Instead, they use all three word catalogs. You have a primary word catalog, which is your "default" method for accessing your catalog of experiences. It is the catalog used most often. People with a visual primary word catalog think in terms of pictures, those with a primary auditory word catalog think in terms of sounds, and those with a primary kinesthetic word catalog think in terms of feelings. Your secondary word catalog is your next strongest method for accessing your catalog. Finally, your recessive catalog is your least used and least developed access method.

You can tell what people's word catalog wiring is by noting the adjectives and verbs they use in their conversations. An adjective is a word used to modify a noun, and a verb is an action word. However, some words can be used as either a noun, verb, or adjective, and this usage will significantly change the interpretation of the word catalog. The sentences in the left-hand column represent a visual, auditory, or kinesthetic usage, while those in the right-hand column do not imply any particular word catalog:

Don't *glare* at me.	The *glare* of the sun was intense.
Map out your account strategy.	Please hand me the *map*.
Please *watch* your mouth.	His *watch* is broken.
Focus on the problem.	The camera has automatic *focus*.

The italicized words in the sentences in the left-hand column are verbs that imply a particular word catalog. Although the same words are used in the right-hand column, they are used as nouns. As you know, a noun is a word that describes a person, place, or thing. In general, nouns do not imply any particular word catalog.

People with a primary visual word catalog will use visual keywords more frequently than auditory or kinesthetic words to describe their experiences. Here are some examples of visual keywords:

Beaming	Demonstrate	Frame	Imagine	See
Bleak	Diagram	Gaze	Light	Shine
Bleary	Diffuse	Glance	Look	Show
Blight	Disappear	Glare	Magnify	Sight
Blind	Discern	Glimpse	Map	Snapshot
Bright	Display	Graph	Murky	Spectacle
Brilliant	Distinguish	Hallucinate	Observe	Spot
Chart	Dreary	Hazy	Outlook	Stare
Clarify	Emit	Highlight	Perspective	Survey
Clear	Expose	Illuminate	Preview	View
Cloudy	Fade	Illustrate	Reflect	Viewpoint
Dazzle	Focus	Image	Scan	Watch

People with primary auditory word catalogs will use auditory keywords like these in their conversations:

Accent	Bark	Denounce	Note	Say
Amplify	Berate	Dictate	Paraphrase	Shout
Articulate	Bicker	Digress	Persuade	Slur
Ask	Blare	Discuss	Plead	Snap
Assert	Boast	Drone	Profess	Sound
Attune	Cajole	Edit	Promise	Speak
Audacious	Call	Giggle	Quiet	Spell
Audible	Chime	Hum	Rave	Talk
Backfire	Chord	Implore	Recap	Tell
Back-talk	Crunch	Loud	Retreat	Vague
Banter	Cry	Noise	Ring	Yell

People with primary kinesthetic word catalogs will use kinesthetic keywords like the following:

Ache	Catch	Hard	Pique	Smile
Bash	Chafe	Heart	Plug	Smooth
Bask	Chew	Heavy	Post	Spit
Bat	Choke	Hit	Press	Squash
Bend	Chop	Hold	Pull	Sticky
Bind	Clinch	Impact	Push	Stink
Bit	Cough	Impress	Queasy	Strike
Blink	Crawl	Irritate	Rough	Taste
Boot	Draw	Kick	Rub	Thaw
Bounce	Feel	Leap	Scratch	Throw
Bow	Friction	Mark	Sense	Touch
Breathe	Gnaw	Move	Sharp	Walk
Caress	Grab	Nip	Smell	Weigh

Although nouns do not usually imply any particular word catalog, there are exceptions to this rule. When a person's communication is dominated by nouns that can be associated with one of the word catalogs, this is a good indication of that person's wiring. For example, if an e-mail has a pervasive or repetitive use of nouns such as "photograph," "picture," or "maps," this would provide additional clues that the person has a primary visual word catalog. If someone continually referred to conversations they were part of, this would suggest he or she has a primary auditory word catalog.

From this point forward, this book will refer to people with a sight-based primary word catalog as Visuals. Similarly, people with sound-based or feelings-based primary word catalogs will be referred to as Auditories or Kinesthetics.

Sales Call Strategy: Developing rapport by connecting with customers is a top priority in every conversation with customers. Knowing which word catalogs customers prefer and speaking to them in their language will help them fall in love with you and your solution. The more stressful or tense a situation is, the more likely people will communicate in their primary word catalogs. People also tend to lie in their secondary or recessive word catalogs.

Your customers are continually telling you in which channel they would prefer you to communicate with them. For example, what do they say to you at the end of a phone call? Visuals tend to say, "See you later" or "I look forward to meeting with you again." Auditories might close with, "I'll talk to you later" or "I'll call you later." Kinesthetics might finish with, "Stay in touch" or "Keep in close contact." Equally important, what do you say to end your phone calls and e-mails? Take a look at the last twenty e-mails you have sent and examine your closing sentence. This short exercise provides the first clue to understanding how you are wired to receive and transmit information. You'll find more a detailed exercise in chapter 16.

16. What Is Your Word Catalog Wiring?

What is your primary word catalog? Here's an exercise that will help you understand how you are wired. Print out the last ten business e-mails you sent to colleagues within your company and the last ten personal e-mails you sent to friends or family. Write the letters *V, A,* and *K* across the top of a piece of paper. In the left column write "Work," "Personal," and "Total." The chart should look like figure 16.1 below.

	V	*A*	*K*
Work			
Personal			
Total			

Figure 16.1 VAK keyword chart

You are now ready to perform a "VAK keyword count." Examine the e-mails and circle each occurrence of a visual, auditory, or kinesthetic word. Remember to circle the word only when it is used in the context of an action or description ("you *light* up my life," not "please turn the *light* on"). As you circle the words, add a tally in the appropriate column. The chart may look something like figure 16.2 when you are done.

	V	*A*	*K*
Work	III	ЖↃ I	III
Personal	ЖↃ	ЖↃ ЖↃ	ЖↃ IIII
Total	ЖↃ III	ЖↃ ЖↃ ЖↃ I	ЖↃ ЖↃ II

Figure 16.2 Sample results of a VAK keyword count and VAK pattern

Did you notice a difference between the tallies from your work and personal e-mails? Most likely, the language in your work e-mails is more androgynous and technical; therefore, the counts will be lower. I like to joke that this is because most communication in the business world is in fact "senseless." Were the counts evenly dispersed or clustered under one catalog? In the example above, the person's word catalog wiring is primary auditory, secondary kinesthetic, and recessive visual. You can do a similar exercise with the e-mails you receive to determine a sender's word catalog wiring.

Sales Call Strategy: The first step to broadening your appeal to a wider audience and becoming more persuasive during sales calls is understanding how you are wired and whether you are a Visual, Auditory, or Kinesthetic. Do not read further until you perform the VAK count exercise above. How are you wired? Are you a primary Auditory, Visual, or Kinesthetic? Did you notice a big difference in keyword counts between your work and personal e-mails?

Now conduct VAK counts based upon the e-mails sent to you by the key contacts for the most important deals you are trying to close. Compare their VAK counts to yours and think about whom you have the best and worst rapport with. Most likely, you share very similar wiring with individuals with whom you enjoy harmonious communication, and you're wired differently from those with whom you have tenuous relationships.

17. Determining the Customer's Word Catalog Wiring

I have spoken at the sales meetings of hundreds of companies. In order to secure the speaking or training engagement, I have to contact and persuade one of five C-level executives to buy: the CEO, the president, the vice president of sales, the chief marketing officer, or the chief operating officer. This is my exact target market.

Before I even consider sending an e-mail or letter, I first study the language used by the executive I am trying to reach. I'll search the Web for video and magazine interviews, company videos he has appeared in, articles he wrote, entries on his blog, and letters he may have written to customers or employees. I'll analyze any language sample that will help me understand how he is wired.

I will also conduct VAK counts when I speak with him in person or over the phone. I suggest you do this by bringing a notebook to your next meeting or keeping one by your phone. Whenever you meet with someone, perform a VAK count to determine the primary, secondary, and recessive word catalogs of the person you are talking with. You don't have to count for the entire meeting or conversation—just until you have a basic understanding of the person's wiring. Better yet, take along your manager or associate to a meeting and have him conduct the count so you can concentrate solely on your presentation. The manner in which your manager or colleague speaks to the customer and whether your colleague emphasizes visual, auditory, or kinesthetic words will indicate the customer's wiring to you.

Another trick is to place customers' business cards inside your notebook and write the VAK counts directly on them (in tiny print). Later, you can review the cards and refresh your memory about people's wiring. The results of your VAK counts will be fascinating. You will begin to be able to identify people's word catalogs in a very short time. You will also spot patterns and similarities among people who share the same word catalogs.

Your ultimate goal is to become aware of VAK keywords automatically without any handwritten counts. You want the process to become a natural part of listening so that, for example, when a customer is explaining his company's needs, you hear not only his content-level words but also the VAK keywords. Therefore, I suggest you start conducting VAK counts for all customers you meet with (and even other people you meet with). Obviously, it's important to know how everyone within a prospective account is wired. Also, people tend to hire those who are similarly wired. In this regard, meeting with the director of technology may help you better understand how the CIO he reports to is wired.

Sales Call Strategy: Analyze the e-mails, letters, or communications your customers may have made on the Internet to determine their word catalog wiring prior to phone conversations or in-person sales calls. Perform VAK counts during sales calls to further understand and validate their wiring.

18. VAK Count Patterns

As you begin to perform VAK keyword counts, you will notice some patterns developing. Figure 18.1 shows VAK counts for three speakers, each of whom made a forty-five-minute presentation. Interestingly, their VAK counts were representative of the three major types of VAK count patterns: balanced, strong secondary, and dominating primary.

	Visual	*Auditory*	*Kinesthetic*
President/CEO	20	17	14
Vice president of engineering	16	20	2
Product manager	5	34	4

Figure 18.1 Sample VAK keyword counts

The president has a visual primary catalog along with strong auditory and kinesthetic catalogs. This is a very balanced pattern. This wiring suits him well in his position. As president, he is responsible for the vision of the company, and it makes sense to have a Visual in that role. Other responsibilities of the president are company communication and consensus building. His well-developed auditory and kinesthetic catalogs help him naturally accomplish these two tasks with people who are not visually wired.

The vice president of engineering has an auditory primary catalog and a strong secondary visual catalog. His kinesthetic recessive catalog is almost nonexistent. The nature of the vice president of engineering's position is both analytical and visionary. He has to be able to give specific direction to the programming teams in order to build products. Since the communication framework by which this is done is a functional specification (a detailed description of the product in the form of words), having an auditory primary catalog helps.

Meanwhile, he has to chart the product road map; therefore, having a strong visual secondary is desirable. Since the vice president of engineering is immersed in the technical specification language (the precise, androgynous, nonpersonal language that uses technical operators to modify general words, as described in chapter 37), a strong kinesthetic catalog is not necessarily needed in this position and, in fact, could even be a detriment.

The product manager has a primary catalog that is so overwhelmingly dominating that the secondary and recessive catalogs are very rarely used. This pattern is called a "dominating primary." In this example, the person has a dominating auditory primary catalog. A dominating catalog could be visual or kinesthetic just as well.

This person's role is primarily technical. One of his main job functions is to create detailed technical collateral, such as white papers, data sheets, and technical content for the company's website. Having a strong auditory primary catalog is helpful in accomplishing these tasks.

Figure 18.2 shows examples of a balanced pattern, strong secondary pattern, and dominating primary pattern. The strengths of the three catalogs in the balanced pattern are relatively close. However, the strengths of the catalogs are different in the strong secondary pattern, where the visual word catalog is far weaker than the auditory and kinesthetic catalogs, and the dominating primary, pattern, where the visual word catalog is strongest.

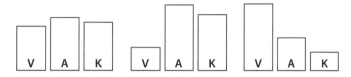

Figure 18.2 Balanced pattern, strong secondary pattern, and dominating primary pattern

Balanced communication is a key attribute of effective persuasion. Balanced communicators create better rapport. They don't limit themselves by speaking exclusively from a single word catalog. They connect with Visuals, Auditories, and Kinesthetics equally. Therefore, a balanced speaker naturally reaches a broader audience.

Sales Call Strategy: People use all three word catalogs, just in different amounts and priorities. For example, a person might use visual words 60 percent of the time, kinesthetic words 25 percent of the time, and auditory words only 15 percent of the time. The strength of each of your catalogs and the order in which you use them can profoundly impact your ability to persuade during sales calls. Therefore, you must know your word catalog usage and determine whether you have a balanced, strong secondary, or dominating primary pattern. Equally important, you must be able to determine the customer's pattern and how it compares to your wiring.

19. Interpreting Sayings and Clichés

Sayings and clichés may be used by people with any primary catalog. However, usually a specific phrase is used more often by people with one particular catalog. For example, "sizzling hot" is most likely to be said by Auditories. They hear the sizzling sound. Upon hearing this phrase, Visuals might picture a grill with something sizzling on it, and Kinesthetics might think of a finger actually touching the grill (particularly if they have burnt themselves in the past).

Let's do another exercise. Below is a list of sayings and clichés. After each phrase, mark a *V* for visual, *A* for auditory, or *K* for kinesthetic. If you think a phrase has multiple interpretations, write the order of what you believe is the priority usage. Here are some examples:

"music to my ears," A   "from their perspective," V

"tough nut to crack," K, A   "that's alarming news," A, K

The answers follow, but don't look at them until you finish the entire list. Also, it's okay to write your answers in the book.

"keep your fingers crossed"   "armed to the teeth"

"down to the short strokes"   "iron out the problem"

"we'll keep pinging him"   "barking up the wrong tree"

"ducks in a row"   "look them in the eye"

"we'll hammer it out"   "banging the phones"

"coin rattling down the pipe"   "see how the smoke clears"

"die a slow death"   "bury the hatchet"

"level playing field"   "a little bird told me"

"hit the nail on the head"   "ear to the ground"

"bite the bullet"   "that's a new twist"

"clear as a bell"   "smoke and mirrors"

"chip on his shoulder"   "quit your bellyaching"

Based on my experience, here is the most likely usage of these phrases matched to the word catalog. Don't worry if your answers don't match exactly because your interpretation is influenced by your own wiring and my interpretation by mine.

"keep your fingers crossed," K	"armed to the teeth," K, V
"down to the short strokes," K	"iron out the problem," K
"we'll keep pinging him," A	"barking up the wrong tree," A, V
"ducks in a row," V	"look them in the eye," V
"we'll hammer it out," K, A	"banging the phones," A
"coin rattling down the pipe," A	"see how the smoke clears," V
"die a slow death," K, V	"bury the hatchet," K
"level playing field," V, K	"a little bird told me," A, V
"hit the nail on the head," K, V	"ear to the ground," A, K
"bite the bullet," K	"that's a new twist," K
"clear as a bell," A, V	"smoke and mirrors," V
"chip on his shoulder," K, V	"quit your bellyaching," K, A

In addition to the VAK keywords, catch phrases, descriptions, and clichés also reveal a speaker's word catalogs. Some individuals use an unusually high number of clichés, for example. These people tend to be strong Auditories, and they actually say a cliché to themselves first before repeating it out loud. In fact, Auditories tend to spend more time listening to themselves speak than do Visuals and Kinesthetics because the volume of Auditories' internal dialogues is higher.

Sales Call Strategy: The sayings and clichés used by customers during sales calls are more than just catch phrases. Pay attention to them and they will help you determine a customer's word catalog wiring and whether he is a Visual, Auditory, or Kinesthetic. Ultimately, they will help you understand and think like your customer. For example, if the customer tells you, "We'll look at the numbers and get back to you," you could reply, "Let me show you a couple of areas of cost savings that might not seem so obvious." When the customer says, "We want more bang for our buck," you might respond, "Tell me what sounds fair to you." If he comments, "We're weighing all the possibilities," you might come back with, "What can we do to tip the scale in our favor?"

20. Speaking Tone, Tempo, Volume, and Pattern Characteristics

Many salespeople pay attention only to the words a customer speaks. They don't pay attention to the person's speaking characteristics—the tone, tempo, volume, and patterns of words. In addition to VAK keywords, you can determine a customer's primary word catalog by his speaking characteristics.

Auditories are actually talking to themselves and tend to speak in repetitious patterns. The pattern could be melodic or more like Morse code. The Morse code–type pattern tends to be monotone. Certain words are enunciated in the pattern. In the following examples, all the "dot" words are enunciated in a similar way, and all the "dash" words are accented in a different way:

- We are committed to your satisfaction.
  (Dot . . . dot . . . dash . . . dot . . . dot . . . dash)
- We guarantee high performance and availability.
  (Dot . . . dash . . . dot . . . dash . . . dot . . . dash)
- Some Auditories speak in a monotone voice.
  (Dot . . . dot . . . dot . . . dot . . . dot . . . dot . . . dot)

Other Auditories have speech patterns that are more melodic. Their sentences are more wavelike; that is, the ends of their sentences will vary in pitch, tone, or even pronunciation from the beginnings.

Auditories tend to be very proficient masters of the technical specification language, the nonpersonal, androgynous, technical talk used in the customer's industry (see chapter 37). Auditories tend to not "leak" or show their word catalogs through the use of VAK keywords as much as Kinesthetics or Visuals. However, when their secondary catalog is kinesthetic, more VAK keywords will be embedded in their conversations. Auditories also tend to quote what they have been told by others. They will also quote themselves in their conversations.

Here are more examples of auditory sentence structures:

- "Our meeting went great. Bob told us, 'We did a great job and everyone is excited to work with us.'"
- "The meeting was going really well and then 'boom, boom, boom,' we were asked some really tough questions."
- "And I started to ask myself, Are they still a partner of ours?"

The speech pattern of a Visual is quite different from that of an Auditory. Strong Visuals are being bombarded with pictures inside their brains. As a result, they have a difficult time keeping the pace of the words being said synchronized with the pictures being created in their minds. This condition is somewhat analogous to a computer's CPU (central processing unit) having to wait for the mechanical movements of the disk drive to be complete before it can further process any information. As a result, strong Visuals are constantly trying to speed up the mechanical process of speaking. Therefore, they usually talk faster than Auditories or Kinesthetics. Here are examples of sentence structures of strong Visuals:

- "WE ARE COMMITTED TO YOUR SATISFACTION."
- "VISUALSHAVEALOTTOSAYANDASHORTTIMETOSAYIT."

To strong Visuals, words are an interruption of the pictures or ideas in their minds. They have to get them out of their internal dialogue as fast as possible because thoughts are constantly getting stacked up. Therefore, they speak with energy and a sense of urgency.

In presentations they tend to speak even faster. Their stream of speech may be interrupted only by the necessity to breathe. Have you ever heard someone insert "um" in every other sentence? Visuals tend to do this more than Auditories or Kinesthetics. This filler word is basically used as a checkpoint to synchronize the images in their minds with their spoken dialogue. The ums are also said at the same speed and tone as the other words.

Conversely, Kinesthetics say "um" much slower and in a deeper tone than the other words they speak. Their ums are actually synchronized with their feelings, and this takes extra time. You also may notice them looking down when they say "um." Meanwhile, the Auditories' ums are not enunciated any differently and blend in with the rest of the sentence. However, Auditories tend to use ums as a part of their editing process to ensure the words they are saying are politically correct. The um provides them additional time to choose their spoken words with more precision.

Visuals tend to talk not only faster but also louder. Visuals are painting a picture for their audience. When they are telling their story, they are trying to make the language represent all the detail and complexity of a picture. You've heard the saying "A picture is worth a thousand words." For Visuals, it's true, and they have to communicate all of the thousand words to convey the picture they are seeing. Therefore, Visuals tend to be the most talkative too!

Having to "always" communicate a thousand words at a time creates a lot of energy. When giving a presentation, Auditories will stand in one place or a small space, and Kinesthetics will shift their weight back and forth. Visuals' arm gestures are more exaggerated since they are illustrating a picture with their bodies. They'll out-stretch their arms as far as they can horizontally (so that they resemble a cross) to make their point. Kinesthetics are more likely to make the same point by holding their hands vertically (with one hand over the head and one hand at the waist). Auditories hold their hands closer to their bodies and will use arm gestures sparingly.

While making a PowerPoint presentation, Visuals will point at the screen frequently and may use an index finger like a laser pointer. Kinesthetics will extend an arm, using the entire hand or palm to point. Auditories will most likely point an arm (in the locked position of a push-up) straight in front of the body or from the shoulder horizontally. You will notice that Visuals' arms are held higher on the body or over the head. Kinesthetics will cradle or hold themselves with their arms and hold their arms lower, at the waist.

Most people wrongly assume that people with a kinesthetic primary catalog are overly emotional, introverted, or extroverted. This may or may not be the case. Kinesthetics simply catalog their experiences in terms of feelings. However, people who are strongly kinesthetic will reflect this in their speech patterns, and in turn their personalities will be affected.

Kinesthetics tend to speak slower than Auditories and Visuals. Their speech is slower because they are frequently checking their feelings while they speak. Their speech pattern may also be frequently accentuated by their breathing, which is deeper than that of Visuals and Auditories. When speaking to a group, they tend to talk directly to a single person in the audience, unlike Visuals, who will constantly scan the audience. When talking about issues, Kinesthetics are more likely to associate a person with the issue or task at hand.

Strong Kinesthetics tend to be more dramatic in their speech patterns. They commonly insert pauses and use voice inflections.

Unlike Auditories with their Morse code patterns, Kinesthetics are "feeling" the words they are speaking. Their tone of voice tends to be lower because they are constantly validating and comparing their feelings with what they are hearing and saying. Here are examples of sentence structures of strong Kinesthetics:

- "*We* are committed to *your* satisfaction!"
- "*I enjoyed* meeting with *you.*"

Every communication with Kinesthetics is personal. The emphasis is on the words "we," "your," "I," "enjoyed," and "you" because they directly correlate with the Kinesthetics' feelings. For example, their interpretation of "we" is actually "my company and I," and their interpretation of "you" is "you and your company." These words represent very personal feelings, so their enunciation is likely to be slower or in a lower tone than the other words in the sentence. Kinesthetics' speech has other patterns. For example, Kinesthetics' voices will tend to rise at the end of sentences or fall and trail off.

The language Visuals, Auditories, and Kinesthetics use reflects the different ways they define their own reality and interact with the real world. Since every company purchase decision usually includes a cross section of Visuals, Auditories, and Kinesthetics, it's obviously important to be able to communicate in each channel.

Keep in mind that people with certain word catalogs communicate better with each other than other combinations. For example, strong Visuals and strong Kinesthetics naturally communicate together better than strong Visuals and strong Auditories. Auditories naturally communicate better with Kinesthetics than with Visuals. Kinesthetics have an intrinsic communication advantage since they are always in touch with their own feelings and are sensitive about the feelings of others. This consideration is incorporated into their communication process.

If you are talking with customers who are wired exactly as you are, you are already mirroring them (see chapter 29). Most likely, these are people you naturally communicate with and who are the easiest for you to sell to. However, it takes skill and effort to communicate with someone who has a primary catalog that is the same as your recessive catalog. Ultimately, you want to become a "communication chameleon" who can adapt to any word catalog.

Sales Call Strategy: If you are a Visual talking to a Kinesthetic, slow down and speak in terms of feelings; this will naturally lower your voice tone and decrease your volume. If you are a Kinesthetic talking to a Visual, speed up and speak in terms of pictures; this will naturally raise your voice tone and increase your volume.

Auditory salespeople face more of a challenge than Visuals or Kinesthetics in presenting their thoughts to customers. If you are an Auditory, you must make a conscious effort to watch the people you are talking to in order to make sure they are grasping what you are saying. What sounds good to you may not look good to a Visual or feel right to a Kinesthetic. Good advice to Auditories is to stop listening to yourself talk and make sure you are hearing what the customer is saying.

Conversely, Visuals and Kinesthetics should adopt auditory speech characteristics when they are speaking. Just as a chameleon changes colors to match its surroundings, your goal is to change your speaking mannerisms to match those of the person to whom you are speaking. To establish rapport, you need to mirror the way customers communicate and enter their world, not make them enter yours.

21. Learning Styles

Your word catalog wiring typically influences the manner in which you like to learn. Here's a quick test to help you determine your learning style. Circle the letter following each question that best applies to you.

1. When driving to a new customer address for the first time, I like to:
    A. View printed directions or watch my GPS
    B. Ask the customer for directions or listen to my GPS
    C. Use my strong sense of direction in conjunction with maps or directions
2. I like to learn about the new products my company is offering by:
    A. Viewing product information and watching presentations
    B. Listening to someone describe the product and talk it through with me
    C. Using the product or having someone demonstrate how it is used
3. To learn the features and benefits of a new product, I like to:
    A. Write them down so that I can refer to my script in the future
    B. Repeat them and practice saying them aloud
    C. Rehearse through role-plays or pretending that I am with a prospective customer
4. At sales training sessions I:
    A. Take notes on important topics so I remember them after the meeting
    B. Like hearing discussions about important information
    C. Like participating in exercises and role-playing

5. When making an important customer phone call:
   A. I may have prepared a list of topics or notes to remind me of what to say
   B. I tend to talk more than I listen
   C. I like to move, walk around, or doodle on a paper during the call
6. When I am writing an important customer letter:
   A. Things I see around me tend to make it hard for me to focus
   B. Noises and sounds tend to distract me
   C. It's hard to sit still and pay attention so I begin to fidget
7. To remember what happened on a sales call:
   A. I remember how someone looked or replay what happened in my mind
   B. I remember what someone said
   C. I remember what someone did or how I felt at the moment

Now add up the number of As, Bs, and Cs you have circled to find your primary, secondary, and recessive learning styles. The As are visual learning style, Bs are auditory, and Cs are kinesthetic. So if you had four As, two Bs, and one C, you would be classified as a primary visual, secondary auditory, and recessive kinesthetic learner.

Sales Call Strategy: Every sales call provides you the opportunity to educate the customer about the benefits of doing business with your company and why your products are better than the competition's. In one sense, you are the teacher and the customer is your student. Therefore, understanding the customer's word catalog wiring also enables you to present your information to the customer in his preferential learning style.

Incorporate the different learning styles into your sales call strategy. Make sure you have a PowerPoint presentation to show visual customers or be prepared to show them how your product works by drawing on a whiteboard. Auditory customers are more likely to want in-depth conversations, so be sure to bring along your colleagues who can answer all of their detailed technical questions. Kinesthetics tend to prefer hands-on demonstrations and trial product evaluations and will become frustrated with vendors who are unable to provide them.

22. Eye Movements and Long-Term Memory

Everyone lives in his or her own world. The world you experience is not the real world but rather your perception of the world. The way in which you perceive your world is intricately connected to the language you use and how you sense your surroundings. You use your senses to define everyday experiences for storage in your brain. Your word catalogs (see chapter 16) are the storage-and-retrieval mechanisms used to access these experiences. They are also responsible for the words you select to communicate your world to others.

I was first introduced to the concept that eye movements are related to long-term memory over thirty years ago. At the time, I had the good fortune to work as a computer programmer for a brilliant doctor who introduced me to neurolinguistics. He had started a medical billing company following many years practicing medicine. He originally studied neurolinguistics in order to better communicate with his patients and understand their mind-sets and behaviors. He also found the principles equally applicable in the business world. Later, when I transitioned my career into software sales, I realized that by understanding my customers' verbal and nonverbal communication, including eye movements, I could predict and influence their future behavior.

You are constantly accessing your short-term and long-term memory. However, it is much easier to access your short-term memory. Accessing your long-term memory is harder and slower. In computer terms, short-term memory is your RAM, while long-term memory is your hard drive. Much like a computer's disk drive, accessing your long-term memory requires some "mechanical" movements, and access to long-term memory can be seen. Conversely, short-term storage is accessed "electronically" and is therefore unobservable.

Amazingly, by observing people's eye movements, you can follow the mechanical movements of the brain that happen when they access their long-term memory. By watching their eyes move, you can determine if they are making pictures in their mind, listening to themselves speak, or experiencing feelings. From this information, you can determine their word catalog wiring and the primary language they use. Most importantly for salespeople, you can learn how to sequence customer questions so specific movements are triggered in order to determine a customer's truthfulness and your future likelihood of winning the deal.

Researchers at the Brain Science Institute discovered that short-term memory is transferred to a different site within the brain to become long-term memory over time and this is directly related to eye movements. To understand eye movements and their relationship to short- and long-term memory, let's pretend you were learning how to play golf and eagerly scheduled seven daily golf lessons. The newly learned skills from your first and second golf lessons would be stored in short-term memory. As you repeat the exercises daily, these new skills would become stored in long-term memory around the fourth day along with their associated eye movements. Here's their physiological explanation (in their technical specification language, see chapter 37): "Command signals that control eye movement are transmitted to the vestibular nucleus in the medulla oblongata over two routes: one direct and the other indirect passway via the parallel fibers and Purkinje cells of the cerebellar cortex. The vestibular nucleus processes the command signals transmitted over both routes and outputs the processed signals to the motor nerves, which in turn, control the movement of the eye."[1]

So now we know that eye movements are closely linked to *establishing* long-term memories, but why are they made when *retrieving* those memories? The brain is a widely distributed neural network with information and memories stored throughout. Eye movements are believed to cause the left and right hemispheres of the brain to better interact with each other. This is known as "hemispheric interaction," and close coordination between the hemispheres is necessary to retrieve certain types of memories. For example, the right hemisphere may maintain information that the left hemisphere requires to retrieve a certain memory. Eye movements to the left activate the right brain hemisphere, and eye movements to the right activate the left hemisphere. Most interestingly, studies have shown that moving the eyes thirty seconds back and forth from left to right improves memory retention before an event.[2] (Try it before your next big sales call.)

Researchers believe that eye movements help activate the areas of the mind that are involved in processing visual, auditory, and kinesthetic information. For example, the left and right temporal lobes (located at the temples) are involved in the processing of auditory sensations. Scientist have recently pinpointed the parietal cortex (at the top of the head in the middle of the brain) as the area that encodes visual information (after it passes from the eyes through the lateral geniculate nucleus to the back of the brain).[3] Brain scans of highly emotional people show increased activity in the anterior cingulate (located behind the eyes deep toward the bottom of the brain).[4] Imaging studies have also proven the anterior cingulate is directly linked to sociability and a person's ability to read and respond to social cues such as facial expressions.[5]

When remembering pictures, people will move their eyes up to the right, keep their eyes straight while defocusing their pupils, or move their eyes up to the left, as illustrated in figure 22.1.

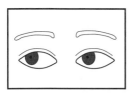 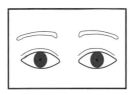 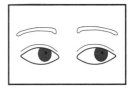

Figure 22.1 Visual word catalog eye movements

When remembering sounds, people will move their eyes straight to their right, down to their left, or straight to their left, as illustrated in figure 22.2.

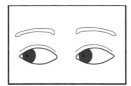 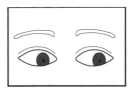 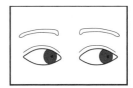

Figure 22.2 Auditory word catalog eye movements

People will move their eyes down to the right when remembering feelings, as illustrated in figure 22.3.

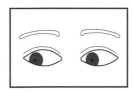

Figure 22.3 Kinesthetic word catalog eye movement

Before we go further, it is important to define the two different types of long-term memories. Some long-term memories can be recalled precisely (precise memories), and some memories are recalled by creating, constructing, and comparing images, sounds, and feelings (assembled memories). Assembled memories will usually cause a different eye movement than precise memories. For example, a Visual might move his eyes up and to the left when asked how many bridesmaids were in his wedding because he's mentally viewing a picture from his wedding album. But the same person may have to look up and to the right when asked to name the church where he was married. Because he couldn't precisely visualize the name, he had to construct the answer and use his imagination to picture the wedding license, the pastor, or the front of the church. Assembled memories require the use of imagination in order to fill the gaps of missing information.

Eye movements reflect the inner workings of the mind. Let's suppose people are asked, What was the best day of your life? Visuals may start searching their memories by looking for stored pictures before finally deciding on a specific day, such as the day their first child was born. To search their memory banks of pictures, their eyes would move up to the right, move up to the left, or look straight ahead with the pupils defocused. Once retrieved, the picture could then trigger the feeling they had of holding the baby for the first time. Their eyes would move down to the right to get the feeling. Finally, to recreate the entire experience, their eyes may move down to the left or straight to the right or left to actually recall the sound of the baby crying.

Have you ever tried to have conversations with people who would not look at you? Perhaps they tilted their heads down and stared at the ground during the entire discussion. Maybe they turned their heads slightly to the right or left so they seemed to be looking at something behind you. Or they could have cocked their heads back, as if they were looking at the sky. These are examples of people who have an exceptionally strong or dominant primary catalog. These people have a single catalog that is so controlling that their heads become an extension of their eye movements. If their heads tilt down and to the right, that indicates they are dominant Kinesthetics, while people who always tilt their heads up are dominant Visuals. When people tilt their heads down and to the left or laterally away from you for the majority of your conversation, you can assume they are dominant Auditories. The person you may have thought of as being shifty eyed or untrustworthy may actually just be an Auditory.

While some people will make very obvious eye movements, other people's eye movements are very subtle and consist of quick glances away from you. Some people have to blink to think. They have to close their eyes for a second to retrieve information. In this case, you will be able to see the bulge of their pupil and iris on the eyelid as the eye moves. The main point here is that you have to pay close attention and look for subtle movements as well as obvious eye movements.

When people search their long-term memories, they will quite often perform a "search loop." Their eyes will initially go to their primary system, then their secondary, then their recessive and repeat the pattern. Their eyes will look like they are going around in circles. They are simply trying to find a mental tag (by sifting through different pieces of information) that will help them bring back the entire memory.

There is also a very rare group of people that I call "Masterminds." One or two out of one hundred people have the uncanny ability to instantly recall exceptionally detailed autobiographical memories and past personal experiences, even though they may have occurred decades before. I surmise that they have more neural pathways that enable their superior memory. Even though most of the Masterminds I have ever met have been Visuals, they don't seem to make any eye movements at all.

The mind is an incredibly complex system, and there will be exceptions to the general rules above. For example, left-handedness impacts eye movements about 50 percent of the time based upon my observations. Since only 10 percent of the population is left-handed, this means that 5 percent of the people you meet will be wired in reverse. Their kinesthetic (down to the right) and auditory (down to the left) eye movements are reversed.

Sales Call Strategy: A longtime salesperson once told me that people are lying when they look away from you to the left while answering questions. Unfortunately, for twenty-five years he had been misinterpreting the eye movements of Auditories. Correctly interpreted, eye movements will help you understand the prospective customer's primary word catalog, thereby enabling you to present information to him in the appropriate visual, auditory, or kinesthetic channel.

When you first meet a customer, ask questions that require long-term memory access, such as When did you start working here? What did you do before you started working here? Where did you grow up? and What was your first job here? The eye movements made while answering these questions will help you get a preliminary idea of the customer's word catalog wiring.

23. Long-Term Memory Eye Movement Test

At this point, you may be skeptical about whether eye movements can really explain what is happening in the brain. Try the following experiment. However, before you start, you will need to find a mirror because this exercise is much more meaningful when you can watch yourself.

Below, you will find a list of questions. All of these questions are intended to make you access your long-term memory. However, some answers are actually stored in your short-term memory. Finding answers in short-term memory doesn't require any specific eye movements. For example, if I ask, When did you wake up this morning? the answer is available instantaneously without much work. However, if I ask you what time you woke up two weeks ago last Saturday, that answer may require some additional thought.

As you read each question, try to follow your eye movements. Specifically, concentrate on where your eyes move first to "search" for the answer and make a notation of it. Use *UL* to reflect upper left and *UR* for upper right. Write *SL* for straight left, *S* for straight center with no eye movement at all, *SD* for straight with defocused pupils, and *SR* for straight right. Write *DL* for down left, and *DR* for down right. Also try to pay specific attention to the exact position of your eyes when you actually "find" the answer.

1. What did you have for dinner last Friday?
2. What was the name of your third-grade teacher?
3. What was your favorite vacation?
4. What was the best job you ever had?
5. What was the best sports event you ever attended?
6. Who is your favorite music group?
7. Where were you when you received your first real kiss?
8. What was the worst sales call you ever went on?
9. What account that you closed are you most proud of?
10. What was the license plate number of your first car?

What happened? Did you have to look away from your reflection to answer a question? Where did your eyes move first? What was the last position of your eyes when you found an answer?

Let's examine the questions further. They are all date dependent and designed to access your long-term memory. However, it's possible that some of the answers were in your short-term memory. It depends on you. If you're reading this book on Saturday, it's easy to remember what you had for dinner yesterday. However, if you're reading it on Thursday, the answer may be in long-term memory. If you had Friday's dinner at your favorite restaurant or ate with a classmate you hadn't seen in ten years, then it would be more likely that the experience would be in short-term memory. If there wasn't anything particularly eventful about the meal, it was probably placed in long-term memory.

I could not tell you who my third-grade teacher was. However, I do know a person who can name each of her teachers, even though she attended school over forty years ago. Not surprisingly, she is now a counselor and has dedicated herself to helping others. Obviously, her teachers had a lasting impact on her, and this information has been stored to reflect its importance.

If it has been a long time since you took a vacation, you probably had to do a complex mental search to determine your favorite one. If you were on vacation last week, you may have recently performed this comparison, and the results are still in your short-term memory. If all of your vacations have been indistinguishable or you had a problem selecting an answer, you may have continued in a "search loop."

It's easy to spot people using their search loop. Their eyes move around in a circle, going from catalog to catalog. They'll start in the primary catalog, move to the secondary catalog, go to the recessive catalog, and then repeat the process. Someone with a particularly strong dominant primary will get stuck with his eyes in the primary word catalog position. When this happens in a sales call, you know the customer is trying to "find" the answer. Since the answer isn't immediately retrievable, the customer's answer will most likely represent his best guess and will need to be validated.

This experiment was intended to make you aware of your own eye movements. This exercise should have helped you understand and validate your own word catalog wiring. Don't be concerned if you were unable to complete every question, as it is hard to track eye movements when you can't look yourself in the eye.

It's very important to note that your eye movements were probably not all the same because you might have had to use your imagination to create part of the answer in order to make a complete recollection. Remembering a precise memory and imagining an assembled memory may have required different eye movements. For example, let's say you are an Auditory. When you answered the question about who your favorite music group is, you could have accessed your long-term memory, precisely selecting your favorite band, causing your eyes to move straight to your left. Conversely, maybe you like a hot new band, but you couldn't recall its name. Using your imagination, you may have had to play your favorite song in your head before you remembered the band's name, and this caused your eyes to move straight to the right. On the other hand, if you had recently attended your favorite band's concert, the answer would probably be in short-term memory, and there wouldn't have been any eye movements.

Two categories of information are kept in your long-term memory: date-dependent experiences and minutiae. Just like a computer's RAM memory, your short-term memory has a limited amount of space. In comparison to RAM, the computer's disk drive (long-term storage) has much more space available. Similarly, your long-term memory is almost infinite. Therefore, your brain is continually optimizing what is kept in short-term memory and "writing," or transferring, it to your long-term memory. As time goes by, the relevance of an event diminishes, causing the event to be reclassified into long-term memory. In addition, your brain will place small details that are considered trivial directly into long-term storage. In this case, the date of the experience has nothing to do with where the experience is stored. It is being stored based solely upon its importance.

Now, take the list of ten questions to some loved ones or friends you know very well. Without telling them why, ask them some of the questions. However, instruct them not to tell you the answers. Rather, at the instant they know the answer, have them say, "Got it!" After each question make two notations—where their eyes went first and where their eyes were when they said, "Got it." You should get a very consistent pattern. Once again, the place their eyes consistently move indicates their primary word catalog. Most likely, it will also be the same place they find the answer.

Sales Call Strategy: The key to successfully understanding the customers' physical layer (see fig. 6.1) is to first establish their baseline movements. Baseline movements are the customers' default nonverbal communication style. For example, at the beginning of a sales call you could ask nonthreatening questions that invoke long-term memory in order to establish the baseline eye movements. These questions could be about date-dependent experiences or minutiae and hard-to-remember details. For example, When did your company go public? What was the highest stock price? and How many employees worked at the company when you started?

Later during the call as you ask more intense qualifying questions about the customer's selection process and perception of competitors (see chapter 44), mentally compare the customer's eye movements to the baseline established earlier. Calibrating eye movements (see chapter 25) will help you ascertain whether or not you are being told the truth.

24. Short-Term Memory Eye Movement Test

Now, let's do another experiment. Pay particular attention to what movements your eyes make as you repeat the questions below, or better yet, ask yourself these questions while looking at yourself in a mirror:

1. What did you have for breakfast today?
2. What color is your car?
3. What is your birthday?
4. What is your zip code?
5. What is your social security number?

Did you notice completely different eye movements compared to those in the previous exercise or no movement at all? While the set of questions in chapter 23 required you to access your long-term memory, the above set of questions probably didn't. Most likely, the answers were already in your short-term memory because the experience happened recently or you use the information all the time. In computer terms, the answers to these questions were cached (held temporarily) in your RAM, while the answers for the long-term memory questions required you to access the hard drive.

Take a minute and complete the following eye movement exercise. Try to hold your eyes in each position for at least ten seconds. After each eye movement, make a mental note on whether the position was more comfortable than the others.

- Up and to the right
- Up and to the left
- Straight to the right
- Straight to the left

- Down and to the right
- Down and to the left

What happened? Did some movements feel strained while others were easy? Suppose that in the analysis of your e-mails you performed in chapter 16, your VAK count indicated that you have a visual primary, kinesthetic secondary, and auditory recessive wiring. Most likely, the auditory eye movements were noticeably more uncomfortable to make than the others. If your VAK count indicated that you are wired with an auditory primary, kinesthetic secondary, and visual recessive, then the visual movements were most likely harder to do.

Sales Call Strategy: When customers answer your questions, try to recognize their short and long-term memory eye movements. This will provide important information about what is going on inside their minds. When you ask a customer different qualifying questions, you should expect the appropriate eye movements or no movements at all. For example, the answer to, What is your budget? should be in short-term memory. This is a very important factual constraint, so you shouldn't see eye movements associated with imagination or long-term memory. If you do, you should assume the customer's budget is not set or it might not be approved.

25. Calibrating Eye Movements to Determine Truthfulness

A polygraph machine measures the body's response (breathing, heart rate, and temperature) of a subject to determine if the person is answering questions truthfully. At the beginning of a polygraph test, the administrator asks a certain number of questions known to be true, such as the subject's name and social security number.

These questions calibrate the response of known answers to the machine's measurements.

Similarly, you can calibrate eye movements of individuals by watching their responses to questions with known answers. By doing this, you can establish a baseline measurement of their truthfulness. For example, here's how you can sequence questions during a meeting with a customer to ascertain whether or not he is telling you the truth. Based on your VAK count, you know he is auditory primary, kinesthetic secondary, and visual recessive.

SALESPERSON: How long have you been evaluating solutions?

CUSTOMER: (*Eyes left, momentary pause.*) Well, we started last . . . November.

Analysis: Since the evaluation started over ten months ago, this question was a date-dependent event stored in long-term memory.

SALESPERSON: When do you plan to roll out the first systems?

CUSTOMER: (*Eyes straight, not defocused, instantaneous answer.*) Our plan is to be up and running by the end of Q2.

Analysis: This is another date-dependent question. However, the answer was in short-term memory. This is probably an important project date, and it is always on his mind.

SALESPERSON: Where will the first system be implemented?

CUSTOMER: (*In a search loop, eyes left, down to the left, up to the right.*) Probably . . . Los Angeles.

Analysis: This question may have caused him to search for an answer. He was actually making his best guess because the decision is not final.

SALESPERSON: What other companies are you talking to?

> CUSTOMER: (*Eyes straight, not defocused.*) We are looking at Acme, Beta Company, and ABC Company.

Analysis: The answer resided in short-term memory. He's probably talking to all the vendors on a regular basis.

> SALESPERSON: Does one of the solutions sound better than the rest?

> CUSTOMER: (*Eyes up to the right.*) No, they all sound the same.

Analysis: This answer is incongruent communication. His eyes were in the visual position as he spoke auditory words.

In the preceding example, the first four questions established the baseline measurements. The decision maker's eyes moved to the left when he accessed his long-term memory. They were straight and centered (not defocused) when he accessed his short-term memory. Any eye movements outside these two ranges must be evaluated in context with the answer.

We can assume that the answers to the first three questions were truthful. The third answer was the customer's best guess. Based on the nonpolitical content of the question, this would be an appropriate assumption. The answer to the fourth question, about which companies he is evaluating, should be in short-term memory. If the answer "Acme, Beta Company, and ABC Company" was given extemporaneously at a quick tempo, then you could assume he was being truthful. If he went into a thirty-second search loop to produce the other vendors' names, he was editing his response, which is another form of incongruence, and this requires further investigation. If you observe very complex eye movements for seemingly simple questions or no eye movement for questions for which you would expect movement, then you need to investigate further to ensure the person is being truthful.

The fifth question is the interesting one. The five questions were purposely sequenced in this order. The salesperson wanted to know if the playing field was level or one vendor was favored. His goal was to find the truth. The first four questions established the baseline to set up the fifth question. While the first four questions provided valuable information about the sales process, they also gave the salesperson a chance to calibrate the answers to the customer's word catalog. The answer given to the fifth question was most likely a lie because it was incongruent communication.

In congruent communication, a person's words and thoughts corroborate each other, and the *entire* body is in alignment when the message is delivered. However, the customer contradicted himself while answering the fifth question. His eyes went up to the right to his visual recessive catalog. This is the first incongruence. Based on the previous questions, we would have expected that his eyes would go to either short-term memory (straight, not defocused) or long-term memory (straight left). Since his eyes went to the visual position instead, it can be assumed he was "imagining" or creating an answer. This is a very important point to emphasize about word catalog eye movements. Imagining something typically requires a different eye movement than recalling something from memory. For example, Visuals' eyes might move up and to the right when accessing long-term memory and up and to the left when using imagination. Sometimes people will have to access an entirely different word catalog to evoke their imagination. For example, Visuals might move their eyes down and to the right, which is indicative of a kinesthetic movement, when they use their imagination.

The second incongruence is that the visual eye movements did not match the layer language used. "No, they all sound the same" is an auditory statement. However, when the customer said this, his eyes were in a visual position. The two incongruencies suggest there is mental conflict and this person is not telling the entire truth. These types of incongruence happen all the time during sales meetings.

Sales Call Strategy: Most salespeople rely on their intuition to tell them they are being misled. However, it can be risky to base decisions solely on gut feelings. The methodology tracking eye movements and matching these movements to customer's spoken words provides you with observable proof points to validate your intuition. Carefully sequence questions you ask customers and be on the lookout for incongruence.

26. Word Catalog and Job Function

People naturally gravitate to jobs that suit their word catalog wiring. On average, more Kinesthetics work in people-related positions like nursing, acting, and teaching. Auditories gravitate toward language-based professions and dominate fields that involve writing, talking, and statistics. Visuals work in fields such as advertising, movies, and designing. Here's the main point: if you sell a niche product, the majority of the people you interact with will most likely be wired in the same way.

Regardless of the industry, you can classify people within a customer's organization into three basic categories of responsibility: product, management, and executive. Most likely, your solution is targeted at one of these categories. Your initial contact with the account and most frequent interactions with the customer will also be within one of these categories. Let's take a moment to define and understand the nuances of these categories.

The *product* category includes those individuals who work hands on with your product. These people use a vendor's products to create a new product for their company. For example, a computer programmer creates an application (product) by using programming tools provided by a vendor. A telephone operator creates communication (product) by using telephone equipment provided by a vendor. A security officer safeguards assets (product) by using surveillance equipment from a vendor. People within the product category may have "administrator," "analyst," "technician," "specialist," or "engineer" in their titles. Or their titles will explain exactly what they do, such as "buyer," "mechanic," or "receptionist."

The *management* category provides direction to each of the various departments of an organization. Departments also may be organized around initiatives or business practices. Typically, people at this level may have "director," "manager," "supervisor," or "leader" somewhere in their titles.

While many different management styles exist, the two fundamental types of department managers are the "domain expert" and the "business expert." Domain-expert managers achieved this position by being the most knowledgeable person within their department. For example, a network manager may have been promoted to a management position because of his troubleshooting expertise. The maintenance supervisor may have been the most talented mechanic. The accounts payable manager may have previously been the most knowledgeable clerk. Domain experts are the "alpha," or dominant, resource that all the other members of the group consult with for technical advice. They pride themselves on being the most proficient technical specification language speaker (see chapter 37).

Meanwhile, business-expert managers are responsible for representing their department to the other departments within the company. They speak the business operations language fluently (see chapter 38), not the technical specification language.

The executive category consists of departmental vice presidents and other company leaders. In larger companies, the executive category is composed of people who have the word "president" or "chief" in their titles, such as the vice president of finance, chief customer care officer, and chief technology officer. In smaller companies, the executive level may also include individuals with "director" or "manager" in their titles.

During my career, I have sold four basic types of software: enterprise application software, systems software, application development tools, and networking/security software. One of the groups I managed sold a product into security departments. The product was specifically targeted at firewall administrators and security analysts (product category), and I was chartered to build the sales team of this start-up business. As I went on more and more sales calls, I began to realize that the percentage of Auditories within the security industry is very high.

In hindsight, it shouldn't have been surprising to find a high number of Auditories in the security area. After all, these product people are responsible for writing and coding the security policies associated with firewalls. The nature of the position naturally attracts people who have an aptitude for words. As a result, I preferred to hire auditory salespeople. Conversely, a group at another company sold to directors and vice presidents of IT (management and executive categories). These people were more likely to have stronger visual and kinesthetic catalogs, so I hired accordingly.

All of these generalizations are not as important as understanding the nature of the market space you sell into. For example, if you are selling a service to sales and marketing departments, that is quite different from selling a product to the engineering departments. Perform the following exercises to better understand your specific market and how wiring varies between the various organizational levels within companies:

- While you are performing the VAK counts on customer calls (see chapter 17), add a notation of whether the person is in the product, management, or executive category. When you have collected data from seven to ten sales calls, chart the VAK counts for each category and see if you can spot a pattern.
- During the next few days, make it a point to spend some time with people within your own organization who conduct different job functions at the lower level, in midlevel management, and at the executive level. Perform a VAK count for each person you meet and total the VAK counts for each category. You may observe patterns within departments as people tend to hire people who are wired like them.

Sales Call Strategy: You should precisely identify the category of responsibility your product is targeted to. This is the main group of people you are trying to sell to (executive, management, or product). For your target category, you need to determine if there is a single pervasive word category. If there is, you need to take this into account in the development of your sales call strategies and how you deliver information to customers.

27. How the Word Catalog Affects the Physical Layer

The physical layer of communication (see fig. 6.1), also known as body language, can be very subtle or more powerful than the actual words being spoken. The physical layer is unique in that it is a three-dimensional language. In essence, the response on the outside of our bodies represents what's going on inside our minds. Our posture indicates our comfort level in any particular situation.

Understanding the nuances of body language is a tricky proposition. First, you cannot assume that each body movement means the same thing for everybody. For example, I worked with an individual who moves his right foot constantly during every meeting. This is his "rapport position," or the position he assumes when he is in a receptive state. He is very different from someone who shows impatience by moving in the identical way. Second, the way to understand the meaning of a physical movement is by observing the movement over time. The time period could be as long as an hour or as short as a few minutes. Finally, the ability to recognize and interpret a person's body language can help you validate the person's word catalog language.

For example, you can learn a lot from someone's handshake. Here are some observations. Kinesthetics tend to shake hands a little longer than Visuals and Auditories. Dominant Kinesthetics will put their other hand on top of the handshake or pat the other person on the shoulder or arm. Visuals tend to shake hands with a faster up-and-down movement. Recessive Kinesthetics tend to not make eye contact when they shake, almost as if they want to end the unpleasant process as soon as possible.

Save a mental imprint of the handshake from the beginning of the meeting and compare it with the handshake at the end of the meeting. Was it more sensual or colder? Longer or shorter? Did the amount of direct eye contact change? Was there more than one handshake? Did the person pat you on the back or touch you in some other way during the latter handshake? Handshakes provide instant feedback about how a meeting went. Like a kiss with your lover before you board a plane, the longer and more emotional, the better. From now on, be conscious of handshakes.

Hand movements will also vary based on a person's word catalog. Visuals and Kinesthetics will use hand movements while speaking much more frequently than Auditories. The position of

Visuals' hands will be high in context with their bodies, usually at the chest or above. Visuals will use their hands to point to things—they want to make sure you see what they think is important. The fingers of their hands are usually straight or pointed out. They have no problem extending their arms and hands as far as they can because they want you to see the "big picture." They will use their hands as imaginary markers to help draw pictures of the content they are trying to communicate. Visuals' hand movements will be quicker because they are exploding with thoughts that must be communicated now.

Kinesthetics will make "deep" hand gestures while they communicate their feelings. That is, their gestures will be lower on their bodies in accordance with their feelings on a subject. The fingers of their hands will be in a closed or interlocked position. They will touch and hold their bodies while they speak. They may use their hands to cradle their heads or use their arms to hug their bodies. Their hand movements tend to be slower and more deliberate than Visuals' or Auditories' because formulating feelings takes more time than creating pictures or assembling words.

Auditories listen to themselves speak. This alone is a full-time job; therefore, they will use fewer hand movements. When they do use them, they tend to keep their hands closer to their bodies. Another term for this is "dinosaur hands" since their arms are being held like the arms of a *Tyrannosaurus rex.* Their hand gestures will tend to be at the middle of the body, lower than Visuals' hand gestures but higher than Kinesthetics'. Their hand movements also tend to keep time with their voice tempo.

Another aspect of the physical layer is breathing. You may not have noticed this, but people actually breathe quite differently from each other. Obviously, people breathe at a different pace depending on whether or not they are performing a physical activity. The aspect of breathing that we are interested in, however, is the changes in breathing patterns that occur while customers are in their normal state (when most business meetings take place), and these changes can be quite subtle. If a customer is wearing a suit or jacket or if glancing at the customer's chest would be considered inappropriate, breathing patterns can be observed by watching people's shoulders rise and fall as they inhale and exhale.

Different breathing paces can be observed by watching different areas of the abdomen. Some people breathe fast and some slow. Some people have a repetitive rhythm to their breathing: deep breath, pause, deep breath, pause. Some people's breaths are quick and shallow. Visuals tend to breathe shallower and higher in the chest, while Kinesthetics breathe deeper and lower in the belly. Auditories' breathing is somewhere in between.

How someone breathes is really not that important. What is important is trying to spot a change in a breathing pattern. A change is a signal that a person's internal communication state has changed and the level of rapport has fluctuated. This is valuable information to help you identify a customer's state of rapport. People experiencing rapport are relaxed and their breathing reflects this.

In the business world, people rarely express their true emotions outwardly. Facial muscles are used more to inhibit the public display of emotion rather than to show it. Therefore, a salesperson only has small variations of a customer's facial expressions to study. Pay particular attention to the following nuances of customers' facial expressions during sales calls. Are the corners of their eyes becoming tight or relaxed? Are their eyebrows rising or lowering? Is their forehead tensed up? Are their lips, chin, and jaw becoming relaxed or tight?

As we discussed earlier, the key to understanding the physical layer is to establish the customer's natural baseline movements early in the sales call and then compare them to the movements as the sales call progresses. Changes between the baseline facial expressions at the beginning of the sales call versus the expressions at the end serve as a visual checkpoint to determine whether or not you have established rapport. Customers' facial expressions will broadcast whether or not you're liked. If they are more tight-lipped and squinty eyed than at the beginning of the call, you have probably lost.

To a lesser extent than facial expressions, skin tone can also give subtle clues to a person's emotional state. In a tense meeting, for example, you may witness the skin tone of someone who is scared or unnerved turn ashen gray. When successful sales calls conclude, the participants' skin tone may seem warmer.

Sales Call Strategy: How do you "read" customers during sales calls? How do you know when the sales call is going well? The physical layer provides a visible feedback mechanism that enables you to continually gauge your level of rapport with the customer. Identify the customer's rapport position and continually monitor when it changes and what topic of conversation caused the change.

Pay attention to "microexpressions" as the customer answers your questions and reacts to what you are saying. Microexpressions are brief nonvoluntary facial movements that last less than a second. They provide a true glimpse into the customer's mind-set and reveal acceptance or rejection. Microexpressions are centered around the eyes and mouth. For example, if the customer displays a quick forced smile before answering your question, he probably rejects its premise or disliked being asked. If the customer tightens the corners of his eyes, he might disagree or is confused with what you said.

28. Observing the Physical Layer in Group Meetings

In sales, we are interested in three main aspects of the physical layer of communication (see fig 6.1). First, we want to interpret people's state of receptiveness to our ideas as exhibited by changes in their rapport position (see chapter 27). Second, we want to observe the physical layer to help validate our assumptions about people's primary, secondary, and recessive word catalogs. And third, we want to match their body language with the content of their spoken words in order to identify congruencies or potential incongruencies.

The sales world normally uses one of three prevalent meeting positions: all the participants at a meeting are sitting, one person is making a classroom-style presentation to a group of people who are sitting, and two or more people are standing in a conversation. These positions cover the majority of sales situations and are worth studying in more detail.

Group dynamics are very complex. In group meetings, the pecking order is reflected in where a person sits. Whether at a round table or in a classroom setting, the person with the most influence will choose a dominant place to sit. For example, at a long, boardroom-style table, these people will be found at the center of the table, and a spot will be left for them there even if they are late. If the table is shorter, dominant people will sit at one of the ends, while their subordinates will cluster around them.

At a round table, the dominant position may be the seat facing the door or the one with the best view outside. In a large classroom-style setting, dominant people will sit in the front of the room or in the most visible position. This is the position that provides the best location to see the presentation and to be seen by the audience. Occasionally, dominant people will sit in the very last row so they can be in the position of leaving whenever they please. Regardless of the setting, where a person sits is of primary importance.

Now that you know where influential people will sit, let's examine their posture. Most meetings start with people in a "closed" posture versus an "open" posture. In a closed posture, the body is folded up on itself. Probably the most familiar closed posture is the arms crossed on the chest. More subtle closed positions are legs crossed, ankles crossed, hands interlocked on the table, and both hands touching the face. A person in a closed position may also face away from the focal point of the meeting or presenter.

A closed posture does not necessarily indicate a negative attitude. Rather, it is a natural position of skepticism that shifts to an open position as rapport is created. The open position represents the best environment in which to communicate your message.

When people change to an open position, it may be as obvious as their uncrossing their arms and lowering them to the table. More likely, the change will be a lot more subtle. They may relax the tightness in the parts of the body that are folded: arms, hands, legs, ankles, feet, and even lips. They could also move their folded arms from their chest to their waist. Or they could switch position, such as going from legs crossed with the right leg on top to legs crossed with the left leg on top. Watch for these subtle changes and make a mental notation of when they happen. Who was speaking? What was the topic? Was there a variation in facial expression that accompanied the move?

People are continually opening and closing their positions throughout a meeting. It's important to identify a person's closed and open state and watch for patterns of reoccurrence during the meeting. Heavy Hitters know they need to investigate why they lost a person's open state and will pause to ask the person if he or she has any questions or try to solicit an opinion on the topic being discussed.

Sales Call Strategy: On a sales call, constantly survey all of the meeting participants to see if they are receptive to your ideas and moving from closed to open positions. The goal is to uncover any confusion and objections as early as possible. You do not want objections to remain hidden until it is too late to address them successfully. Even if someone else from your company is presenting, do not relax but carefully and continuously examine everyone's physical state. Try to be the first person to enter the meeting room so you can take the position that affords you the best viewpoint to observe all of the meeting participants.

29. Pacing, Mirroring, and Leading

I drive to the local mountains to vacation during the summer and winter. The trip takes several hours each way. While I am driving, my pace will be determined by several factors besides the speed limit. Usually, I will drive at the pace of the car in front of me, keeping a distance between that car and mine that I feel comfortable with. I will automatically maintain this distance until the pace of the car in front of me becomes too fast or too slow.

Sometimes, I will keep pace to the music on the radio and find myself speeding up to the tempo of the song. Suddenly, I'll be jolted into action upon realizing that I am driving faster than the legal limit.

Pacing can be thought of as the natural process of adjusting your tempo to your environment. In both of the examples above, my behavior was being influenced by something else (the car in front of me and the music), and even though I am mindful of how

I am driving, I'm not concentrating solely on it. It's as if I have passed the responsibility to my subconscious mind.

On remote roads, cars tend to cluster together instead of being evenly dispersed. It seems that the cars act together as a group and will accelerate or slow down together. I like to drive in these groups because I believe it reduces my odds of getting a traffic ticket. Therefore, when I drive on long stretches of highway, I will adjust my speed to fit into one of these groups of cars. This is mirroring, which can be thought of as the conscious act of modifying your behavior to fit your surroundings. As opposed to pacing, where your subconscious mind is in control, mirroring requires a physical effort at the direction of the conscious mind.

The car in front of me is also "leading" my behavior. Let's assume I have been mirroring the car in front of me for the last ten minutes. Suddenly, the driver swerves to the right. I will follow his lead and prepare to swerve to the right, even though I have not actually seen the danger. Leading is the process of influencing another person's action by yours. In this example, if the other driver had been driving erratically as if under the influence of alcohol, I would not have swerved. However, for the past ten minutes he had demonstrated he was a capable driver. He created a "driver's rapport" so that when he swerved, I followed. This is an important point: leading requires rapport.

Heavy Hitters use pacing, mirroring, and leading to gain rapport with their customer. They are constantly monitoring the customer's physical communication—handshakes, hand movements, breathing, facial expressions, and body posture. They know that by changing the style to match the customer's, they will create more effective communication because the customer is more comfortable, relaxes, and lowers his defensive guard.

When we watch someone else perform an action, mirror neurons in our minds fire off and respond as if we were doing it ourselves. Mirror neurons help explain why laughter is contagious, why we grimace in pain for people we don't even know, and why we feel like crying when we see others cry. However, not everyone has the same amount or strength of mirror neurons. Therefore, we need a strategy to put ourselves in the "mental shoes" of the customer and help lead him to understand the value of our company, products, and ourselves.

Mirroring breathing styles is the first step in helping you create rapport because it makes you recreate the customer's world with your body. If someone breathes slowly, you have no choice but to slow down the pace of your speech and movements along with your breathing. If a person breathes faster than you, your actions will naturally speed up.

Mirroring body posture is accomplished by making a subtle reflection of the customer. The most obvious mirroring is a direct reflection, like the opposite image in a mirror. For example, when someone sits with legs crossed, you sit in the identical position with your legs crossed oppositely. Or you cross your arms tightly to your chest, in the exact opposite position of your counterpart during a conversation while standing.

However, this type of mirroring is too obvious and can potentially be perceived as patronizing. Rather, the mirroring we want to use is much more discreet. Instead of crossing your legs to directly mirror someone, cross your legs at the ankles or even cross your arms. Instead of standing with your arms tightly folded, cross your arms in a looser fold at the waist or stand with your legs crossed.

Let's think about handshakes in the context of mirroring. You start a handshake using a medium grip and instantaneously react to the other person's actions. If the other person's grip is firmer, you grip harder, and vice versa. The length of the handshake and degree of hand motion you use are also equally matched to the other person's. You have instinctively been doing this mirroring for your entire career.

Assuming you have been successfully mirroring your customer, now it's time to test whether you have rapport by leading. Leading can be thought of as the process of using your actions to guide another person's behavior. Let's assume that you are fifteen minutes into a meeting. You have been successfully mirroring the customer's breathing and body positions. You feel you have gained rapport and now want to test if this is true. Slowly, you start varying your breathing, and the other person follows your lead. Slowly, you change your body position, and the other person changes as well. If you are doubtful about leading, think about how contagious yawns are during meetings.

Through the process of leading, you can determine the level of rapport that exists between you and your customers. However, if they don't follow you, it doesn't necessarily mean there's a problem. It's normal for people to fall in and out of rapport during meetings. Simply start mirroring again.

Most importantly, through the process of leading, you can influence a person's state to be more open or receptive to your message. In chapter 28, we discussed how people are continually opening and closing their body postures throughout meetings. You should constantly be scanning for closed positions. When someone is closed, you should becomes curious and want to know why. Initiate an investigation by asking questions or soliciting the opinion of the person in the closed position. The goal of this questioning is to understand what the person's internal dialogue is saying.

The ability to consciously develop a formalized process of pacing, mirroring, and leading and integrating these actions naturally into sales meetings is an extremely powerful sales tool. Most likely, you don't have a formalized process to accomplish this. It comes naturally. Salespeople with strong kinesthetic catalogs do this instinctively. However, this process can be learned by anyone with any word catalog.

Sales Call Strategy: You can perform exercises to help build the skill set necessary to pace, mirror, and lead customers during sales calls. At your next meeting, choose one person and spend the entire meeting mirroring and leading the breathing of that person. Similarly, in other meetings, pick a body position, such as the position of the person's hands or feet, and mirror it along with the person's breathing through the entire meeting. Continually add new layers of sophistication to your mirroring and leading. You can even mirror how a person speaks, including his tone, tempo, and volume.

30. Dominating Sales Call Vignettes

During a sales call, the salesperson wants not only to *present* information about his company and solution to sway the customer to buy but also to *uncover* information about the politics and biases inherent in every selection process. Gathering, presenting, and uncovering information results in interactions between customers and salespeople that can be thought of as circular vignettes.

Vignettes are small dramas, short interchanges between a customer and a salesperson. Usually they focus on one topic or one conversational theme. They are considered circular because every vignette will come to an end and close as the topic of conversation is exhausted, as shown in figure 30.1. During each vignette, the salesperson is either in a dominant position, in control, or in a submissive position, trying to regain control.

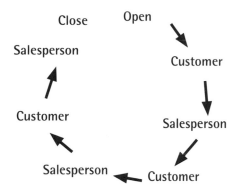

Figure 30.1 Customer interaction vignette

Vignettes typically change when the subject changes or when an implied agreement on the current topic of discussion is reached. The implied agreement may or may not mean that the issue is resolved. Often, it is an agreement to move on for the sake of time. Unfortunately, unresolved vignettes don't go away by themselves and almost always come back to haunt salespeople later.

A sales call is a collection of these circular vignettes. Since the use of PowerPoint is so pervasive in sales presentations today, most vignettes last as long as one slide or a series of several slides (one to five minutes). A typical sales presentation will begin with individual vignettes about the company's history, milestones, and customer references before moving into vignettes explaining specific technical features of the product.

Similar to a tennis match, a sales call is a psychological rally between the customer and you. Unfortunately, all meetings start with you in the submissive position. You can move to a dominant position only if you establish rapport and can successfully answer the customer's questions and concerns. Once in the dominant position, you have earned the right to ask about the dynamics of the decision process. You can ask questions to get a better understanding of the knowledge, credibility, and influence on the decision process that your main customer contacts have. However, you will quickly move back into the submissive position when the customer uncovers a weakness with your company and solution or asks a question you can't answer.

Choosing the moment to take control of a vignette is critical. For example, after you have proved the legitimacy of your company and product, you can change the subject and ask sensitive questions about the decision-making process. To do so earlier would alienate the customer and violate business etiquette. Although the conversation may seem natural and free flowing, your goal is to maintain dominance by guiding the interactions to topics you feel will positively influence the customer's perception of your solution.

Throughout the course of a sales call or presentation, the relationship between the customer and salesperson is continually being recalibrated. Dominance shifts from one side to the other, and the dynamics of the relationship can change quickly. A salesperson who thought he had found his soul mate at the beginning of a sales call could be quickly disappointed when he learns that the customer is really in love with another vendor.

Meeting participants perform internal and external assessments during vignettes. In internal assessments, information is analyzed solely within one person's mind. For example, the salesperson listens to the customer's response and determines the next course of action in his mind. Likewise, the customer listens to the salesperson's response and determines privately what to say next.

External assessments are spoken aloud by the meeting participants. Therefore, the complexity of a vignette is also directly related to the number of sales call participants.

For example, the customer's selection team members may have a discussion in front of you to determine what their response should be to one of your questions. When this happens, you should listen intently. Recognize this as a valuable opportunity to learn about the dynamics of the decision process and get a better understanding of people's knowledge, credibility, and importance in the decision process.

The sales team may also perform external assessments. A salesperson and his technical engineer may have a conversation about a technical detail in response to a question from the customer. Together, they use the vignette to make their points. Most importantly, the salesperson should manage all the vignettes as part of his tactical plan to complete his strategy for the call. In other words, don't let one of your colleagues hijack and seize control of the sales call.

Sales Call Strategy: Every sales call will have several critical vignettes that determine whether the call is a success or failure. While every vignette will close, the issues associated with some vignettes will remain open. These unresolved issues will come up again later in the sales cycle, usually when you least want an objection. Therefore, always try to address these awkward points early. You want them out in the open. You want to know whether an issue will inhibit the purchase of your product, and you want to know as soon as possible.

Following every sales call, think about the critical vignettes that determined the call's outcome. Ideally, you should write down the topic of conversation, what you said to successfully close the vignette, or what the customer said that caused you to lose control of the sales call. History will most likely repeat itself on future calls, so you must develop offensive and defensive statements (see chapters 46 and 47) to overcome objections and maintain momentum.

31. Lexical Dictionary and Dead Words

We connect with people through the words we speak, the way in which we say them, and the congruence of the words to our demeanor. However, the words we use are complex objects that don't mean the same to everyone. To understand this, let's do a word association exercise. For each of the following words, what is the first thought that comes to mind?

- Dog
- Cat
- Sports
- Church
- Marriage
- Children

If you have a dog, you probably thought of your dog. A picture of your dog may have come to mind, and you may have said your dog's name to yourself. If you are a "cat person" who dislikes dogs, you probably wondered how anyone could like those drooling, unruly beasts. Conversely, the word "cat" evoked positive feelings or a positive receptive state. The word "sports" may have caused you to think about the sport you played in school because words are anchored to our memories. The word "church" could elicit many different responses, ranging from a sense of purpose to a resistance to authority, depending upon your orientation. Meanwhile, marriage is to some a blessing; to others, a dream; and to the unlucky, a nightmare. So your reaction to the word "marriage" is likely based on your experience.

All of these words have something in common. In order to be understood, they must be interpreted into something meaningful: familiar thoughts and terms. This process occurs in three steps: determining the lexical meaning of a word, translating the word into personal meaning, and finally, forming a psychological impression determined by how the word is cataloged.

The first step is comprehension, checking whether or not the word can be found in the personal dictionary you keep inside your mind. Your lexical dictionary determines your word comprehension. The average person's dictionary contains about fifty thousand words.

After your lexical dictionary has defined a word, personal meaning is associated with it. For example, your lexical definition of the word "children" might be "kids between two and twelve." In your mind, children are not teenagers or babies. Your mind then tries to derive personal meaning from the word "children." If you have children, you might immediately think of your son, your daughter, or all your children. You might think of a child playing or even a schoolroom. Thus, another level of personal interpretation occurs. The deepest level of meaning occurs inside the mind's word catalog, where the word is associated with psychological meaning. While your lexical dictionary defines the basic meaning of words, your word catalog links that meaning to your past experiences. For example, you may have felt a sense of pride when you thought about your children and a specific memory, such as a school graduation ceremony or sporting event they competed in.

New words are continually being added to your lexical dictionary. For example, you may not know the meaning of the word "amorphous." However, you can derive its meaning when you hear it used in a sentence such as "The customers gave a vague and amorphous answer when asked when they would make a decision."

New words are also continually introduced into the English language. They pass through periods of introduction, adoption, and then widespread use when they are universally known and called "general words." Then they are subject to "linguistic inflation" from overuse. For example, the word "green" as it refers to

environmental friendliness is in a period of linguistic hyperinfla-
tion and is quickly losing its value. At the end of an overused
word's life cycle, its meaning is deadened from the word's excessive
use. This is what has happened to the words "powerful," "reliable,"
and "scalable." Overused words that have lost impactful meaning
are called "dead words."

Sometimes the terms your marketing department believes are
so important and persuasive actually detract from your credibility.
I have probably reviewed more than one hundred corporate
PowerPoint presentations in the past year alone. Not only do they
all look the same, but they all use the same general words to
describe their company's unique advantages. Open your corporate
presentation and see how many of these terms and phrases you can
find:

World leader	Increase revenues	Scalable
Market leader	Reduce costs	Manageable
Best-in-class	Competitive advantage	Reliable
Best-of-breed	Greater productivity	Powerful
Cost effective	Improve customer satisfaction	Easy to use
End-to-end solution	Better visibility	Dynamic

These dead words have been so overused that they actually
have a negative impact or no impact at all. So while you're thinking you are saying something profound to customers, they're roll-
ing their eyes and saying to themselves, "Here we go again!"

As opposed to dead words, "rich words" evoke a deeper personal meaning, importance, and even caché. For example, the
word "painter" can be replaced with rich words like "artist" and
"artisan." A "salesperson" can also be called an "account manager"
or a "client specialist." Rich words can be used to describe product
qualities like "intelligently" designed, "straightforward" operation,
or "ingenious" craftsmanship.

Sales Call Strategy: Whether you are talking with a CEO or a receptionist, the first step of communication is to check comprehension—whether or not your spoken words can be found in the personal dictionary that is kept inside his or her mind. Don't assume the customer understands the lexical meaning of the words you're using just because everyone in your own company does. Avoid using dead words that detract from your credibility and actually decrease rapport. Instead, use distinguishing rich words that impart significance.

32. Specific and General Words

Suppose I go to a fast-food restaurant and order a cheeseburger. Regardless of the way I enunciate the word "cheeseburger," whether enthusiastically, soberly, or abruptly, I will still be served a cheeseburger. The phonetic layer (see fig. 6.1) has little impact on the content of my message. I could drive up to the drive-through window and yell, "Cheeseburger please!" and the server would know what I want. In this example, cheeseburger has a specific meaning. A "cheeseburger" specifically has a bun, cheese, and a beef patty.

Now suppose I decide to go to a pizza parlor. When I am asked for my order, I say, "Pizza." The server will give me a blank stare. Do I want a deep-dish, regular, or thin crust? Do I want toppings? Unless the restaurant has only one pizza on the menu, "pizza" is a general word. A general word requires the use of additional words for the message to be received accurately. These additional words, called "operators," are used in conjunction with the general word to change the meaning, as shown in figure 32.1.

General word: pizza

First-level operator	Regular, deep-dish, or thin crust
Second-level operator	Pepperoni, mushroom, olives, etc.
Third-level operator	Large, medium, or small

Figure 32.1 Examples of general words with operators

When I introduced the concept of ordering a pizza, the first picture to enter your mind may have been a thin-crust cheese pizza. This would have been your own specific interpretation of the word "pizza." Let's say I was imagining biting into a deep-dish pepperoni pizza. This would have been my specific meaning of the word "pizza." Obviously, they are not quite the same.

Unless I add more operators to the word "pizza," the server won't know what type of pizza I really want. Also, in this case I can place the operators in any order and still have my message be correctly understood. I could order by saying, "I'll have a large, deep-dish, pepperoni and olive" or "I'll have a pepperoni and olive, deep-dish, large." They both mean the same thing. However, sometimes the order of the operators can change the meaning. Going to the lumberyard and ordering a six-foot-long two-by-four board is very different from asking for a four-foot-long two-by-six board.

Since the interpretation of a general word's meaning is up to the receiver of the message, such words have been used by psychics, fortunetellers, and astrologers for centuries. Look at the following examples with the general words in italics. Try to determine if any of these apply specifically to you and whether the astrological sign is yours.

- Astrological sign: Members of this sign are admired for their *generosity* and *sensitive* nature. They often make excellent businesspeople or salespeople because of their *honesty, skill,* and *genuine* communication.

- Psychic hotline: Someone you know is having *troubles.*
- Fortune cookie: You will *soon* receive *good news* from a *faraway place.*

What happened? When you were reading these sentences, you most likely added your own operators to gain some personal meaning. As you read about the astrological sign, did you think it was your sign? Nearly everyone wants to be admired for his or her generosity and honesty. You may have even thought of a specific person (spouse, child, or friend) or an event (giving a donation) to validate the idea that you are generous and honest.

The psychic understands that everyone knows someone who is having troubles. "Troubles" could be anything ranging from a flat tire to a life-threatening disease. The fortune cookie leaves you to interpret what "soon" means. Is it hours, days, or months? What is considered good news? How far is the faraway place? Basically, it is impossible to prove these statements to be false since they apply to almost any situation!

So why are pizza, horoscopes, and fortune cookies important? Because sometimes you want to use general words during sales calls and let the customers add their own meaning to them. For example, if you are meeting with an unsophisticated buyer, then general words can be used effectively. However, buyers today tend to be more sophisticated, so general words used by themselves are, in fact, meaningless. If you tell a customer your solution is "fast and reliable," what have you communicated? It's through the use of operators that specific meanings are added and meaningful communication is completed. If you tell a customer your solution is "fast and reliable, will print two hundred pages per minute, and has a 99.99 percent uptime rate," you have communicated something meaningful.

It's important to recognize the difference between general and specific words. In sales, general words are used predominantly to describe and market product advantages. Probably three of the most regularly used terms are "performance," "reliability," and "scalability."

The phrases below were taken from the website home pages of three prominent high-technology companies:

- "ABC Company enables organizations to exceed performance and reliability expectations."
- "DEF Company combines power and scalability to meet your business needs."
- "XYZ Solutions automatically and intelligently delivers the best possible performance and availability."

Other popular general terms include "new and improved," "flexibility," "manageability," "powerful," and "price performance." Little meaning can be derived from these product claims unless operators are added. Here's the point: when speaking with buyers, always validate the general claims about your products with specific features or specific examples to give credence and meaning to your statements.

Sales Call Strategy: Not all words are equally persuasive. General words such as "performance," "reliability," and "quality" by themselves are not influential. Operator words, words that improve the persuasiveness of general words, must be added to influence a customer's mind. Adding "nine hundred pages per hour" to define "performance" adds a comparison-point meaning. Adding "one hundred thousand hours mean time between failures" to specify "reliability" helps makes the general word more convincing.

Believability is improved when "lifetime guaranteed replacement" is associated with "quality."

33. Do You Have Congruence?

How people speak is a good indicator of congruence, the truthfulness of their communication. When people aren't telling the truth, their tempo speeds up or slows down, their volume gets louder or softer, and their tone is higher or lower than normal. For example, Visuals may slow down their speaking, Kinesthetics may speak faster, and Auditories may change their tone. In addition, people's choice of words will change when they are not telling the truth. People telling the truth will talk in a straightforward manner using ordinary terms. When creating misrepresentations, their word selection is more careful, and they tend to use more sophisticated words. They also speak with precision and are mindful not to repeat the same word twice, unlike in natural conversation.

Congruence is at the heart of persuasion. How can you improve your congruence during sales calls? First, you should know your product inside out. This alone will build your credibility. You can't believe in what you don't understand. You need to understand your company: its history, what makes it unique, how it compares to others, and its future direction. You need to understand the customers you sell to and the problems they face, and you need to understand yourself. Why would someone buy from you? What are your strengths and weaknesses?

Congruence is attained when thoughts and language are aligned to communicate the same conscious and subconscious message. Do you have congruence? Here's a short exercise to test your congruence. Take a moment to answer the following questions:

- Do you honestly believe customers are better off when they choose your product over your competition's?
- Do you think your company is the best in your industry?
- Do you truly believe in yourself and that you are in the right profession?

What were your answers? Do you exude conviction about your product, your company, and your profession? If not, why would you expect someone else to believe in you?

Sales Call Strategy: Consider what motivates you. If your fundamental concern is fortune and fame, each of your various layers of communication will reek of it, regardless of how well you think you have concealed or camouflaged your motives from the customer. On the flip side of the coin, if you honestly put others' interests before yours, you will subliminally send this important statement about relationships. You can still be competitive, aggressive, and forceful, so long as you're acting in the customer's best interests.

34. Mastering the Seven Sales Call Languages

Customers today are smarter. Information is not only easier to find but available in greater detail than ever before. In addition, technology has become a way of life. Via the Internet, customers can research products, prices, and opinions. Our cars, appliances, and toys have become computerized tools. Collectively, this has raised the level of sophistication (and skepticism) of the customers we must converse with and sell to. Power is definitely in the hands of today's buyers and the situation will only continue to get worse.

The orientation of customers has also changed. Customers are more self-accomplished and self-reliant. Not so long ago, the gas station attendant would pump your gas and the bank teller would handle your deposit. Today, you fill the tank yourself and bank online.

Your competitors have not sat idly by either. They've educated themselves about your products and sales tactics, and they're more focused on defeating you than ever. Fortunately, they usually believe the best way to defeat you is by frontal attack based upon their product features, when in reality, using language to build customer relationships is the winning strategy.

This strategy requires differentiating yourself from the competition by building a stronger relationship with the customer than the competition through the words you speak. Customers can think of you as a salesperson who is trying to sell something, a supplier with whom they do business, a strategic partner who is of significant importance to their business, or a trusted advisor whose opinions on business and personal matters is sought out and listened to. Obviously, a trusted advisor enjoys significant advantages over a salesperson.

The nature of conversational themes depends upon the nature of your relationship. Salespeople engage the customer in friendly conversation, suppliers talk about their products' capabilities and attributes, strategic partners discuss business matters, and trusted advisors talk about future plans along with the people and politics behind them.

In addition to conversational themes, you need to master the seven different languages used by salespeople and customers during sales calls. These languages can be divided into two categories. The lower-level languages are responsible for the personal connection between people and consist of the word catalog language, internal dialogue language, and physical language. The higher-level languages are logic and psychological appeal languages. They consist of the intersecting activity language, technical specification language, business operations language, and confidential language. Figure 34.1 represents these languages and their associated conversational themes.

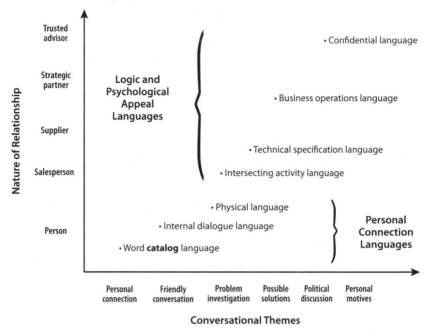

Figure 34.1 Ideal progression of languages during sales calls

When you strike up a conversation with customers you probably believe that everyone is speaking a common language. However, no universal language exists because everyone's mind is so distinct. People actually talk in many diverse languages. Therefore, if you want to communicate persuasively and learn how to make lasting impressions, you need to learn to speak each of the different languages.

Sales Call Strategy: To differentiate yourself from the competition, you must speak more impactful languages with your customers. The ideal progression during sales calls is to quickly establish a personal connection with the customer and then progress through the higher-level logic and psychological appeal languages with the ultimate goal of having the customer speak the confidential language with you.

35. Determining Your Sales Call Goal and Personal Outcome

The first step toward conducting a successful sales call is to determine your goal and outcome for the meeting. The ultimate goal for the sales call is simple: you want the customer to expose his internal dialogue to you. You want him to honestly explain what he is trying to accomplish and why he is doing it from a business and, more importantly, personal standpoint. You want him to tell you about his personal needs and career desires along with how he plans to fulfill them. You want him to speak the confidential language with you (see fig. 34.1).

You are not there to sell anything. Your goal is to become a trusted advisor by asking questions and intently listening to the answers so that you can apply your expertise to solve the customer's business problems or complete his initiatives. As figure 35.1 shows, the conversational theme starts with establishing a personal connection, and is followed by investigating the problem and discussing possible solutions. Ideally, the conversation flows into an off-the-record talk about the politics of his organization and his ulterior motives.

You might be worried that this important sales call may be your only chance to meet with the customer; therefore, you feel you *must* explain to him how wonderful your company and products are. However, if you go into this meeting with the intention of selling something, you'll be proven right: it will be the last time you get on his busy calendar.

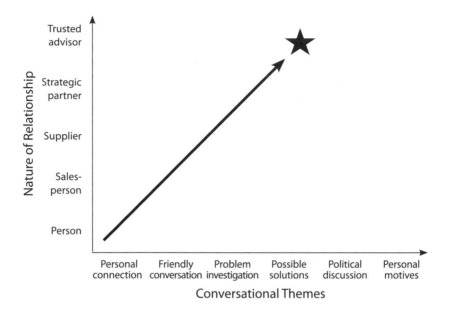

Figure 35.1 Trusted advisor goal

Never forget, that although you are excited about the meeting, the customer isn't that excited about your products and not all that interested in your marketing pitch. He's seen them and heard them before, and they all seem the same. You will be granted continual access if you can demonstrate how you can help solve his business problems and help him achieve his personal ambitions.

Unfortunately, the majority of sales call conversations never reach the confidential language. The discussion gets stuck at the technical specification language or the business operations language. Usually, this is because the salesperson is too busy talking about his products and what they do instead of what the customer wants to change. At other times, this is by design because the customer doesn't trust and believe in the salesperson enough to speak frankly and share his thoughts with him.

Moreover, too many meetings end without any definitive results. First meetings are short and the time passes quickly. Therefore, it is important to identify a specific personal outcome of the meeting beforehand so you can judge whether you have achieved your goal.

Professional athletes understand personal outcomes. Sprinters will visualize an entire race and see themselves on the winner's stand receiving the gold medal. College basketball coaches will ask their teams to mentally rehearse cutting down the net after they win the national championship.

Athletes describe their field of vision narrowing while they are focused on their personal outcome. A professional baseball player will see the stitches on a ninety-mile-per-hour fastball. Golfers surrounded by the gallery won't hear or see the crowd while they focus on the next putt.

Your personal outcome may be to have the customer tell you at the end of the meeting, "It sounds great. Send me your contract!" In this example, you create a mental picture of the person and hear those words being said as he shakes your hand. You can measure the success of the call based upon what actually happens and how closely that matches this visualization.

The tactical objectives for the meeting can be quite diverse. The objective could be to *gather* information and find out how you are perceived versus the competition or other details about the selection process. It could be to *impart* information about your products or make a special pricing offer. It could be to *create* relationships or *influence* opinions. It could be to *negotiate* terms and conditions.

Whatever the tactical objectives for your meeting may be, you should define the words the customer must say to know that they have been achieved. You want to hear the customer say something definitive like, "You are our preferred solution" or "Yes, we have a deal," not "We are still evaluating options" or "We'll consider that." Only when you hear the customer say the words that validate your meeting's outcome have you actually achieved it.

Sales Call Strategy: The most important difference between you and your competitors is not your products, your company, or the services and support you offer. It's you and your ability to build a deeper relationship with prospective customers. The proof of a successful sales call comes when the customer speaks the confidential language with you and shares the unedited thoughts of his internal dialogue.

Prior to every sales call, think about the exact words you would like the customer to say that proves he respects you. What would he say to show he trusts you more than the competition? What commitments would he make to you at the close of the meeting? Most importantly, how would he communicate the sales call was a success and he likes you and wants to see you again?

36. Intersecting Activity Language

All people have outside interests, hobbies, and personal pursuits by which they display their personalities, beliefs, and values. Think about all the potential non-business-related subjects you can discuss with your customers: cars, movies, wine, college, dieting, music, pets, investments, marriage, horse racing, golf, books, firearms, professional sports, raising children, and cigars.

Each intersecting activity also has a unique content layer language. In order to have a meaningful conversation about an intersecting activity, you need to understand its language. For example, a conversation about horse racing requires an understanding of terms such as "exacta," "furlong," and "maiden race." If you are talking with someone about wine, being able to discuss the difference between varietal and Meritage wines makes your participation in the conversation credible. Through the use and understanding of these common terms, rapport is established.

You can easily identify intersecting activities of customers by observing how they have decorated their cubicles or offices. Pictures of family vacations, mementos, awards, degrees and other personal artifacts convey their interests and the attributes of their personality.

Sales Call Strategy: Always engage the customer in a personal conversation about the intersecting activities you have in common. By doing so, you develop rapport with the *entire* person, not just the *business* person—building the foundation of a personal friendship that sets you apart from the competition.

37. Technical Specification Language

Every industry has developed its own language to facilitate mutual understanding of terminology and an exact meaning of the words used throughout the business. The technical specification language consists of these abbreviations, acronyms, business nomenclature, and specialized terms. Whether you are selling airplanes, computer chips, telephone equipment, or real estate, you need to know the terms and nomenclature of your industry. For example, if you sell telephone systems to businesses, you need to understand what "PBX," "PDC," and "ACD" mean. Since it is one of the primary languages your customers speak, you must be able to speak it fluently.

Technical specification languages have four major characteristics. First, unlike normal day-to-day language, words within a technical specification language have very narrow meanings. The language is precise and exact. For example, "100 Mbps" means "100 megabits per second," not 99 or 101. Second, the meaning of general words can be completely changed by the addition of operators. For example, a general term like "car" dramatically changes in meaning when "sports" or "luxury" is added in front of it and keeps changing in meaning when additional operators such as "BMW" or "Jaguar" are added. Third, the language is completely androgynous. In general, no reference is made to feminine or masculine characteristics. Finally, the language is usually nonpersonal. After all, it's referring to products, not people.

Unfortunately for salespeople, the technical specification language usually is adopted by customers as the default standard for all of their communication. This presents salespeople with a significant problem. They are trying to create a personal relationship with the buyer. However, the buyer is communicating in an androgynous, nonpersonal, technical language. More importantly, given the use of this unusual language, salespeople must somehow decipher the underlying meaning and intent of the customer's words.

In addition, the technical content of the language is the yardstick by which a customer's technical peer group (the team selecting a product) measures a person's relevant knowledge. Outside of formal titles, it's another way members of the peer group will establish a hierarchy. It's also how they will validate the sales team's value to them. Conversely, it is how the sales team members will present their product's features and the technical reasons for selecting their product.

It's the language C-level executives use to communicate with their subordinates and instruct them what to do. For example, the CIO may instruct the vice president of infrastructure that he would like to "Replicate the SAP IBM server data in New York to the NOC in Los Angeles." Obviously, a computer salesperson who doesn't understand these terms will have a difficult time winning the company's business.

Sales Call Strategy: The technical specification language is one of the primary languages that is used during sales calls. Therefore, you must know the technical specification language of your products and industry. You cannot expect to conduct successful sales calls and drive account strategy if you don't understand one of the fundamental languages your customers speak!

You must internalize the technical specification language and speak it fluently. Role-playing with your company's technical experts can help you practice and test your knowledge. Stay on top of the latest industry news. Start your own blog to demonstrate to prospective customers that you know their industry. Include the blog's URL on your business cards and in the signature line of every e-mail you send.

38. Business Operations Language

The business operations language is the language executives and managers use to run their organizations. A popular misconception is that you have to be a subject-matter expert to speak effectively with a C-level executive. For instance, you have to know financial accounting standards inside and out before you should even think about meeting with a CFO, you have to be a shop-floor control expert to meet with the vice president of manufacturing, or you must be an expert on corporate branding to hold an important conversation with a CMO.

While having a deep domain-area expertise is the ideal situation, in reality, all C-level executives, midlevel managers, and lower-level managers perform the same basic duties associated with running a company. They are either creating something new or controlling an ongoing process. These duties fall into "create" and "control" categories. The business operations language consists of these create and control descriptions:

CEO: Creates corporate direction through top-level business goals.

Controls which departmental initiatives will be undertaken to accomplish these goals.

VP of Sales: Creates revenue through customer relationship strategies.

Controls sales force behavior through compensation plans and sales forecasts.

CFO: Creates the financial plans to run the business.

Controls money through budgets, accounting practices, and company policies.

The orientation of the business operations language varies by the level of the organization you are selling into. First, the higher levels of the organization are responsible for short- and long-term organizational planning. Next, the lower levels of the organization are responsible for the execution of the plan as defined by management. Finally, the higher levels of the organization are responsible for the measurement of the execution of the plan by the lower levels as well as the plan's overall success. As a result, the create and control languages are spoken differently. People in the lower levels will tend to talk about their specific jobs and what they are trying to create, while people in the higher levels will speak about department goals. Successful customer communication is based upon providing relevant information and the language you use to send your message must be tailored to the person's organizational role and responsibility. Figure 38.1 illustrates these differences.

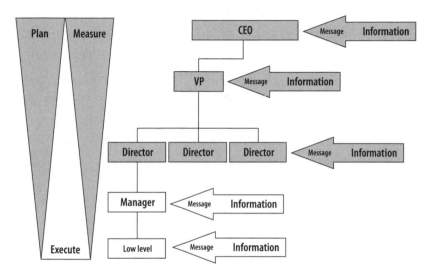

Figure 38.1. Business operations language differences by organization level

Think about the seniormost executive you met during a very important recent sales call. Check each of the following create and control functions that are applicable to that person's role in the organization.

Create
___ Prepare and present the fiscal budget.

___ Provide forecasts.

___ Implement new programs and policies, and provide their general administrative direction.

___ Develop and execute departmental best practices.

___ Sign financial agreements and long-term contractual agreements.

___ Provide justification for all recommendations and decisions on capital expenditures.

___ Conduct new business development activities to promote growth or decrease costs.

___ Foster departmental and company communication.

___ Build positive relationships with customers, the press, trade associations, and industry organizations.

___ Develop and maintain relations with employees, customers, and the community.

___ Maintain responsibility for the selection, appointment, and retention of key management personnel.

Control

___ Administer the management of daily operations.

___ Analyze operating results versus established objectives.

___ Take appropriate steps to reverse unsatisfactory results.

___ Work closely with other departmental executives to ensure the company is functioning smoothly.

___ Supervise budget performance throughout the year.

___ Ensure that the growth of the company is in accordance with identified goals.

___ Maintain the desired quality of products, customer service, and professionalism.

___ Ensure that the company is in compliance with federal laws and local regulations.

___ Operate the organization in a profitable manner.

___ Provide oversight of and make recommendations for business initiatives.

___ Resolve all departmental business and human relations problems.

___ Ensure that the company's policies are uniformly understood and administered by subordinates.

__ Establish standards for managerial performance.

__ Recommend staffing and compensation changes within the organization.

__ Approve all personnel promotions and staff reductions, and oversee the hiring/firing processes.

__ Conduct periodic performance and salary reviews of personnel.

Let's assume that you sell network performance management software and are meeting with the chief information officer at a new account you are trying to close. Before the call, you write down five create and control attributes of your solution that you plan to discuss using the business operations language.

Create

1. Improve the perception of the information technology organization within the company.
2. Improve responsiveness to the company's changing business needs.
3. Improve systems uptime and availability.
4. Maximize the existing infrastructure's life span.
5. Use staff more effectively, focusing on highly visible company projects.

Control

1. Reduce departmental staffing costs.
2. Control unexpected capital outlays.
3. Eliminate crisis situations that defocus daily operations.
4. Reduce IT project delays.
5. Control the demands of remote device support (smartphones and tablets) on IT.

Ideally, you should prepare offensive call statements (see chapter 46) for each of the create and control points above. The offensive call statements explain how you accomplish the create or control objective using meaningful terms, specific benefits, and proof points.

Since a sales call is based upon the exchange of information, it is critical to tailor your message and deliver it corresponding to the person's level in the organization. Let's assume you are meeting with a low-level network engineer at the same account as the CIO above. The create and control points you discuss will be focused on the engineer's ability to better execute his daily job duties:

Create

1. Improve daily effectiveness by quickly identifying the source of performance issues.
2. Make troubleshooting of network problems easier.
3. Proactively test and audit network performance.
4. Create network readiness prior to new technology deployment.
5. Increase the speed of network performance and throughput.

Control

1. Reduce network downtime.
2. Reduce the number of open support tickets.
3. Reduce escalations.
4. Reduce travel time to remote sites.
5. Reduce the number of network analysis tools used.

Now it's time for you to conduct a short exercise. Write down the title of the person you typically meet with on sales calls. Then list five create and control points the person would find important. Go ahead and write in the book, or list your ideas on a piece of paper.

Title:

Create		Control	
1. _____		1. _____	
2. _____		2. _____	
3. _____		3. _____	
4. _____		4. _____	
5. _____		5. _____	

Congratulations. If you completed the exercise, you now officially know how to speak the business operations language.

Sales Call Strategy: The create and control discussion will vary depending upon the organizational level of the person you are speaking with. People in higher levels will be more interested in planning and measurement, while people in the lower levels will focus on tactical execution. Certain features and functions of your solution are associated with create and control tasks. Be sure to adjust your message and the manner in which you speak to mirror the business operations language of the customer you are meeting with.

39. Selling Value

Customers spend far more time living with their decisions than they do making the decisions. In fact, the decision to start a project or buy a particular product is usually made before the official decision-making process even begins. Unfortunately, I have some very frightening news to share with you based upon thousands of interviews with customers as part of the win-loss analysis studies I have conducted on behalf of my clients.

Approximately 30 percent of the time, the winner of the sales cycle was determined before the "official" selection process started.

Another 45 percent of the time, customers had already made up their minds about whom they were going to buy from about half-way through the process. That means 75 percent of the time, customers had made their decision by halfway through the process. Only 25 percent of the time did customers make their final decision at the end of the selection process. Therefore, if you are not clearly in the lead at the midpoint of the selection process, the odds are that you are going to lose. Figure 39.1 illustrates this point.

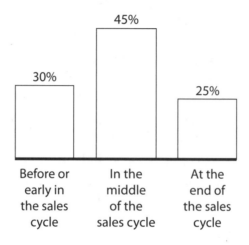

Figure 39.1 When customers made up their minds

Here's another frightening fact. In almost every case, the decision wasn't even close between the top two choices. Even though customers had made up their minds, they still caused all the other salespeople to jump through a series of hoops for nothing, wasting their valuable time, resources, and mental and emotional energy.

The customer's evaluation criteria could be extremely well documented. A request for proposal (RFP) may be three hundred pages long, with descriptive narrations about the customer's environment and very detailed questions about the vendor. However, this is only the external aspect of product selection. The internal, political part of product selection isn't publicly revealed. Establishing rapport is the only way to learn the true inner workings of a customer's selection process. In order to build customer rapport, we must demonstrate the value of our products, our company, and our self. We must be able to convince the customer of the unique psychological value, political value, operational value, and strategic value we provide.

Psychological Value

At the root of every decision is one of four psychological values. People buy products they believe will help them fulfill deep-seated psychological needs: satisfying the ego, being accepted as part of a group, avoiding pain, and ensuring survival. All the other outward appearances of a customer's decision-making process—the analysis, return-on-investment calculations, and other internal studies—are the means to achieving an overriding psychological goal. Therefore, the psychological value is the most important value when it comes to purchasing decisions.

I have interviewed thousands of customers as part of the win-loss studies I conduct for my clients. The most important finding from these studies is that human nature is the ultimate decision maker for every major decision. While the customer may have publicly recited a laundry list of rational reasons to justify the decision he made, he truthfully revealed in private that politics, self-interests, and personal emotions were responsible for the selection in the end.

Customers do not establish vendor relationships based upon the best business judgment; rather, they judge vendors based upon who establishes the best business relationships. A CIO I interviewed said it best: "We made it clear that we weren't buying a brochure or data sheet. For that matter, we weren't even buying a product. We were buying a long-term relationship with another company and, equally important, the team of people from that company whom we would have to work with on a day-in, day-out basis."

Political Value

The second most important value, political value, involves organizational power. Many people think that power is dependent upon title and that the way work gets done in organizations is through hierarchical authority. However, this is not usually the case. Power is the ability to influence the environment for your own benefit. It is often used to get your way when diplomacy, consensus building, and negotiation fail. For example, while I have parental authority over my children, they have their own types of powers and associated strategies to get their way. Sometimes they will band together and recruit their mother to support their cause in order to override my authority. Companies operate in much the same way.

Your product provides customers the opportunity to achieve political power. It may enable them to increase their authority, help them become indispensable to the company, allow them to satisfy an internal powerbroker, or enable them to maintain authority. Interdepartmental coordination always involves the use of power. Your product can make someone more powerful, or for those seeking to become more influential, it can provide much-needed visibility that enables them to be in contact with the company's powerbrokers.

Operational Value

The third most important value is operational value. People's success in an organization is dependent upon the success of their department's operations. Therefore, every department has inherent pressure to accomplish projects that successfully add operational value.

The ways that operational value is determined are quite diverse. An ambitious manager might consider your product's operational value the ability to successfully complete the department's project that enables his department to proliferate its services throughout the company. Another customer might prize satisfying internal customers in other departments, and operational value to some might be found in products that enable them to resist change. For example, a bureaucratic IT department might add a new Internet interface to its existing mainframe rather than replace the entire system.

You can also think of operational value in terms of the customer's résumé—a list of all his successful projects and accomplishments. After the customer purchases your solution, what accomplishment or milestones would he add to his résumé?

Strategic Value

Strategic value, the fourth value, is based upon the appearance of rationality and impartiality. However, customers do not seek information that will help them make an objective strategic decision; they amass information that helps them justify their preconceived ideas of strategic value. In other words, your product's strategic value comprises the reasons and arguments evaluators give to senior management and others in the company as to why the product should be purchased, regardless of whether the reasons are real or imagined.

The seven basic types of strategic value enable customers to

- Gain a competitive advantage (increase market share, enter new markets, defeat competition)
- Increase revenues
- Decrease costs
- Increase productivity and efficiency

- Improve customer satisfaction
- Improve quality
- Standardize operations (increase ease of business)

Some customers will say that a purchase provides a competitive advantage or will enable them to increase revenues. Others might argue internally that a purchase will save money in the long run. Some will show how customer satisfaction will be improved or detail improvements in operational efficiency.

Sales Call Strategy: Before every sales call, write down your psychological, political, operational, and strategic value to the customer. During the sales call, present your solution to the potential buyer based upon these four values. You must communicate that *you* and *your solution* can help solve critical department problems, help the customer become an expert and an internal source of knowledge, and help him become successful and more powerful, and that you are providing a safe, long-term solution.

40. Confidential Language

The most important language spoken during sales calls is the confidential language. While the business operations language (see chapter 38) is a process-based language about what customers do on a daily basis, the confidential language is a personal language based upon what they want to do in the future. It's the language associated with the human nature of self-promotion and leading a group of people to accomplish a specific objective.

The confidential language is the most significant language spoken on sales calls. It's the language of strategic planning because it provides the customer's personal motivations for pursuing a project, the internal politics of the organization, and the unedited truth about the customer's real goals.

The confidential language has two variations, and sometimes it's easy to confuse the two. Companies and the executives who run them have a natural need to protect their images. The "public" confidential language is spoken when the customer is toeing the company line about why he is doing what he is doing. This is the official version for public consumption versus the off-the-record truth. When he's speaking the public confidential language, he is telling you the same thing he is saying to your competitors.

The "true" confidential language is spoken when the customer treats you like a confidant and shares his personal reasons why he is initiating a project and what he hopes to personally gain when it succeeds. Like a close friend, he discusses his private matters and problems with you. However, he will speak the true confidential language to only one of the salespeople competing for his business. He doesn't want to run the risk of having his true motives publicly known.

Quite often, salespeople mistake the public language for the true confidential language. In the following exercise, try to determine whether each statement below is the public or true confidential language:

1. "Let me be honest with you: if this project doesn't succeed, we'll probably have to cut two thousand jobs at our Dallas operation."
2. "The strategic goal of this project is to improve our workforce efficiency during the next twelve months."
3. "Our win rate is decreasing and the CEO keeps pointing his finger at me, telling me to fix it now."
4. "Our goal is to increase sales by 10 percent, and this will require great changes to the company."

5. "Our employees act like they work for the post office. Our new CEO and I are on a mission to change this antiquated monolithic organization into a state-of-the-art customer-driven company."

The odd-numbered sentences are examples of the true confidential language. They are personal revelations that would not typically be shared with someone who wasn't trusted. They reveal the customer's off-the-record opinion, personal dilemma, and ulterior motives, as well as the stress he is under. They aren't statements that would be made in public for everyone to hear. They would be said only to a salesperson who was trusted. The even-numbered sentences are examples of the public confidential language. They're generic statements that could have been said to all the salespeople because they aren't personally revealing.

In order to achieve your ultimate goal of speaking the true confidential language, you must be able to speak in each of the seven different sales call languages summarized in figure 40.1. By doing so, you will establish credibility and trust and use common languages that are at the foundation of meaningful communication.

Sales Call Strategy: Always keep the following principles in mind regarding the confidential language. First, you must be able to distinguish the true confidential language from the public version. Otherwise, your sales strategy will be based upon false information. Second, customers will speak the true confidential language to only one of the salespeople they are selecting from. Therefore, you should always assume they are speaking it with one of your competitors if they are not speaking it with you. Finally, confidentiality is not freely granted by customers. It is earned through multiple interactions over time. This requires you to speak in all seven of the sales calls languages and prove you can be trusted.

Confidential language	The most powerful trust-based language by which the customer explains his personal needs, desires, and plans along with the strategy by which he hopes to fulfill them
Business operations language	The language that is specific to the daily running of the customer's business and his role in the organization
Technical specification language	The androgynous, nonpersonal, and technical communication that is based upon the nomenclature and technical terms of the customer's industry
Intersecting activity language	Interests, hobbies, and personal pursuits by which the customer displays his personality, beliefs and values
Physical language dialogue	Also known as body language, the nonverbal communication that is constantly being emitted by the customer's body posture
Internal dialogue language	The never-ending stream of communication inside the mind that represents honest, unedited, and deep feelings
Word catalog	The mind's method for receiving, interpreting, and transmitting information based upon the three sensory channels—visual, auditory, and kinesthetic

Figure 40.1 The seven sales call languages

41. Sales Call Themes

The objective of every sales call is to build deal momentum. You should always be gaining momentum with the account and need to have tangible evidence that the deal is moving in your direction. Evidence of this movement includes the elimination of other vendors, meetings with upper management or people involved in procurement, and other buying signs such as contract reviews. The three underlying sales call themes that enable you to build deal momentum are your personal demeanor, your communication style, and the messages you deliver, as shown in figure 41.1.

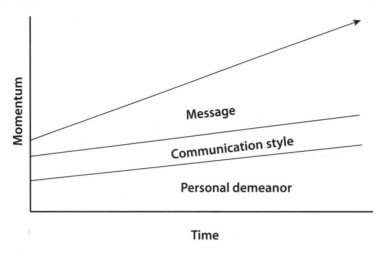

Figure 41.1 The three underlying sales call themes

You can think of personal demeanor as your physical presence. For example, some salespeople have such a lighthearted presence that customers will buy almost anything to keep them around—they're attracted to a humorous type of presence. Other customers want to associate with someone better than themselves, a person who has a character trait they feel they lack. For example, they may want to be around someone more outgoing, confident, charming, attractive, or worldly.

Our communication styles vary, depending upon whom we are presenting our arguments to. For example, persuading a child to eat peas is much different from persuading your company's board of directors to pass your resolution. However, during sales calls, many salespeople become like Shakespearian actors on center stage. They feel compelled to prove they know every line of their company's sales script. Giving long orations about your product will not win over the customer's heart, whereas speaking passionately will.

Honest enthusiasm for your company and its products will permeate your customer's mind. The most persuasive salespeople are passionate about the company they work for and what they do for a living. However, their passion is not ostentatiously displayed like a cheerleader's pompoms. It is displayed in the confident way they demonstrate their product knowledge, the ease with which they talk about their company, and the cheerful disposition with which they approach their job.

Tailor your message to individuals rather than using a one-size-fits-all approach, reciting the same pitch to every prospect. Instead, you want everyone you meet with to take away his or her own personal message from your presentation. You want each person to have a positive feeling about your solution and how it will impact his or her role in the company. We'll cover how to structure messages in further detail in chapter 42.

Remember that everyone has a primary, secondary, and recessive word catalog (see chapter 15). When you construct and communicate your message by speaking with words matching the customer's primary catalog, moving to his secondary catalog, and ending in his recessive catalog, you will have a profound impact on your listener. This persuasion technique is called the "recessive word catalog access technique." It requires that you understand your customer's word catalogs explicitly and are able to establish and maintain intense rapport.

The primary catalog is the catalog most frequently used by the conscious mind during daily conversation, while the recessive catalog is the least used and can be thought of as being "closer" to the internal dialogue. Assuming rapport is present, as you access each progressively weaker catalog, the listener's internal dialogue becomes more relaxed. The consciousness of the internal dialogue starts to diminish, and it is lulled into an inward thought process as it disengages from the conversation. If you execute this technique correctly by patiently moving to the recessive catalog in a natural manner, you will ultimately put this person into a hypnotic trance.

Have you ever had conversations with people who mesmerized you? As they spoke, you could feel yourself slipping away, but you didn't fight it; in fact, it felt good. It wasn't so much the content of their words but their manner of speech that made you feel so relaxed and at ease. It was almost as if your ears were being tickled and your mind was being massaged. If this has ever happened to you, whether in person, over the phone, or even while watching television, most likely the speaker had a primary word catalog that was the opposite of yours and was naturally accessing your recessive catalog.

Sales Call Strategy: Regardless of how long you have been in sales and how accomplished you believe you are, you need to regularly evaluate your personal demeanor, your communication style, and the messages you are sending during sales calls. Therefore, I strongly suggest you make a video of yourself giving a fictitious sales presentation. In addition, use your smartphone to record your side of the conversation for the next five phone calls you make. Then while watching your video and listening to your calls, ask yourself this important question: If you were the customer, would you buy from yourself?

42. Sales Call Structure

From a sales linguistic perspective, each of the underlying sales call themes introduced in chapter 41 (personal demeanor, communication style, and message) has three stages, and each stage requires different linguistic strategies. The opening stage comprises the few minutes at the beginning of the call, the main stage is the longest period of interaction between the salesperson and customer, and the closing stage is time at the end of the call. Each of the stages has different linguistic components, as shown in figure 42.1.

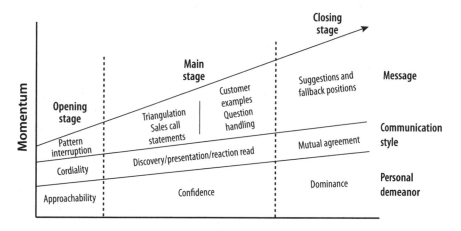

Figure 42.1 The stages and linguistic components of a sales call

Your personal demeanor should vary at each stage, moving from approachability (not overfriendliness) in the opening to confidence when talking about your company's products and answering questions in the main stage. At the close, you want to establish dominance, where the customer follows your opinions and advice.

Your initial communication style should be cordial initially (courteous and genuine). In the main stage of the call, you first conduct discovery by asking questions and using a communication style based upon curiosity. Next, you present ideas that are tailored to the customer's benefactions. Your "reaction read" is how you gauge the verbal and nonverbal reactions (acceptance, rejection, or indifference) the customer transmits after hearing your call statements. It's also your overall opinion of the customer participants in the meeting. Who is for you? Who is against you? And who can be swayed? The closing stage communication style is based upon mutual agreement where both the customer and salesperson are saying the same thing.

The opening message you deliver at every sales call should be a pattern interruption, which differentiates you from the competition. The main session consists of triangulation to ensure you are receiving accurate information, sales call statements, customer examples specifically selected for the customer, and an individualized question-handling strategy. During the sales call close, you offer the customer suggestions and have prepared fallback positions in case your suggestions are rejected by the customer. We'll cover each of these linguistic components in more detail in the following chapters.

Sales Call Strategy: How do you plan your sales calls? If you cannot articulate your plan aloud, you don't have one. Break every sales call into stages and take the time to choreograph each stage beforehand.

43. Using Pattern Interruption and Cowcatchers

Put yourself in the position of the customer for a moment. You've sat through hundreds of different sales presentations through the years. Because these presentations have been based upon marketing propaganda, one of your primary objectives is to delineate fact from fiction. Therefore, you are skeptical.

You've also met hundreds of salespeople and have found many of them to be friendly, courteous, and professional. Each of them also wants to build a personal relationship with you. You can't let this happen. You aren't going to build a friendship with everyone when you know you are going to select only one person to do business with. That wouldn't be practical or comfortable. Therefore, you are reserved and on guard and you keep your distance.

You also have met your share of truly obnoxious salespeople who were pushy, arrogant or just plain incompetent. Some salespeople lied straight to your face and broke their promises. They overcommitted what their products could do and misled you about what they couldn't. You don't want anything to do with liars. As a result, you initially treat every salesperson you meet with extreme wariness.

Now if you're the salesperson meeting this customer, the first step of your call should be to perform a pattern interruption to break the customer's mode of thinking and stand out from the competition. The pattern interruption starts the process of building rapport, engages customer interest, and provokes open-mindedness. It successfully sets the stage for the remainder of the sales call.

But what exactly is a pattern interruption? Let me explain with the following analogy. An Apple iPod can store thousands of songs. We have several iPods in my household, and I frequently listen to my teenage daughter's to check out the latest hits. As I thumb through her playlists, each song has just a few seconds to capture my attention. If the introduction isn't interesting, different, or exciting, I immediately move on to the next song. The term I use to describe this critical lead-in is "cowcatcher."

Most people associate the term "cowcatcher" with the metal grill on the front of a locomotive. However, "cowcatcher" has an entirely different meaning in the entertainment industry. It's a show's opening moments in which the performers try to grab your attention and cause you to stop and look. The best meetings and presentations start with a great cowcatcher.

A great cowcatcher engages the mind, appeals to the imagination, and helps the presenter gain credibility. For example, I worked at a company whose core technology was originally developed by the California Institute of Technology and funded by a grant from NASA. Explaining the origins of the company during presentations—not with one simple slide with a few bullet points but using highlights of the project and its results set against the black backdrop of outer space with its millions of stars—was a great cowcatcher. We differentiated ourselves and gained instant credibility.

Another company I worked for was the top-rated NASDAQ stock for a period of five years. In fact, during one two-year time frame, $32,000 worth of this company's stock grew to be worth $1,000,000. I always opened my presentations with a chart of the stock price and some facts about the stock's appreciation. The customers would be more than intrigued; they were downright fascinated and eager to learn more. Many would buy my company's stock that very day!

Sales Call Strategy: Customers are not only skeptical, they're nervous. Meeting someone new is a stressful experience, and the customer's internal dialogue is on high alert. One of the biggest challenges you face is establishing a sufficient level of customer rapport to ensure your message is received in an open and honest manner. This is why you must interrupt customers' patterns of negative thinking and lower their natural defenses.

From this point forward, begin every telephone call, every sales call, and every customer presentation with a pattern interruption. Differentiate yourself and your product from other attention-getting solutions using a unique cowcatcher that engages the listener's internal dialogue. Never forget, that in order to stand out, you have to be long-remembered.

44. Finding Your Position with Triangulation

You and I filter information consciously and subconsciously all the time. While most salespeople operate in a world of incomplete or incorrect customer information, Heavy Hitters have a different strategy, called "triangulation." Triangulation is the process of identifying your position by using three or more data points. Heavy Hitters constantly try to triangulate their position by answering these questions: Is there a deal? Am I winning? Whom do I have to watch out for, and what can ruin this deal?

The following discussion shows how you can carry out the triangulation process. It is based on the metaphor of a baseball diamond, shown in figure 44.1. (After all, Heavy Hitters are trying to score a home run!)

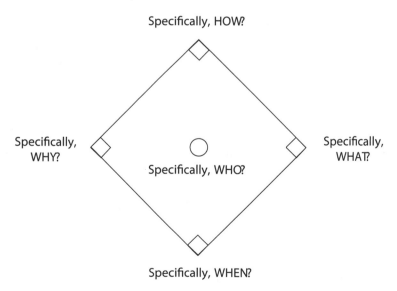

Figure 44.1 The triangulation diamond

First Base

On the triangulation diamond, first base is the "what" base. What are the content-level words being spoken by the prospects? What specifically do these words mean? You are trying to determine as specifically as possible what the customers mean when they speak. Questions asked on first base include the following:

- Specifically, what are you trying to accomplish?
- Specifically, what business problem are you trying to solve?
- Specifically, what technical problem are you trying to solve?

As the customers answer these questions, you're trying to decipher their high-level requirements into very specific targeted needs. For example, let's say you sell a financial application and are meeting with prospects who are unhappy with their company's accounting system. You need to help them define exactly what is making them unhappy. Is it functionality, performance, ease of use, support, or flexibility? Suppose it's functionality. Is it accounts payable, accounts receivable, human resources, or integration? Suppose it's accounts receivable. Is it customer creation, payment application, or delinquent accounts reporting?

You are trying to get to the very specific cause of pain or dissatisfaction, the more detailed the better. Members of the customer team participating in the meeting will each have his own prioritized list of pain points, and these should be understood in detail. Since you have been on hundreds of similar sales calls before, you must fight the urge to assume you know what the pain points are. Treat every sales call like a one-of-a-kind experience. Once you have triangulated with the group about the pain points, put them in writing so you can uniquely explain how you and your product solve each individual's pain, particularly in comparison with other solutions being evaluated.

Second Base

Second base is the "how" base. Use second base to understand how the customers will take action. Again, try to determine in as much detail as possible how the sales process will happen by asking specifically how the customers will accomplish a task. Questions asked on second base include the following:

- Specifically, how will you make a decision?
- Specifically, how will you implement the solution?
- Specifically, how will you determine if it is successful?

You will want to know the prospects' evaluation criteria, the steps of the evaluation, and how they will determine if the evaluation is successful. Members of your triangulation team will gather this information from their respective contacts. Together, they will compile and assimilate the results. From this exercise, you will identify areas of product strength, weakness, and information you don't know. Once again, don't assume anything. Rather, you want the customer to provide clear verbal answers to your questions.

Third Base

Now that you know specifically what customers are planning and how they intend to accomplish their goal, you need to understand why. Third base is the "why" base where you want to understand the following from the company's perspective:

- Specifically, why is the company evaluating a new financial system?
- Specifically, why is our product a better fit than our competitor's?
- Specifically, why would the company select our product?

The second element of "why" is the personal agendas of the individuals involved with the initiative. Items on these agendas are called "benefactions," personal benefits that come from taking a particular action (see chapter 2). Our definition of "benefaction" is "an advantage that contributes to one's well-being, such as happiness, esteem, power, or wealth, and that results in influencing the way the person behaves during the sales cycle." At the personal level, ask the following questions about each participant in the customer's selection process:

- Specifically, why is this particular person on the evaluation team?
- Specifically, why would this person endorse our product?
- Specifically, why would this person oppose our product?

Home Plate

After rounding third base, you are headed for home plate. Home is the "when" base. Even if you reach third base every time you hit the ball, you don't score until you reach home. All the work the Heavy Hitter has done on the account is moot if the customer doesn't have a time frame to evaluate, decide, and purchase. On home plate, the questions include the following:

- Specifically, when will the evaluation start and finish?
- Specifically, when will a decision be made?
- Specifically, when will the customer buy?

The Pitcher's Mound

In baseball, the pitcher can throw the ball to any base at any time. The pitcher's position represents "who." "Who" can be applied to each base to determine who decided on the criteria, who will perform the evaluation, who will make the decision, and who will buy.

Triangulation is a technique for comparing multiple data points to determine your true position. Ideally, we want to identify and validate information using different customer sources. The various members of the customer's evaluation team are going to give contradictory information. Since we all have our own perception of reality, this isn't surprising. The intent of the triangulation process is to identify these subtle or obvious differences. Areas of contention or contradiction require further investigation and analysis.

Think of triangulation as the rule of three. Ideally, you want to ask every qualification question from the triangulation diamond at least three times, in three different ways, with at least three different members of the customer's evaluation team so you can compare the various responses from each person.

Sales Call Strategy: While the topics of discussion during every sales will vary greatly, every sales call provides an opportunity to triangulate your position and the customer's true motives by asking questions. The triangulation strategy is based upon the metaphor of a baseball diamond. By associating triangulation with a baseball diamond, your mind is able to visualize and more easily remember the steps of the qualification process. The analogy of running the bases creates mental tags that will help you recall which line of questions should be asked while the sales call progresses.

The triangulation diamond also serves as an important reminder that the dynamics of every sales call are completely unique. If you are a senior salesperson, you've probably participated in thousands of sales calls. After so many customer interactions, the mind tends to generalize the experience. Many times, you are actually going through the motions of account qualification. You assume information that isn't true, ignore important details, and misinterpret critical facts. Occasionally, you will be jolted back to reality when you are blindsided by a surprising loss. A quick review of the qualification diamond before important sales calls will remind you that you must never take any sales situation for granted and that discovering reality is a main objective.

45. Asking Questions to Discover Reality

There's no such thing as reality; it doesn't exist. Most likely, you find this statement hard to believe. After all, you are a real person reading a real book. However, please allow me to explain why this is actually the case.

While absolute reality—the world as it truly is—does exist, no one is able to experience it. We don't know exactly what absolute reality is because we each experience our own individual version of reality. Your reality is based upon your conscious and subconscious minds' perception, and my reality is based upon my minds' perception. And since every mind is different from the next, people's perceptions of reality vary. Therefore, if everyone's interpretation of reality is different, reality doesn't actually exist.

Perhaps an analogy will help you better understand the concept of individual reality. Pretend for a moment that you are in an airplane en route from New York to Los Angeles in seat 9B. You're wedged between two larger passengers and quite uncomfortable because they are using both armrests. The passenger to your left in seat 9A is peacefully sound asleep, and you can hear his slow, deep snoring. The businessman to your right in 9C is concentrating on his laptop. He's making last-minute adjustments to the Power-Point presentation he'll give tomorrow. The retired couple sitting in front of you are poring over sightseeing maps of Los Angeles. They are chatting excitedly about attractions they plan to see. You peer into the first-class section and notice that the passenger in seat 6D is comfortably enjoying his fourth glass of wine.

The reality is that all of these passengers are on an airplane heading for Los Angeles. However, each of them is having a completely different experience from the others. Each is in a completely different set of mental, physical, and emotional states. Just as each has an individual seat number, each has an individual reality. As a result, no one of them can experience absolute reality.

The same is true when you are meeting with a customer. While both of you are physically present at the meeting, you each have a different mental orientation, level of attentiveness, and way of sensing the world. Therefore, the overall success or failure of a sales call is determined by your ability to adapt yourself and your use of language to access the customer's reality. In order to adapt, you must ask questions to discover the customer's unique point of view. For instance, if the passengers in first class were asked about their flight, they would probably give a much different answer than if they were seated in coach class.

One of the most important parts of the sales call is at the beginning of the main stage when you have the opportunity to ask questions (see fig. 42.1). This is your "discovery" part of the sales call, and the customer's answers help you determine his word catalog wiring and find intersecting activities in common. The questions you ask also provide the opportunity to demonstrate your command of the technical specification language (see chapter 37) used in your industry and show the customer that you understand how his company runs by speaking the business operations language (see chapter 38). Successful discovery is the first step toward building a foundation of trust and respect that leads to the customer speaking the confidential language (see chapter 40).

Remember, everyone operates in his or her own individual reality. While you may have had twenty meetings with low-level and midlevel personnel within the company you're meeting with, the goal of asking the questions is triangulation. Triangulation is the process of checking multiple data points of information about an account with various decision makers to ensure the information is accurate and true. In order to identify true reality, these data points should always include information from C-level executives.

Suppose we sell enterprise software to banks and we have our first meeting with the CFO of Acme Bank, one of the world's largest banks. We are competing against Archrival Software. We assemble our sales team and make a list of all the possible questions we can ask the CFO. The five types of questions to ask customers are based upon the triangulation diamond (fig. 44.1) and asking what, how, why, when, and who. Here are some of the questions we could ask:

> What would you say the top five most significant challenges are?
> What has prevented you from addressing these business challenges in the past?
> What metrics does your CEO tend to be most interested in?
> What is the toughest part of your job?
> What are the three most important qualities you look for in a business partner?
> Why are you looking for new software?
> Why wasn't this project started a year ago?
> Why are these problems getting attention now?
> Why is your budget $10 million for this project?
> Why are you in charge of this decision, as opposed to the CIO or COO?
> How long have you worked at Acme? Where were you before?
> How familiar are you with us and the solutions that we offer?

How do projects get prioritized, and what is this project's priority?

How do we stack up against the competition?

When will the evaluation be complete?

When will the contract approval process start, and how long would it take to get the project approved?

When can we show you a demonstration?

Who prioritizes projects like this, and how are they prioritized?

Who else are you looking at right now?

Who will be part of the evaluation team? Why have they been selected?

With whom should we work in each step of the evaluation process?

Are you aware that Big World Bank is now moving to our solution because of our superior service and track record?

What are the most important questions to ask? It depends. Aside from qualification questions, the best questions to ask are called "hypothetical questions" and "leading questions."

Hypothetical questions enable you to gauge the strength of your personal relationship and include questions like below:

Would you like to meet with our president next Thursday when he is in town?

We usually partner very closely with our customer executives and have regular advisory council meetings. Would you like to attend one?

Would you like to make site visits to other financial institutions that are using our solution?

Would you like to attend the Super Bowl with me next weekend?

Leading questions are planned in advance so that the customer's answers guide the discussion to your product's unique strategic and operational value. For example, you could ask, "What metrics does your CEO tend to be most interested in?" in order to provide the opportunity to explain the unique metrics your executive dashboard provides. Take a moment to complete the following exercise. Write down five leading questions you could ask on your next sales call.

1. _____

2. _____

3. _____

4. _____

5. _____

Sales Call Strategy: Obviously, you won't be able to ask a hundred questions during a brief sales call. Therefore, you must prioritize your list beforehand to ensure it includes your top ten most important qualification and leading questions. Even though you may have asked the same questions many times of low-level and midlevel personnel, you need to ascertain reality according to the C-level executive in charge. The C-level executive's perception of the pain, problem, and future plans may be vastly different than the reality that has been presented to you by his staff. Finally, ask hypothetical questions to ascertain the level of customer rapport you have developed.

46. Using Offensive Call Statements

After the salesperson has been allotted a certain amount of time by the customer to ask introductory questions, the natural flow of the sale call shifts to the call statements phase. You may recall that I made this statement in chapter 8, "When you make a sales call, you are not talking to people. You are actually talking to their internal dialogues." The purpose of call statements is to talk to and guide the customer's internal dialogue. The structure of call statements is very important because as listeners receive information, they check with their internal dialogue to verify a statement's accuracy.

Here are a couple of exercises to familiarize yourself with internal dialogue. First, start counting backward from one hundred to one. As you are counting, try to sense the specific number at which your mind starts to wander. At that point, try to sense when your internal dialogue starts another conversation with itself or when it turns inward and becomes lost. Note that as it turns inward, you are still aware of your surroundings. So you may have to close your eyes while you try to focus on the task at hand, counting backward.

Overwhelming people's word catalogs causes their internal dialogue to start an intense conversation with itself and turn inward. When turning inward, the internal dialogue changes from being externally focused on the outside world to internally focused within the mind. The point of reference of the senses changes from outside the body to the exclusive conversation with oneself. This also happens when people pray, meditate, chant, or engage in activities that require intense concentration, such as painting or drawing. One way to think of it is as self-hypnosis.

Now try a slightly different experiment. Say the alphabet backward. You will notice it is harder to do since there isn't a sequential relationship or pattern between the letters. Therefore, you may have had to first say the alphabet forward in order to reverse it. This requires more concentration and creates a more engaging task for your internal dialogue so it cannot turn inward as easily. When it does, it is more likely to be from frustration rather than the boredom associated with counting backward.

The point of these two exercises is to prove to you that the structuring of information can have a profound influence on the customer's internal dialogue and mental state. The way you say something can guide customers to accept your thoughts or it can frustrate them.

As we discussed earlier about generic words (see chapter 32), little meaning can be derived from standard product claims unless operators are added. Here's how to incorporate operators into call statements. Start with a high-level statement and then continue to define the statement into meaningful terms, specific benefits, and proof points:

We	help save you money
	increase your revenues
	provide better technology
	offer a more comprehensive solution
	provide better functionality or ease of use
Because of our	superior technology or functionality
	quality, people, customer service, or support
	ease of use or breakthrough paradigm
In comparison to	the way you conduct business today
	how the competitor's product operates
	how your existing process functions
As a benefit, you will	increase revenues by 30 percent
	save 25 percent
	improve your output by 3,000 units
	achieve 45 percent improvement

For example	ABC Company implemented our solution and has saved $750,000 in the first six months
	DEF Company increased revenues by $10 million in the first year
	XYZ Company improved production by 400 units per day
Final proof point	I would be delighted to introduce you to John Smith at ABC Company.
	If you like, I could arrange a visit to DEF Company.
	Here's the case study on XYZ Company for further reading.

Use offensive call statements to clearly articulate your competitive differences. The demeanor and communication style you use to deliver them should be based on confidence, not arrogance, and perhaps a sense of urgency.

Sales Call Strategy: Using call statements is a more sophisticated strategy for talking to your customer's mind. By guiding the internal dialogue of your customers, you can deliver a message that will be understood and interpreted as true. Instead of barraging the customer with point-by-point facts and figures, structure your arguments in a logical way using a storyline that builds momentum while you deliver it.

47. Using Defensive Call Statements

Many times salespeople are asked underhanded questions by customers. This questioning is disguised as information gathering but in reality only serves the selfish motivations of the interrogators. Unfortunately, novice salespeople fall into the trap and try to respond to questions to which there are no correct answers. Anything that is said is used against them.

Defensive call statements are specifically structured responses to the toughest questions customers ask. You create them by writing two to four high level talking points followed by a short written script. Since it's common to be nervous on important sales calls, talking points serve as mental tags to help you remember your script. Here's an example of one of my defensive call statements that I use with reporters and prospective customers.

"Steve, there are thousands of books about sales. Why is yours any different?"

- Talking Points
  - It is written for senior salespeople with five, ten, or fifteen-plus years of experience.
  - It is the first book that truly explains how to master sales linguistics.
  - It provides advanced real-world strategies and tactics.
  - Its goal is "Right words at the right time."

- Written Script
  Well, I think there are three major differences. First, it is written for senior salespeople who have been in the field for five, ten, or fifteen-plus years. Most sales books are intended just to teach beginning salespeople how to sell, so they rehash Sales 101 techniques that senior salespeople already know. This is also the first book that truly explains how to master sales linguistics, the new field of study of how the customer's mind uses and interprets language during the selection process. Finally, it provides advanced real-world strategies and tactics to close more business in today's tough times. The goal of *Heavy Hitter Sales Linguistics* is to help

salespeople say the right words at the right time to persuade customers to buy.

The demeanor and communication style used to deliver defensive call statements is calm, collected, and matter-of-fact. However, you want to build momentum as you make the statement and finish on a high note. This is called a "buildup." Whenever you speak to a customer, you want to confidently peak during the final sentence of your paragraph. You don't want your voice to trail off, signaling uncertainty or lack of conviction.

The talking points in the example above are sequenced according to whom the book is for, what it is about, and how the reader will benefit. The last talking point is to remind you about the buildup and to close the vignette on a high note. It summarizes the book's value in an interesting and assertive way.

Sales Call Strategy: A critical aspect of the sales call is not necessarily what you have planned to say. Rather, it is how you handle the tough questions the customer asks you. Your question-handling ability is what separates you from the pack. Prepare defensive call statements in advance to protect yourself as you answer uncomfortable questions about your products, company, customer, and competitors.

48. Choosing Customer Success Stories

Salespeople love to tell stories. Of all the stories we tell, none are more important than the metaphors (or examples) about the customers that are successfully using our products and services. The personal connection between a customer example and its relevancy to the prospect's experiences will determine to what extent the salesperson's claims are accepted. Therefore, the pertinence of the example chosen is very important. Presenting a company that closely mirrors the prospect's business or technical environment will make the statements more powerful. Presenting a company that the prospect doesn't recognize will have less impact. In reality, it may actually hinder the argument because the prospect might think the product is not pervasive or popular.

At the lowest level of relevance, the example used could be a well-known organization, such as Coca-Cola or Shell Oil. Certainly, these are companies that would be known by the customer. The level of relevance improves when the example company is known for its past innovations, such as FedEx or Intel, or is well respected for its quality and brand, such as Mercedes-Benz or Nordstrom. By providing examples of customers that have a dominant position in an unrelated business, such as Microsoft, Amazon, or Starbucks, you also receive implicit approval since it is highly likely the prospect has successfully used the services or products of these companies personally. Therefore, the prospect makes the logical assumption that the salesperson's product works successfully.

The company example could also include a technical environment similar to the customers. In this case, the company's name or business is de-emphasized while its technical environment is highlighted. Let's assume the prospect is using Hewlett-Packard computers and Cisco network equipment. By providing a customer example that identically matches this combination, the salesperson is able to validate his technical claims that his product works in the prospect's exact technical environment.

Geographic proximity is a very compelling attribute of a reference. If the customer's company is based in New York, a reference to a company that is based in Los Angeles is not nearly as strong as a reference to one that is based in New York.

The ideal reference is a customer's direct competitor. This example provides the highest level of relevance and the most persuasive argument to use the salesperson's product. The best customer reference of all is a company in the same business, in close geographic proximity, and with the same business initiatives.

Be careful with name-dropping. Once you offer a customer's name, you have obligated yourself to give the customer's contact information should it be asked for, and you have given the prospect the right to call the customer as a reference. Never forget, anytime you insert another person into the sales cycle on your behalf, it adds an element of risk.

One exception to this rule is when you give prospects the name of a company that is a direct competitor. Generally they will not call the rival company, and you do not have to provide contact information. In fact, two direct competitors almost never share information about a critical project. What makes this type of customer example so useful is that you can validate your product claims without adding risk to the sales cycle.

Using customer anecdotes and references is a powerful way to add credibility to your product claims. Think for a moment about the last major personal purchase you made, such as a car, a boat, or even a vacation. Most likely, you wanted to talk to someone who already owned the product or had been to the destination you were considering.

Sales Call Strategy: Whenever you have an initial sales call, whether it is over the phone or in person, review your entire list of customers beforehand. Select five to ten customers from your list who share similar characteristics as the potential customer. The potential customer may be in the same industry, a user of these companies' products, or a direct competitor. For each of the customers you have selected, prepare a call statement that validates your product claims and tell a customer success story that helps you connect with the customer's subconscious mind, as discussed in the next chapter.

49. Structuring Customer Success Stories

Customer success stories (a specific type of sales metaphor) play a very important role in influencing customers to buy. The power of customer success metaphors lies in their individual interpretation. While the conscious mind is listening to the content of the surface-level story, the subconscious mind is deciphering its own message. On the surface, explaining how a customer is successfully using a product is a story the conscious mind will follow logically. Underneath this story, a message can be sent to the customer's subconscious mind that it is in his personal interest to select your product.

The average person will hear only seven and a half minutes of a one-hour presentation and remember only half of the words he or she hears.[1] In essence, we don't listen to and we reject far more words than we actually hear. However, the subconscious mind acts as a reservoir for this overflow of information. Therefore, a metaphor's structure is critical.

An effective method of structuring customer success stories is to break them into four parts: history and situation, options, evaluation process, and decision reason and results. Below, you will find an example of each part and descriptions of ideally what message should be sent to the conscious mind and the connection to the subconscious.

Part 1 describes the history and situation.

- *Conscious message.* Describe the business problem or condition the customer was trying to solve or improve and the situation that created it.

- *Subconscious connection.* Specifically identify the people involved in the selection process, including their names, titles, and backgrounds. These are people the customer can identify with. When you provide these names, you are also offering them as references. Therefore, your examples should always be based upon happy, referable customers.

- *Example.* "I would like to take a moment to tell you about one of our most difficult customers, ABC Company. Their requirements were so complex that they were unsure whether any off-the-shelf product would work for them. Frankly, we had never seen a business that processed so many transactions. Their CIO, Bob Smith, was also one of the most meticulous and demanding customers I have ever met."

Part 2 presents the options.

- *Conscious message.* Describe the different products or methods that could have solved the problem or improved the customer's situation.

- *Subconscious connection.* Explain the impact of these circumstances in terms of the decision maker's job, career, or emotional state of being.

- *Example.* "Bob decided to bring in the top two products, ours and XYZ's, for intensive evaluations, even though he honestly believed that neither product would handle their requirements."

Part 3 delineates the evaluation process.

- *Conscious message.* Outline the process the customer undertook to determine the best solution.
- *Subconscious connection.* Describe the personality, preferences, and motivations of the evaluation team members.
- *Example.* "Bob tested every aspect of the solutions: installation, ease of use, performance, and technical support. One month into the pilot test, Bob stopped testing XYZ's product because it just wouldn't scale. He spent another two months verifying every feature of our product. He wanted to make sure everything worked precisely as advertised."

Part 4 describes the decision reason and results.

- *Conscious message.* Describe the final selection and its impact on the decision maker or company.
- *Subconscious connection.* Translate the outcome into personal terms.
- *Example.* "When Bob was completely sure of his decision, he finally purchased our solution. Today, Bob is one of our happiest customers and their project has been a complete success. I would be delighted to introduce you to him."

Sales Call Strategy: When you meet with a customer, you know you must establish trust and demonstrate competence in order to reduce the customer's personal angst. Customer success stories are valuable tools for proving that you and your company are the authority on solving the customer's problem. With this proof, you gain dominance. You should always include customer metaphors on your sales calls and in your presentations so you can become the dominant authority during the sale cycle.

50. Handling Questions

One of the hardest things to do in all of sales is handle tough questions from skeptical prospective customers. After interviewing thousands of customers as part of the win-loss studies I have conducted, I can tell you with certainty that answering customer questions successfully is often the difference between winning and losing. Here are six points to consider when answering questions:

- *Clarify the question first.* Customers ask two basic types of questions. Some are very specific questions about a feature or issue, while others are more general about a broad topic or your opinion. In both instances, make sure you understand the question before answering it. Either rephrase the question in your own mind using your own words and repeat it to the questioner aloud or ask the questioner to further explain what he meant before answering. Many times, salespeople are too eager to give an answer to a question that wasn't even asked.
- *Show your domain expertise.* If you intimately know your industry, company, and products and how they compare against the competition, you need not fear even the toughest question.
- *Make sure everyone understands.* Since most sales calls are conducted with groups of people, you should give a little background information with your answers to ensure everyone understands the topic of conversation. Don't assume everyone understands your company's buzzwords or nomenclature.
- *Provide an expert point of view.* Never forget, your customer would rather do business with a trusted consultant who has intimate knowledge of the industry than an ordinary salesperson who simply understands how the product works.

- *Remember: demeanor speaks volumes.* The most powerful response to the most difficult question isn't solely the answer you give. It's also how you say it! Regardless of the question, keep a calm and confident demeanor. Most of all, do not get defensive. Stay positive. This is a critical lesson. When confronted by someone who disagrees with your opinion, it's okay to disagree without being disagreeable.
- *Redirect inane and unfair questions.* Don't get flustered when you are asked an inappropriate question. Simply redirect the question by saying something like, "The question you really should be asking is . . . "

Sales Call Strategy: Behind every question customers ask is an ulterior motive. They may want to validate a bias or throw you off track. That's why you shouldn't be too eager to answer or say yes to every question you are asked. The first step is to quickly theorize why the question was asked. Then formulate your response strategy to demonstrate your industry and business expertise in order to command respect. Sometimes, it is best to address inappropriate questions by providing an answer that guides the customer to a different topic. Most importantly, maintain your composure at all times.

51. Preparing for Selection Pressure

When a customer asks you a question, you will provide either an instantaneous answer from your short-term memory or a calculated answer that involves your long-term memory. The instantaneous answer is available immediately since it involves the recall of a logical fact or the recollection of a flashbulb episode. Logical facts include details committed to rote memory, such as product specifications, features, and performance details. Flashbulb episodes are emotional, physical, or cerebral experiences that were so overpowering that they are permanently imprinted in short-term memory. For example, when someone says "9/11" you might immediately think of the twin towers of the World Trade Center. Both logical facts and flashbulb episodes reside in your short-term memory, which is accessed faster than your long-term memory.

Giving a calculated answer is akin to solving a mathematical equation in your mind by searching for and selecting the right answer or creating an appropriate answer based upon a set of rules learned from prior experiences residing in your long-term memory. Three types of calculated answers are constructed in long-term memory. The first type uses a key access to search previous experiences. An example of a key access search would be entering a person's last name into a database in order to retrieve their contact information. An example of a key access search during a sales call would be recalling previous meetings with CEOs in order to help you answer a question being asked by a CEO.

The second type, pattern recognition, requires a more complex calculation involving multiple attributes. Let's say you were asked by a skeptical, detail-oriented COO how your product is different from your major competitor's. The creation of your answer is based on previous encounters with this particular circumstance. Pattern recognition can be thought of as trying to find the what-when-where response—*what* you should do *when* you are in this circumstance *where* you need to respond to a question or execute a sales-related action.

Finally, sometimes you are presented with situations you have never encountered before and you have to use your imagination to create an answer. Making a best-guess answer requires a pattern recognition search to find closely resembling experiences plus additional hypothetical reasoning to create a new model. Obviously, this process takes the most time. In fact, psychological testing has proved it takes 30 percent longer to imagine something than to recall the truth.[1]

Customers expect you to respond to their questions within a certain time frame. When you are face to face, this time is measured in seconds, and there is a penalty for delay. If the expected length of time is exceeded, customers will perceive that you don't command the facts, or worse yet, that your answer is untruthful. When this occurs, it is difficult to establish that you are their equal because you have lost their trust. As a result, they will not speak the confidential language with you. Figure 51.1 illustrates the impact of selection pressure during the sales call.

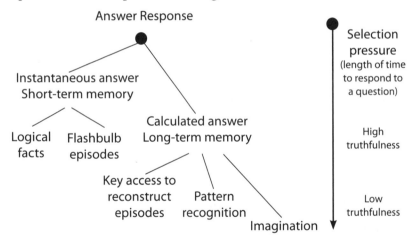

Figure 51.1 Question handling and selection pressure

The main point of this discussion is that you need to anticipate the questions customers will ask and have answers prepared and internalized in advance. Create a list of all the toughest questions you could be asked and then rehearse your answers out loud until they are smoothly and quickly delivered. The answers should not be more than forty-five seconds long and should succinctly answer, not evade, the question. Referring to the example from chapter 45 where we are selling enterprise software to banks and meeting with the CFO of Acme Bank, here are some of the tough questions we should be prepared for:

Why should we do business with you?

What makes you different?

Why are you so expensive?

Why aren't you a publicly traded company (or why is your stock so low)?

How do you plan to be successful when your competition is twice your size?

Your ROI is way too high. Are you sure it's right?

Who is your unhappiest customer and why?

Why did ABC Bank switch from your solution to Archrival Software Company's?

You claim your technology is a big differentiator. If so, then why do your competitors run some of the world's biggest banks?

What's the biggest deficiency in your solution?

Why is your market share smaller than Archrival Software Company's?

Can you tell me a little bit about yourself?

The selection pressure on salespeople forces them to produce answers promptly. Quite often, when salespeople lie to a customer, it is more likely because of the pressure to produce an instantaneous answer, rather than a conscious decision to mislead. In any case, the customer will determine if your statements are true or false depending upon your congruence. Congruence can be thought of as "truth in communication," while incongruence suggests a person is not telling the entire truth. Be forewarned, the customer will always spot lies. Whether he calls you on them publicly depends upon how he perceives himself and the role he takes during the decision-making process, which we will discuss in detail later in chapters 95 through 98.

Sales Call Strategy: When you have a private moment immediately following every sales call, write down the toughest questions you can remember being asked. Then grade your response to the customer from A to F based upon the customer's reaction. Next, analyze whether each response came from your short- or long-term memory. Typically, the hardest questions require long-term memory (key access, pattern recognition, and imagination). Your answers to these are the ones you probably graded lowest. By repetitively practicing these answers aloud ten to twenty times, you effectively transfer them into short-term memory, which will improve your believability and persuasiveness.

52. Improving Sales Call Memory

One of your goals is to continually build your personal knowledge base of your sales call experiences. Obviously, taking insightful notes during sales calls will help you recall the meetings. However, during the next sales call, you won't have time to search through your notes to find the "right" answer to a customer's question. You must make information available instantaneously by committing it to memory. Here are six principles to help improve your sales call memory:

- *Sensory information.* During the sales call, consciously gather as much information as possible from your sight, hearing, and touch senses. A vivid event is more likely to be memorized than a dull one. For example, the customer wore an ugly shirt or had on too much cologne.

- *Association.* Thoughts and experiences are more readily recalled when they are linked to a specific association. A very simple association would be the success or failure of the call.
- *Specifics and details.* The persistence of a memory is directly related to the precision of details that are input at the time of the experience. For instance, the customer said the budget was $132,500.
- *Unique events.* Many sales calls are free-flowing events that lack a strict organization of facts. Therefore, it is easier to remember any unusual and unique aspects of a sales call.
- *First and last.* Most salespeople are quick to remember how a sales call began (the big opening) and how it ended (the grand finale). This is a natural characteristic of memory, whereby we tend to remember the information that is presented first and last more than the details in between. This particularly applies to longer sales calls, those more than an hour. One way to help remember all of the in-between information is to mentally break the sales call into smaller segments (or chunks) either by time, presenter, or topic of discussion.
- *The good, the bad, and the ugly.* Your brain has been trained to block out unpleasant images. It even releases chemicals to lessen the strength of bad memories. However, it is critical that all information during a sales call, both good and bad, be stored.

Sales Call Strategy: Memory plays a fundamental role in determining the strength of your sales intuition. Never forget that how you remember something will determine how much you remember.

53. Identifying the Bully with the Juice and the Emperor

Four different characteristics of the people involved in the product selection process can be measured as displayed in figure 53.1. The vertical axis shows a person's insistence that things be done his way. This is called being a "bully." A bully will get his way at any and all costs.

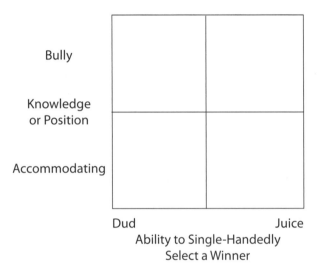

Figure 53.1 Characteristics of evaluators

A "bully" is not necessarily a negative term, nor does it mean that the person is physically intimidating. It is simply a description of a person who will tenaciously fight for his cause in order to get his way. People are more likely to be bullies when they have an elevated status within the evaluation team. The status could be the result of their domain expertise or their title and the authority it commands.

At the other end of the spectrum are people who are accommodating. They are apathetic about whatever solution is purchased. The degree to which people are bullies or accommodating depends on the effect the purchase decision has on them personally, their span of control, their position in the company, or their ability to perform their jobs.

On the horizontal axis are the concepts of "juice" and the "dud." Simply put, juice is charisma. But even this definition is too simple. Some people are natural-born leaders. They have an aura that can motivate and instill confidence. That's juice. Juice is fairly hard to describe, but you know it when you see it.

People who have juice do not necessarily act like superheroes, nor are they always the highest-ranking people involved in an evaluation. Instead, they are the ones who always seem to be on the winning side. Only one member of the customer's evaluation team has the juice. Single-handedly, he imparts his own will on the selection process by choosing the vendor and pushing the purchase through the procurement process. He can either finalize the purchase terms or instruct the procurement team on the terms that are considered acceptable. With large enterprise purchases, the bully with the juice is usually at the senior management level. To succeed, you will need sponsorship at this level.

Duds are named after the ineffective fireworks they represent. Sometimes the fuse of a firework will burn down, but nothing will happen. Other fireworks may be very big but produce disappointing results. Duds talk big but take little action. "Accommodating duds" are people who do not take an active role in the sales process. Even worse are "dud bullies," who pretend they have juice but don't. You may not realize who they are until it's too late.

For all the people involved in the sales selection process, you need to calculate their amount of juice and their propensity to be bullies. For example, John, Jim, Karl, and Rich are plotted by a salesperson who sells large-scale computer data storage equipment (see figure 53.2). John is the senior purchasing agent. Jim is a network administrator. Karl is the director of information technology, and Rich is the CIO. They are going to make a $350,000 purchase.

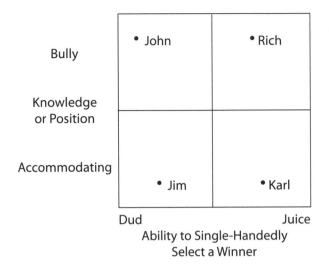

Figure 53.2 Plotting individual assessments

As shown in the figure, John is a dud bully, Jim is an accommodating dud, Rich has the juice, and Karl is accommodating to him. Even though Jim and Karl might conduct the vendor evaluations, their decision can be overridden by Rich. While they might have a vested interest in ensuring that their favorite vendor wins, you can assume their recommendation will match Rich's preference. His will may be imposed on the evaluation process through brute force or by finesse. Either way, his preference is "bullied" into the decision.

However, Rich, the CIO who has the juice, probably doesn't care which toner cartridges are purchased for the company's laser printers. He will be accommodating and support the decision of the people who make that decision. Someone else has the juice for the procurement of toner cartridges.

Now let's assume Rich is making a $3.5 million software purchase. Once again, he is the bully with the juice, and the evaluation team's recommendation matches the vendor he wants. However, he can't make a purchase of this magnitude by himself. It must be blessed by the "emperor."

In ancient Rome, the emperor would decide whether or not a beaten gladiator would live by gesturing with a thumb up or down. Today, the life or death of enterprise purchases is decided in much the same way by a company president, CEO, chairman, board of directors, or capital expenditure committee that has no personal attachments or vested interests in the purchase. This individual or group will decide whether the funds should actually be spent. This emperor will give a thumb up or down to release the funds to make the purchase, even though an exhausting evaluation of many months or even years may have been conducted by lower-level personnel.

Sales Call Strategy: Two of the most important people in every sales cycle are the bully with the juice and the emperor. These people will ultimately make and approve the decision. Therefore, it is imperative that you truly understand the decision-making process. Who is the bully with the juice? Will an emperor have to ultimately approve the decision? Whether you are selling a product in only one or two sales calls or two dozen or more, you must always validate who the bully with juice and the emperor are.

54. Aligning Value During Sales Calls

Here's an important mantra to always keep in the back of your mind when meeting a new prospect: the purpose of the sales call is to talk about *his* problems, not *your* products. A successful sales call is not based upon how much product propaganda you impart but how much information you collect about the customer's problems.

The conversation will be conducted using the technical specification language and the business operations language (see chapters 37 and 38). It will typically take place in two phases during the main stage of the sales call (see fig. 42.1). The first phase is your discovery of the problem: understanding the customer's specific problem, its cause, the goal that will be realized when the problem is solved, the possible options and vendors being considered to solve the problem, and the employees who will assist him in solving it.

The second phase is the customer's discovery of your solution. Once the problem is understood, you then define how you might solve the problem by explaining how you have helped companies in similar situations. You accomplish this by providing real-world examples that equate your solution to the four different types of product value we reviewed in chapter 39. While these examples straightforwardly explain the strategic and operational values, the political and psychological values are suggestions that are inferred by the customer when listening to the stories. Finally, you will describe the unique features and functions by which your solution achieves the customer's strategic and operational values.

Here's an example to help you understand and apply this concept. Let's assume you work for a software company that provides workforce productivity software—the Laborsaver 3000—and you are meeting with the COO of a large food-processing company. The sales call starts with your asking questions to discover the COO's problem. In this case, the CEO has mandated that all departments cut their budgets by 20 percent. The COO will comply with this request by cutting raw material, labor, and shipping costs. He determines that half of the cost savings will have to come from reduced labor costs. However, he dreads laying off people and wants to avoid across-the-board pay cuts and employee reassignments. He would rather drive the labor cost savings through less-intrusive methods that don't hurt employee morale.

After you conduct your discovery, you frame your solution based upon examples about how other large food-processor customers, Dole Food Company and Kraft Foods, have reduced labor costs 10 percent through more efficient and more accurate scheduling of skilled employees against actual demand. We discussed customer examples in chapters 48 and 49. The metaphors to be used are important and should be chosen with care. These stories show the COO how he can accomplish his reduction goals and achieve strategic value (he can tell the CEO he's cut labor costs 10 percent) and operational value by improving his department's efficiency. Politically, he has satisfied the powerbroker CEO, and psychologically, he has gained the approval of his employees for preserving their livelihoods.

As the conversation progresses, the executive wants more details about how the solution works and is implemented. You then describe the relevant features and functions of the Laborsaver 3000 software that specifically explain how the strategic and operational values are achieved. The structure of the main stage of the sales call is represented in figure 54.1.

Sales Call Strategy: One major mistake salespeople make during sales calls is to talk too much about topics that aren't important. Your solution has a laundry list of benefits and many interesting features and functions. However, the only ones that merit mentioning are the ones that lead to the specific business benefit of achieving the customer's goal and communicate your strategic, operational, political, and psychological value. Don't waste the precious minutes you have on nonessential topics.

Problem	Cause	Goal	Possible options	Applicable solution	Strategic and operational value	Political and psychological value	Product
I have to reduce department costs that consist of raw materials, labor, and shipping	Sales are down and the CEO mandates 20% budget cuts	Realize a 10% labor cost savings with minimal impact on my employees' lives	1. More efficient workforce 2. Employee reassignment 3. Pay decreases 4. Layoffs	Improved workforce planning and labor budgeting	A 10% labor reduction at Dole and Kraft	Satisfy CEO while maintaining department morale	Laborsaver 3000 features and functions that create the labor cost savings benefits

Customer converses in business operations language   Salesperson converses in business operations language

Salesperson discovery: asking questions   *Customer discovery: asking questions*

Figure 54.1 Aligning value during sales calls

Prepare for the main stage of a sales call by dividing it into two parts. The first part is your discovery based upon asking questions that cause the customer to respond in the business operations language. The second part begins once all the possible options the customer is contemplating are discussed. This is the presentation of your solution, discussion of its value, and answering of the customer's questions in the business operations language. Be careful to avoid a mismatch of languages between you and the customer. Even the most experienced salespeople have a tendency to recite product features and specifications when nervous. A good rule of thumb is to only speak the technical specification language when the customer does.

55. Getting to the Confidential Language

In the example in chapter 54 about the sales call with the COO, the conversation may have never reached the confidential language, but the call still could have been deemed successful. The executive thought your solution would solve his problem and you felt great about your performance. Everyone left the meeting excited about the prospects of doing business together, with you being the most excited of all.

However, the sales call had four major problems. First, the CEO is the emperor, while the COO is the bully with the juice. The CEO will ultimately approve the method the COO uses to reduce costs. Even though the COO may decide to go with the Laborsaver 3000, the CEO might not want to spend the time or money implementing it. He wants layoffs instead. So even though you met with the highest-ranking departmental C-level executive, you might not have a deal here after all.

Second, one of your competitors might outflank you and reach the CEO first. When the COO presents his recommendation about how he intends to cut costs and the vendor he intends to use, he'll be overruled. The third problem is that the COO has several meetings with other competitors scheduled in the days ahead and could easily change his mind.

The biggest problem with the sales call with the COO was that the true confidential language wasn't spoken. The true confidential language is a personal language a customer uses to explain what he wants to do and why (see chapter 40). The language is based on accomplishing future objectives to increase or retain power. The sales call conversation stayed at the business operations level and never approached confidentiality, where the COO's true motivations would be revealed.

An example of the true confidential language would be if he had said, "Our CEO is a really mean SOB, and he told me that it would be my hide if I didn't cut costs 20 percent." Furthermore, the COO did not enlist you to help him execute his strategy of avoiding layoffs. The COO could have confided to you, "This will be a tough sell to my CEO. Is there any way we could arrange a meeting between him and the CEO of Kraft to talk about how they are saving money during these difficult times?" So even though plenty of enthusiasm was exhibited by both sides, real trust wasn't established.

Sales Call Strategy: How do you establish the level of trust necessary to get to the confidential language? The answer isn't simple. You know you must understand your products, the industry, and the operations of the customer's business. Three additional factors greatly determine your ability to establish trust. They are your question-handling ability, the congruence of your communication, and your personal presence and its impact on the customer's conscious and subconscious minds.

We have discussed how you should understand your strategic, operational, political, and psychological value to the customer. However, in reality, you and your competitors will make very similar statements about how much money the customer will save and how departmental efficiencies will be improved. The key to reaching the true confidential language is communicating your political and psychological value to the customer. Think about the different things you can say to make the customer feel more powerful and all the examples that show how your products guarantee career success.

56. Structuring the Sales Call Close

Remember the last time you were being pressured into doing something you didn't want to do? Whether the pressure came from a boss, colleague, spouse, or child, your natural response was to resist and push back. It's human nature to resist high-pressure tactics. So, how should the closing of the sales call be structured? The answer is to create a primary closing strategy, utilize fallback positions, and select an appropriate delivery technique as represented in figure 56.1.

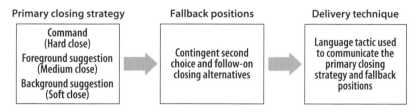

Figure 56.1 Sales call close structure

Your primary closing strategy should be based upon securing the main objective for the meeting. The objective could be to be granted a follow-on meeting, have the customer start a product evaluation, receive approval to conduct a site survey, or negotiate final purchase terms. You also need fallback positions, alternatives you prepare ahead of time to present should the customer reject your primary closing strategy.

Your primary closing strategy and fallback positions are based on choosing to issue a command or presenting foreground and background suggestions. A command is an instructional statement that creates a binary type of yes or no response from the recipient. It is typically associated with a hard close and "take it or leave it" mentality. Foreground suggestions (medium close) are explicit, but they deflect the source of the request from the demander. Background suggestions (soft close) lead recipients to believe they are acting of their free will when in fact they have been directed to follow a message.

Let's pretend I am a passenger in your car and I feel you are driving too fast. A command would be "Slow down!" A foreground suggestion would be "You know the speed limit is forty five miles per hour and police ticket a lot of speeders here." A background suggestion would be "A speeder was in a horrible accident last week in this exact spot." While the background suggestion may be more subtle in its delivery, it can trigger a more profound reaction.

In a sales situation, a command might be "We always recommend you benchmark the products you are evaluating." A foreground suggestion might be "*Consumer Reports* gave our product the highest rating and recommended it as the best buy." An example of a background suggestion is "One of my customers tried the other company's product and recently switched to ours."

After you have determined your primary closing strategy and fallback positions, select the delivery technique to be used during the meeting. Here are some examples, assuming the main sales call objective is to close the business deal:

- *Time-based technique.* This technique incorporates a time-based deadline.
  - *Command (hard close).* "This is the last time we'll be able to extend this offer and we need your answer now."
  - *Foreground suggestion (medium close).* "My boss told me that this pricing expires December 31 at midnight."
  - *Background suggestion (soft close).* "Think it over tonight and I will call you at 10 o'clock tomorrow morning."

- *Linkage.* This technique connects different events, subjects, or ideas.
  - *Command (hard close).* "If we give you those terms, then you must have our contract signed by the end of our quarter."
  - *Foreground suggestion (medium close).* "I'll talk with my boss and if he okays the terms, could we have the purchase order by month end?"
  - *Background suggestion (soft close).* "Our implementation team will be fully booked starting in September, so to complete your project by year end, we'll need to have the contract signed in the next couple of weeks."

- *Power of Print.* This technique leverages a document or printed company policy.
  - *Command (hard close).* "Our new price list is coming out in thirty days, and I can't hold these current prices for you after that."

- *Foreground suggestion (medium close).* "Here's our volume discount schedule. If you spend another $100,000, you'll receive an additional 10 percent off the entire order."
- *Background suggestion (soft close).* "Should I send you a formal quotation that details the purchase price and terms?"

If you are a senior salesperson, you've already closed your share of business and know many different closing techniques. You also understand that your closing strategy must vary depending upon the customer's background, your competitive position, and the circumstances that are unique to the sales cycle. Sometimes, you need a commanding hard close for your meeting—for example, if the sales cycle for the products you sell involves only one or two customer interactions. With experienced buyers, consider a softer close because how many times do you think they have heard "this is our best and final offer" and every other type of hard close before?

Sales Call Strategy: Maintain control of the sales call so you can employ your primary closing strategy and be prepared with fallback positions should your primary closing strategy fail. You can sequence your primary closing strategy and fallback positions with commands (hard close), foreground suggestions (medium close), and background suggestions (soft close). For example, your primary closing strategy might be based upon a hard close; first fallback position, a medium close; and final fallback position, a soft close. Or, your strategy could be completely opposite depending upon the circumstances and the type of person you are meeting with.

57. Establishing Dominance

The drive to take command of a situation is instrumental to a salesperson's success. Some salespeople have such a strong dominance instinct that they think of customers as naturally inferior people who deserve to be taken advantage of. In the world of sales, these salespeople are known as "sharks." Sharks don't build rapport: they only know how to take advantage of people.

Even if you are not a shark, at times everyone must act like one. Just as a doctor must sometimes prescribe a painful treatment to heal a patient, in some sales situations you must control the customers for their own good. For example, I remember threatening a team of unsophisticated customers, telling them we would not sell them our solution unless they purchased the associated implementation services. Although they said they would be fine, I knew they didn't have the wherewithal to be successful on their own.

Conversely, salespeople with a weak dominance instinct are never quite in control of an account. They operate under the direction of customers or are at the mercy of the competition. Every account has an equilibrium point of dominance versus submission. It's the point where the customer respects your conviction and is not offended by your persistence. Even though you promote your agenda with determination, you are not considered pushy or overbearing.

Dominance is gaining the willing obedience of the customer. The customer listens to your opinions and advice, internalizes your recommendations and agrees with them, and then follows your course of action. Your personality greatly influences the way in which you establish dominance during sales calls. Take this short test to determine your natural tendencies to dominate group settings. Score your answer after each question with zero, one, or two points.

1. *Assertiveness within groups.* Are you someone who prefers to stay in the background (0), occasionally lead (1), or usually be in charge of the group (2)?

2. *Conformity within situations.* Are you someone who usually defers to others (0), occasionally challenges others (1), or usually challenges others when you believe it is necessary (2)?

3. *Self-consciousness around people.* Are you someone who is easily embarrassed (0), occasionally embarrassed (1), or seldom embarrassed when your ideas are challenged (2)?

4. *Straightforwardness and candor around people.* Are you someone who guards and edits your words (0), tactfully speaks your mind (1), or is completely frank and open with your thoughts (2)?

5. *Modesty and humility around people.* Are you someone who is genuinely humble (0), generally believes you are equal to others (1), or usually thinks you are superior to people around you (2)?

Total your score for all questions. A score of six or below indicates you have a low natural tendency to establish dominance in group settings. A score of seven or more indicates high natural tendencies.

Sales Call Strategy: There are two basic approaches to establish dominance during sales calls. The direct approach is based upon personal prowess, while the indirect approach is based upon finesse. The approach you should use depends upon attributes of your personality. If you scored a high level of dominance, you are typically well suited to use a direct approach. This approach is based upon first establishing yourself as the focal point of the purchase. In essence, the customer is buying your credibility, your personal experience, and your ability to help them accomplish their goals.

If you scored a low level of dominance, you are more likely better suited to use an indirect approach. This approach is based upon establishing your product and the capabilities of your company as the focal point of the purchase before you start selling yourself. For example, a salesperson with low dominance who transitioned his career from a technical position into sales can have an equally dominant presence as a seasoned sales veteran. However, he has to use a different approach. Instead of projecting a powerful presence in person, his deep-rooted technical understanding of his product draws customers to follow him. We'll discuss additional strategies to gain dominance in chapter 71.

58. Recognizing the Customer Placebo

One vendor is almost always preferred going into the selection process. However, customers are in a predicament. They still want to collect information from the other vendors to be 100 percent certain they are selecting the right vendor. Or they may want to complete the evaluation process to show others within or outside their organization (management, colleagues, consultants, or government agencies) that their evaluation was thorough and fair.

As a result, they offer the other (losing) vendors a "customer placebo." The customer placebo consists of false information and all the types of lies described earlier in chapter 5. This is an entirely different kind of fear from the kind that salespeople normally experience—this is false evidence appearing real, or FEAR.

The customer placebo occurs in every sales cycle. One vendor is in a unique position of receiving information from the customer that the others don't receive. As this favored vendor and the customer spend more time together, they develop a higher level of rapport. While this is happening, the customer is presenting misleading information to the other vendors about their position in the deal. Customers give salespeople false buying signs that they are more interested in the product then they actually are. Conversely, they may not share critical information or access to other people in the company as they do with the leading vendor. Unfortunately, the other vendors continue to spend additional resources and time on the account when a decision for one vendor has, for all intents and purposes, already been made.

In reality, the only two positions to be in at the end of the deal are first place, as the winner, or last place, as the first loser. Salespeople who are proud of a second-place finish are a detriment to their company. Figure 58.1 illustrates this point.

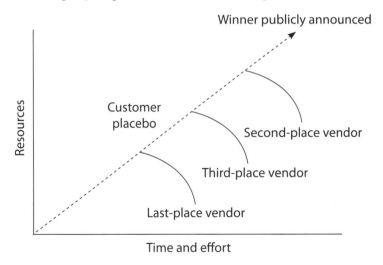

Figure 58.1 The customer placebo

As the sales cycle progresses, the losing vendors try to escalate FUD (fear, uncertainty, and doubt) in the customer's mind about the wherewithal of the competitors' companies and the capabilities of their products. For example, competitors will try to sabotage one another with facts such as unfavorable performance metrics, missing functionality, and tales of unhappy customers.

In turn, the attacked competitors will provide the customer with believable information that contradicts the original attacks. Therefore, the sales cycle naturally disintegrates into a "he said-she said" type of quarrel. This can leave company leaders not only confused but sometimes in "analysis paralysis" due to receiving too much contradictory information. This scenario helps set the stage for no decision to be made. The bickering tends to turn off potential buyers. Do you like watching people argue? Probably not.

But the biggest problem in the sales cycle is not FEAR or FUD. It's that the difference between products is extremely small. Compounding this problem is that everyone is presenting the same message to the customer. Take a moment and visit the home page of your company's website and those of your two biggest competitors. You'll see that the words and claims are interchangeable. Because all the competing products share the same basic features, functions, and benefits, the final decision to purchase is based upon customers' personal preferences and individual biases.

Sales Call Strategy: Never forget, the only two appropriate positions to be in at the end of the deal are first place, as the winner, or last place, as the first loser. Every place in between is the result of a judgment error. Every sales call presents you the opportunity to determine whether you are leading and will be the winner or lagging behind in second, third, or fourth place, destined to become the ultimate loser.

You should take two actions during every sales call to determine if you are a victim of the customer placebo. First, determine whether the customer knows the truth. Use triangulation (see chapter 44) to validate statements from the customer against those from other members of the evaluation team. Second, determine whether you are being told the truth. As you ask questions, calibrate the customer's eye movements (see chapter 25) and watch for incongruent communication where layers of human communication are at odds (see chapter 33).

59. Finding a Coach

Salespeople know they need a constant, accurate source of information that reveals the internal machinations of the customer's selection process. For many years, the term "coach" has been used by all types of salespeople, selling every conceivable product, to define the person who provides this inside information. Coaches are individuals who provide accurate information about the sales cycle and competition to you.

Salespeople sometimes believe they have a coach when in reality they don't. Heavy Hitters know they have a coach when the person not only provides them with accurate information but also helps them by fighting for their cause. A true coach will represent and promote a salesperson's solution to his colleagues and, even better, to senior executive leadership. Finally, the information coaches provide is accurate. Figure 59.1 below shows the five different types of coaches and their respective value to a salesperson.

A frenemy is someone who befriends you so that you think he is a supporter. In reality, the frenemy is only acting the part and is truly an enemy who is against you. Frenemies are extremely dangerous because they lull you into a false sense of security that you are winning when they are really coordinating a plan to defeat you.

A well-wisher talks to you on an intimate, friendly basis. He provides information that you consider proprietary. However, the well-wisher is an extremely amiable person and is providing the same information to all the salespeople competing for the business.

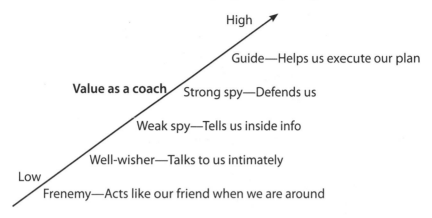

High

Guide—Helps us execute our plan

Value as a coach Strong spy—Defends us

Weak spy—Tells us inside info

Well-wisher—Talks to us intimately

Low

Frenemy—Acts like our friend when we are around

Figure 59.1 Types of coaches

Coaches can be either weak or strong spies. Weak spies are observers who provide you information about the internal machinations of the selection process. They report the thoughts of the various selection team members and the movements of other vendors. Strong spies are not only observers but disseminators of information as well. Strong spies have a deeper, more personal connection to you than weak spies do. They're more akin to confidants than acquaintances.

Guides are trusted friends who will courageously defend you and your solution when you are not around to do so yourself. Guides are considered your best friends. Not only are they confidants who provide all the inside details about the internal politics of decision making, but they also help you plan and execute your strategy to win the business. Guides are usually seasoned employees. They've worked at the company for quite some time and understand how to get things done. They have the business acumen and the experience to provide adept advice on how to win the deal and get the contract signed. Most importantly, after helping devise the winning game plan, they play an integral part in executing it.

The ideal coach is the person with the highest authority or influence involved in the selection process. When this person becomes the coach, you will enjoy a unique advantage. For example, let's assume Rich, the CIO who is making the $350,000 purchase of storage technology (see chapter 53), is your coach. Since he is the bully with the juice, you win! The next best scenario is when your coach can influence the bully with the juice.

However, the coach could be anybody inside the customer's company or even outside the company, such as a consultant working on the project. All of these advisors share a common characteristic. They have a selfish reason for wanting you or your company to win. This reason may range from the simple fact that they like you to the complicated nature of internal politics, where your solution helps them gain power, prestige, or authority.

Quite often, salespeople mistake someone for a coach when in fact the person isn't a loyal compatriot. You should always have a certain level of paranoia about your coach. Is he secretly coaching the competition? Is he acting as your eyes and ears when you are not around? Is he truthfully telling you about what the other vendors are up to and about the preferences of the various selection committee members? Is he providing privileged and proprietary information to you that the other vendors aren't receiving?

Sales Call Strategy: One of the most important sales call goals is to develop a trusted coach—hopefully, a guide. Obviously, the more coaches you have inside an account, the better the quality and quantity of information you will receive. The information you receive from these coaches can be used to determine your standing in an account and help determine your course of action. Being at the mercy of a single person is a risky position to be in. What if your coach is wrong?

60. Questions to Ask Your Coach

A successful sales call depends on your understanding the complete environment and the interactions between the audience members. The optimum way to conduct a sales call is through holistic interactionism, a person-centered approach that combines concrete thought processes (facts, features, and functions) with abstract thought processes (politics, environment, feelings, and benefactions).

The holistic view of personal behavior acknowledges the inter-action between people (their thoughts, emotions, and personalities) and the world that surrounds them at the same time. The situational nature of this theory helps explain why some customers don't want to disappoint salespeople during the sales call so they tell the salespeople what they want to hear. Meanwhile, other customers seek to avoid face-to-face confrontations so they tend to keep their objections to themselves.

The process of holistic interactionism starts with an investigation before the call to ascertain what the meeting environment will be like. Will you be interrogated Spanish Inquisition–style or attend a Woodstock-like love fest? While it is easy to find out who is attending and what their official titles are, understanding the internal machinations of the customer's decision process requires a coach. Only a coach can tell you who is for, against, or ambivalent to your solution. Only a coach can prepare you for the various objections that will be raised during your sales presentation, objections that could you throw you off track. Involving your coach in the creation of the presentation topics, finding out what points to cover and what to avoid, is critical. Previewing the presentation with your coach is ideal.

Let's assume Mitch is your coach during this selection process. He's been providing you with accurate, proprietary information about the decision-making process and has actually told you he wants you to win. He is guiding you through the sales process and has arranged a meeting with his boss, Bob, the C-level executive who is the emperor. Mitch is a great source of information about what you can expect from Bob during your upcoming meeting, and you want to ask him questions that will help you prepare for them in advance, such as the following:

> What is Bob's background, and how long has he been with the company?
> What's it like to work for him?
> Is he outgoing with a sense of humor, or is he more serious and sullen?
> Is he big picture or detailed oriented?
> What kind of work hours does he keep?
> What are his personal hobbies?
> What projects has he promoted, and were they successful?
> Is he well liked by the other company leaders?
> What are his perceptions about my company and me?
> How does he typically treat salespeople, and what should I watch out for?

These are just a few of the many questions you could ask your coach to understand the C-level executive's conscientiousness, gregariousness, and clout within the company.

Sales Call Strategy: Knowledge is power. You must secure proprietary knowledge about the accounts you are trying to close to obtain the power you seek. You must have a coach to win a deal.

Without one, you will never know the true nature of the organization and who has the real power to make the decision.

Ideally, you want to develop your coach into a guide because the most effective method of meeting senior executives is for mid- and lower-level personnel to introduce you to them. And the best coach is always the seniormost executive of the account you are trying to close.

61. Building a Participation Pie

Group dynamics are very complex and often revealing. One way to identify the bully with the juice is by observing people's behavior during presentations and meetings. In chapter 28 we reviewed how a pecking order is communicated by where people sit during meetings. Whether at a round table or in a classroom setting, the person with the most juice and greatest ability to bully will usually take the dominant seating position.

This dominating behavior is also evidenced in meeting interactions. To explain this, we need to introduce the concept of the "participation pie." The participation pie, shown in figure 61.1, illustrates the amount of time each person interacts in a meeting or presentation.

Usually, the person who interacts the most will be the bully with the most juice (see chapter 53). This is particularly true when the bully with the juice is a domain-expert manager who is very technical: he is in charge and wants everyone to know it. Be fore-warned that you may observe a different behavior when the bully with the juice is a business-expert manager. He may choose to remain silently hidden in the back of the room.

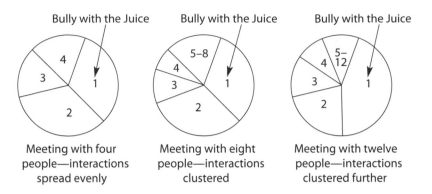

Figure 61.1 Participation pie charts

Dud bullies (see chapter 53) will be very active meeting participants. However, the more they participate, the more it becomes obvious that they do not have the stature or expertise they think they do. We have all been in meetings where people like this are contradicted or even publicly chastised by members of their own team. Dud bullies confirm the old adage "It is better to keep your mouth shut and be suspected of being a fool rather than open it and confirm suspicions."

Another key aspect of the participation pie is how the number of attendees affects the level of participation. In meetings with up to four members, the amount of time each person spends interacting and asking questions is relatively equal. As the group grows to eight people, the interactions become clustered around several people. In larger groups, up to twelve people, the majority of interactions are usually among a few individuals.

Sales Call Strategy: Every group meeting presents the opportunity to understand the internal machinations of the customer's selection process. Pay attention to who is dominating the conversation and build a participation pie as the meeting progresses.

62. Setting the Tempo

The decision on whether or not to pursue an account can be a difficult one. One deciding factor is who has set the tempo in the account—you or another competitor. This is particularly important when your product has a long sales cycle that requires a large investment of your time and your company's resources.

Basing the decision on an honest assessment of competitive strength is critical. For example, you should pursue accounts where you have established personal relationships. If you enjoy product and personnel advantages, you should almost always pursue an account, even if you are late into the deal. If you have product and personnel disadvantages, you must be first into the account to win. If you are on equal footing with the competition, you must be on time at the start of the evaluation process in order to build a relationship advantage. Figure 62.1 illustrates the tempo rules (when you should arrive in accounts) when your products and personnel have an advantage over, are equal to, or are at a disadvantage to your competitors'. For example, if you have product and personnel disadvantages, you must be the first salesperson in the account to establish relationships and set the buyer's criteria.

Obviously, many combinations are possible. The decision to work on an account or walk away from it shouldn't be made solely by the salesperson; it's always wise to get outsiders' opinions. The best people to help you make this call are your sales manager and the other members of your team who would work on the account with you. Not only is the personnel attribute a comparison of you against the salesperson you are competing directly against, but it also involves the availability, quality, and commitment of your team members (technical presales support, consultants, and management) to win the account. Therefore, it makes sense to get their buy-in before you move forward on any account.

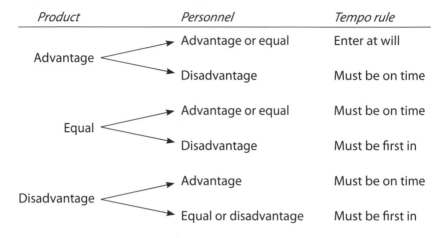

Product	Personnel	Tempo rule
Advantage	Advantage or equal	Enter at will
	Disadvantage	Must be on time
Equal	Advantage or equal	Must be on time
	Disadvantage	Must be first in
Disadvantage	Advantage	Must be on time
	Equal or disadvantage	Must be first in

Figure 62.1 When to pursue a deal

Once you're engaged in the deal, setting the tempo takes on a new meaning. While a good defense may keep you in the deal, the only way to win is to be on the offensive. Salespeople who are on the defensive will make it to the next step of the sales cycle at best, but they won't win the deal.

Sales Call Strategy: Setting the tempo is the first step in winning the business. Knowing how your products and personnel measure up against your competitors' will help you determine whether or not you should invest time in the account. Ideally, you want to be the first one to call on the customer in order to set the buyer's criteria for their selection process. Conversely, only the salesperson that has a clear advantage can arrive later during the sales cycle and have a chance to win.

63. Using Investigative Research to Penetrate New Accounts

Before you attempt to send an e-mail or letter or make a cold call to penetrate a new account, you need to research the business and the person whom you are trying to gain an initial meeting with. Old-fashioned detective work is still vitally important today. Fortunately, the Internet makes information more readily available than ever. Study every page of information on the customer's website as though your life depended on it. Read the annual report, press releases, and product information, and scan all the various financial documents. From these documents you can derive your initial thoughts about your product's strategic, operational, political, and psychological value (see chapter 39).

Another type of investigative research has a profound impact on whether or not your efforts will be successful: you must find the "right" people to contact within the account. You can find out who's who in any company in several ways. First, the company's website probably has an "about the company" page that may list senior executives. If the company is public, senior executives will be listed in the financial reports that can be found on its "investor relations" page. You can also search financial websites such as Yahoo! Finance (http://finance.yahoo.com) and the Securities and Exchange Commission website (http://www.sec.gov) for financial filings.

However, this information is far from complete for the purpose of penetrating the account. Ideally, you want to collect four critical pieces of information. First, knowing the date the company's fiscal year ends will help you coordinate your efforts to penetrate new accounts. Three to six months before the fiscal year ends, C-level executives will start thinking about their next year's goals along with the initiatives to accomplish them and the budget associated with each initiative. This is a crucial time to be gaining "mindshare." Budgets begin to be shaped through an iterative process with the CEO, CFO, or entire executive team. They become set in stone after the budget has been approved by the board of directors, usually before ninety days into the new fiscal year. Remember, there are certain points in the year when a strategic conversation is academic and other times when it's relevant.

Second, you want contact information about employees at all levels of the organization (midlevel managers and lower-level project people along with all the executive-level leaders). For example, if you were selling security software, you would like contact information for the chief information officer, chief technical officer, chief security officer, and vice president in charge of networking or infrastructure. You also want contact information for midlevel managers (director of information technology, director of security, manager of global networks) and key lower-level personnel (senior firewall administrator, IT security specialist, and lead network engineer). There are many different providers of this detailed information, including Hoover's, Dun & Bradstreet, Salesforce .com's Jigsaw, ZoomInfo, LinkedIn, InsideView, and CardBrowser.

Third, you need each person's precise title. There's a big difference between finding out that someone is the "vice president of global manufacturing applications" versus knowing someone who goes by the more nebulous title "vice president of information technology." Knowing the more detailed title will help you send better targeted messages.

Finally, you need accurate and complete contact information. You need the correct spelling of each person's name and his or her personal usage (whether someone goes by Charles or Chuck, for example), as well as the person's mailing address, direct phone number, and, of course, the all-important e-mail address.

Sales Call Strategy: It can be well argued that the first sales call with a prospective customer is the most important. Before you pick up the phone to make a cold call, fire off a letter, or press the button to send an e-mail, research the company and the employees within it that you are trying to contact. This is the first step toward creating a tailored message that will elicit a positive response.

64. Communication Vehicles

If selling is about speaking the language of the customer, then there are as many varieties of languages as there are customers. However, you have only three basic communication vehicles at your disposal to reach new customers: cold calls, letters, and e-mail. While you can use any of these three communication vehicles to secure initial meetings with customers, let's take a moment to review the pluses and minuses of each method.

Cold Calls

I recently conducted a win-loss analysis for a high-tech company that had a marvelous telemarketing team. These guys were relentless and pounded the phones day in, day out. As a result, they uncovered a lot of new opportunities for the outside sales reps in the field. These prospective customers were in different stages of evaluating vendors, ranging from midway in the sales cycle to nearly complete.

The results of the study were fascinating. The loss rate for these cold-call-driven opportunities was greater than 95 percent. In other words, only fifty out of one thousand actual opportunities the telemarketing team uncovered were ever closed. Conversely, the win rate of the outside sales reps and their field-driven opportunities was over 75 percent. The reason for these results is that the company had product and personnel disadvantages, and the tempo rule (see chapter 62) mandates that you must arrive early in the account when facing this situation. Most importantly, the combined revenue that resulted from those fifty wins generated by telemarketing was less than the costs of the telemarketing department to produce them. This is one example of how the positive impact of cold calling can be misinterpreted.

I receive a lot of cold calls from salespeople who are trying to sell me everything—sales force automation software, productivity tools, search engine optimization, online meeting solutions, marketing services, trade show events, business insurance, and the list goes on and on. Almost all the time these salespeople don't reach me and are forced to leave a voice mail.

Sometimes the funniest part of my day is listening to these voice mails. Here are a few of my observations. First, many salespeople are either nervous, bored, or both. Most of the time their tempo is too fast for me to understand what they have said. I like to pay attention to how they say their phone numbers. Since the number is given at the end of a long-winded speech, it is said the fastest. Is someone really going to replay the voice mail three times to get your phone number right?

Some salespeople assume I already know exactly what they do. Just because they have been saying the same thing all day doesn't mean I understand their terminology. At times I'm tortured as they ramble on and on about something in a dreary, unexciting way. Why should they expect me to have any enthusiasm for what they're selling when they don't show any? I feel like a judge on *American Idol* with my finger poised over the Delete key. There's no way they're going to finish their audition.

But here's the really bad news. In the past ten years I have never returned a cold call from a salesperson. Not once. The C-level executives I have spoken to about this have said the same.

Also, I've had salespeople cold call me for weeks or months at a time. I guess they think their persistence will win me over, but because I have to listen to their voice mails to get to my more important messages, I actually begin to hate them and will never do business with them. In one sense, these salespeople are infringing on my personal time and space.

By the way, I have a very different attitude about e-mail because it is a cafeteria-type communication channel. Voice mail is a serial communication channel. I have to go through messages in order, one at a time. E-mail is different; I can pick and choose which e-mails I open and do so in whatever order I want. Therefore, it doesn't bother me when someone sends me an occasional unsolicited e-mail. I can always add the person to my Block Sender list if the frequency gets too intrusive.

Should you cold call senior executives? Yes, cold calling does have a specific purpose during the sales process. However, it should be used only as a follow-up device after an e-mail or letter has been sent. And it should be used sparingly. However, I have a totally different attitude toward cold calling lower-level and mid-level personnel: Life's short. Go for it! Phone away!

Here's the most important point about cold calling. You have a small chance of actually speaking with the prospective customer. You're going to voice mail most of the time, so you must be able to leave a succinct message. In no more than twenty seconds you must identify who you are and why the customer should call you back. Your message must be delivered in a clear, commanding, yet approachable tone. Therefore, every time you plan on making cold calls you should rehearse leaving the voice mail. I suggest that you call your own voice mail three to five times and practice leaving the message you plan to use. Listen to your voice mail, put yourself in the customer's place, and ask if you would call yourself back.

Letters

Letters sent by snail mail must meet one important condition: the letter and associated marketing collateral that is sent to the customer must be totally unique. The people in your marketing department believe that the product brochures they have created are something truly unique. After all, they painstakingly selected the colors, fonts, graphics, and words to be used. However, product differentiation is at an all-time low and you could very easily substitute the name and logo of your archrival on your marketing collateral. That's why I am not a big fan of sending executives brochures and literature packs. Whereas lower-level personnel might look through them, executives will almost always place them in the circular file (trash can).

The material and message you send should vary according to the level of personnel in the account you are trying to penetrate. Senior executives should receive short, high-level summary information, such as press articles, one-page reviews, and case studies about their competitors whom you are doing business with. Save the company brochure, white papers, data sheets, and other detailed information for the midlevel and lower-level personnel.

Think about all the different types of items you can send to a potential customer other than a standard letter of introduction. You can send interesting news clippings and serious-sounding industry updates that help validate your marketing claims. You can send company tchotchkes such as T-shirts, baseball caps, and mouse pads that carry your company's name and logo. Most of the time these items are taken home and given away to family and friends, and it's great advertising when Junior parades around the house wearing your company's T-shirt. Remember, whatever you send should be as unique as possible while still promoting a professional image. For example, if I cold call a vice president of sales to introduce myself, it's highly unlikely my call will be returned. However, when I send a personally inscribed copy of one of my books first, I will almost always hear back from him.

One of the most common problems with letters and e-mails is they're too long and recite an unbelievable list of reasons why a product is so wonderful. I call this the "it slices, it dices, it juliennes" syndrome. This phrase was made famous by Ron Popeil, the first infomercial personality, as he described all the incredible features of the Ronco Chop-O-Matic. A senior executive is a sophisticated buyer, and describing your product like a carnival pitchman won't earn you a meeting. Such pitches actually do more harm than good.

E-mails

One of the first lessons every new salesperson learns is to "call high," to try to reach the most senior-level executive. Therefore, it's not surprising that senior-level executives are continually harassed by salespeople. When you try to call the CEO, president, or vice president of a company, you face a monumental challenge because the entire organization is designed to protect him from you. Most likely, you will be screened by an assistant or directed to an underling whose most important job function is to say no to you. The letters you send to executives tend to suffer the same fate. Given this reality, the preferred vehicle of communication is e-mail.

The subject line is the single most important part of the e-mail. Its sole purpose is to catch someone's attention and motivate the person to open the e-mail. The best e-mails start with a great cowcatcher (see chapter 43). Here are some actual examples of bad subject lines from e-mails I have received.

- *Subject: Increase Revenues 1000%!* This overpromising subject line means the e-mail will immediately be considered spam and deleted before it has a chance to be read.
- *Subject: Business Proposal Information.* This subject line incorrectly sets readers' expectations. They'll feel deceived when they open the e-mail and see it is from a stranger trying to sell them something.
- *Free White Paper.* A C-level executive doesn't want to waste time reading this.
- *Would you be interested in XYZ Product?* The answer is no when the question is presented this way.
- *Don't Break the Bank! Product of the year saves money and eliminates network bottlenecks.* It's just too long to bother with.

The hook is the catchy part of the e-mail. It's the first few sentences that deliver a punch and motivate you to keep reading. The cowcatcher and the hook work together synergistically. Great e-mails have an interesting cowcatcher and a provocative hook. Here's an example of a terrible e-mail exactly as I received it with my critique immediately following.

Subject: Please advise

The pressure is on to grow revenue faster. How will you adapt business to reach goals?

XXXX can help you gain a strong competitive edge. Let me show you can use XXXX to:

- Drive better results.
- Increase customer satisfaction and loyalty
- Expand your market share.

Do you have time this week or next for a brief discussion about your business needs? Please reply with the best time for me to contact you.

Best regards,
XXX XXXXXX

This e-mail has the wrong subject line. It is titled "Please advise," which gives the reader the impression it is from someone the reader knows about a business issue the sender needs advice on. When the reader opens the e-mail and sees that it is spam, it creates a "negative receptive state" because the reader feels deceived. If this e-mail was intended for a vice president of sales, a better title would have been "Increase revenues by increasing sales calls." If intended for a CFO, "Five tips to decrease your cost of operations" could have been used. These titles set the readers' expectations and create a "positive receptive state."

The e-mail suggests the sender is a simpleton. It also has typos and grammatical mistakes. In chapter 30, we discussed the roles of dominance and submission during communication. This submissive e-mail is written at the level of a fifth grader when scored by the Flesch-Kindcaid test (see chapter 70). Is a senior-level executive really going to want to meet with an elementary school student? This e-mail actually demeans the recipient by inferring the reader is at the same communication level.

The e-mail is also too generic to grab the reader's attention. It uses strategic terms like "grow revenue," "competitive edge," and "increase customer satisfaction" generically without any explanation. These terms are so overused by everyone in sales that they are "dead words"—they have no meaningful impact.

Finally, the sender didn't conduct any background research so that he could craft a message that would appeal to the recipient. You can differentiate your solution using strategic value, operational value, political value, and most importantly, psychological value (see chapter 39). The best way to tap into these values is by tailoring your message directly to the intended recipient based upon the person's role within the company. A one-size-fits-all e-mail is less effective because the vice presidents of marketing, sales, and finance face very different day-to-day challenges.

Sales Call Strategy: The Internet is fundamentally changing the way people communicate. You must take advantage of one of the most important communication developments of your lifetime. You must master how to use e-mail to penetrate new accounts. Your success will increasingly depend upon it in the future. You'll never get an initial face-to-face meeting if your introductory message doesn't connect with its intended target.

65. The "1, 2, 3, Rest, Repeat" Campaign

I have spent my entire career selling to C-level executives. For nearly two decades I sold enterprise software to CEOs, CFOs, CIOs, CTOs, and vice presidents of engineering. For the better part of the last decade I have sold my keynote presentations, training workshops, and consulting services exclusively to senior decision makers. In order of priority, the executives I target are the chief sales officer (vice president of sales), chief marketing officer (vice president of marketing), CEO (president and chairman), and COO (vice president of operations).

My philosophy about contacting senior executives and other employees of an organization is probably different than you think. I believe that every company will become a customer of mine because I honestly believe I can help improve every sales force. Essentially, it's just a matter of time before I connect with the executives and we work together.

My philosophy is based upon three important points. First, you must believe in what you're doing. Your efforts cannot be based upon half-hearted motivations. You must have a conviction that you, your products, and your company are the only true solution for the customer. When you have this mind-set, it is impossible to consider yourself an obnoxious telemarketer or discourteous e-mail spammer. Rather, you are on an urgent mission to save the customer from making an ill-advised decision that will create a less-than-perfect workplace.

Second, your attempts to contact a customer will take time. In essence, you are running a political campaign that will take several months and in many cases over a year. While you obviously want to generate immediate interest, you need to set your own expectations so you don't get frustrated by a lack of results and stop campaigning. The campaign ends only when the customer buys your solution or specifically tells you to stop contacting him.

Third, the reason why the customer doesn't respond to your message is not that he's disinterested or too busy. Do not misinterpret a lack of response and assume he doesn't want your product. Rather, consider it your fault because you didn't send him the right message. While you didn't get the message right this time, you should also know that you will get it right over time. Therefore, you should never be bashful about contacting the customer again. However, you must send a different type of message or history will surely repeat itself.

I call the strategy to penetrate new accounts the "1, 2, 3, Rest, Repeat" campaign. It is based upon sending a series of three unique messages that have different structures and intentions. These actions are followed by a period when you go quiet and do not make any attempts whatsoever to contact the customer. Once this time frame is over, you start another campaign with a series of different messages. Here's how the campaign works:

Step 1—Send an initial credibility message. This introductory message identifies in an interesting way who you are and what you do.

Step 2—Send a tactical offer message. This message is centered upon a business problem or industry theme.

Step 3—Send a final message. This message is the culmination of the campaign.

Step 4—Rest. During this period, you do not contact the customer.

Step 5—Repeat. After the rest period has ended, you start another campaign with a series of three entirely new messages.

Most companies and salespeople make two critical mistakes when they try to reach customers. They either contact them once and stop if they don't get a response or contact them way too much. They mistakenly believe they are gaining mindshare by sending a newsletter or announcement every other week or once a month. The exact opposite is true. They are devaluing and diluting their message.

Your strategy to penetrate a new account should not be a one-time action. Instead, it requires an ongoing campaign that can utilize all three communication vehicles at your disposal: e-mail, telephone cold calls, and letters (direct mail). Ideally, you should coordinate the order in which you send the communiqués. For example, you could send a letter in step 1, follow up with an e-mail in step 2, and cold call the customer a few days later.

Here's why you will gain psychological benefits by sequencing your messages. The customer has had many interactions with salespeople over the years. At both work and home, he receives telemarketing calls and is barraged by all types of spam and junk mail. Each of these communications is a stimulus that requires a response. Usually the response is negative (hang up on the tele-marketer, throw away the junk mail, etc.).

When you send a customer an e-mail or make a cold call, you too are creating an unexpected stimulus that requires him to respond. Based upon past negative experiences, the customer's nat-ural tendency is to automatically respond from his "hot emotional system" and immediately disregard your message. In other words, the customer acts quickly without thinking and deletes your e-mail or voice mail because of negative associations from the past.

In order to reach the customer, you want to elicit a response from his "cool cognitive system." This is his neutral and more thoughtful system for responding to stimuli. Therefore, you need your messages to stand out, to create a different psychological response, and to be respectfully sent. Typically, the time frame to accomplish the first three steps should be between sixty to ninety days. If you try to shorten the contact period, your messages will run the risk of being considered a nuisance.

The rest period should be at least twice the time it takes to execute steps 1 through 3. For example, the two sequences I typi-cally use to reach C-level executives are e-mail, letter, e-mail and e-mail, e-mail, e-mail. I will sequence these messages on a once-a-month basis over a three-month time frame. I also use a longer rest period up to nine months before I will attempt to contact the executive again.

Sales Call Strategy: What is your philosophy to penetrate new accounts? If you're like most salespeople you probably don't have one. Rather, you reflexively increase your prospecting activity when your pipeline is empty. While the sudden burst of activity makes you feel better about your future, the disappointing response rate means you need a new strategy. The 1, 2, 3, Rest, Repeat campaign leverages sales linguistics to secure initial meetings with executives, midlevel managers, and lower-level personnel. Follow the steps explicitly and you will achieve even greater sales success.

66. Structuring Messages for the 1, 2, 3, Rest, Repeat Campaign

Because people have different motivations, they have different perceptions of a product's value. The perceived value depends on the psychological, political, operational, and strategic value it provides the evaluator.

Psychological value is the most important value in terms of motivating purchasing action. As we discussed in chapter 39, at the root of every decision is a desire to fulfill one of four deep-seated psychological needs: satisfying the ego, being accepted as part of a group, avoiding pain, and ensuring survival. Therefore, you should understand your product's psychological value and how it applies to the person you are trying to reach.

Political value involves organizational power. Your product can make someone more powerful outright, or it can provide much-needed visibility that enables a person to be in contact with the company's powerbrokers.

People's success in an organization is dependent upon the success of their department's operations. You can think of operational power in terms of how your solution impacts a person's résumé.

Finally, strategic value is the reason evaluators give to others in the company as to why they are purchasing a product. Strategic value includes gaining a competitive advantage, increasing revenues, decreasing costs, increasing productivity, improving customer satisfaction, improving quality, and standardizing operations.

The message you send to customers should be based upon these four values. You must communicate to potential buyers that you can help them solve critical department problems and help them become experts and an internal source of knowledge, thereby making them powerful. To see how this can be done, let's look at an example of a generic e-mail for a marketing campaign targeted at senior executives in the automobile industry.

Subject: Increase Profitability and Maintain Dealer Partnership Loyalty!

Dear Mr. Smith,

My name is John Johnson from XYZ Corporation. We are the leader in providing solutions that help accelerate time to market and improve customer communications. We're helping customers such as Ford, Toyota, and Honda automate their relationships with their distributors, dealers, and parts suppliers.

In a recent strategic implementation, we were able to deliver Ford a robust solution that allowed them to communicate more effectively with their worldwide dealer distribution channel, drastically increasing customer service and loyalty. XYZ Corporation can help you

- Improve communications with critical partners
- Speed time to market and increase dealer retention
- Implement a "best practices" approach for all enterprise communications

For a free evaluation of our robust solutions, please call or e-mail me at your earliest convenience.

Best regards,
John Johnson

What follows is my version of the same e-mail. While the main message isn't changed significantly, my goal is to employ a better cowcatcher (see chapter 43) and hook and to tap into all the different types of customer value.

Subject: How Toyota Maintains Critical Dealer Relationships

Mark,

Q. How do Toyota, Ford, and Honda maintain near-perfect dealer relationships?
A. XYZ Corporation has helped them automate and streamline all aspects of partner communications.

For example, Toyota distributes thousands of unique messages and memorandums to its worldwide dealer distribution channel on a daily basis. Toyota has drastically reduced turnaround times while increasing customer service using XYZ's solution. As a result, they have cut overhead costs by 9 percent.

If you would like to learn how you can improve relationships with all your important business partners, call or e-mail me at your earliest convenience. Finally, please expect my call next week to discuss our free dealer communication analysis program.

Thank you,
John Johnson

John.johnson@XYZcorporation.com
(123) 456-7890

The most important aspect of the e-mail is not the bullet points of benefits; rather, it is the psychological impression it creates on the reader. When salespeople try to penetrate a new account, they are considered enemies, so they are met with disdain and fear. Salespeople must turn negative resisters into positive accomplices. In the above example, I was trying to make the e-mail recipient become psychologically attached to the sender.

One recipient might envision starting a grand project like Toyota's for his own personal gain. Another might want more information so he could impress others with his expertise. Someone else might have criticized his company's dealer communications in the past and thought, "If it is good enough for Toyota, it should work for us." He just wants this painful problem solved.

The purpose of your investigative research (see chapter 63) is to enable you to tailor your cowcatcher and hook. For example, if the company you're contacting has recently gone public, you might title your e-mail to the CEO "How to maintain profitability after an IPO." If it made a recent acquisition, you might use "Revenue strategies from acquisitions." Such e-mails are more likely to be read and less likely to be considered spam because they are personalized around a timely event.

Another key reason for conducting research is to help you determine the different values your solution offers. Reading the CEO's letter to the stockholders in the company's annual report will help you understand the state of the business and the major initiatives planned for the new year. Reviewing the 10-K financial report will provide you with details about the business challenges the company faces. Press releases announce new programs and company crusades that are being undertaken. Meanwhile, industry analyst reports explain how the company is faring compared to the competition.

Take a moment to complete this exercise by answering the following questions:

- What is my solution's psychological value?
- What is my solution's political value?
- What is my solution's operational value?
- What is my solution's strategic value?

Notice how my e-mail doesn't recite a list of product features and benefits. It explains real-world results in a plain-spoken way without buzzwords.

Take a look at the last sentence of the closing paragraph, "Finally, please expect my call next week to discuss our free dealer communication analysis program." This sentence employs two linguistic strategies. First, the sender *grants* himself permission to contact the recipient next week. Let's examine the e-mail from the recipient's perspective to understand this concept. This e-mail was written respectfully. It created a positive receptive state when the reader opened it, provided valuable information, and at 125 total words didn't take too much of the reader's time. It also established credibility via customer metaphors and employed an interesting cowcatcher and hook. It was well-written from a grammatical perspective, which confirmed the sender's professionalism. As a result, the recipient would not be offended if the sender followed up next week with an introductory phone call. However, the call must be made! If not, the momentum and credibility of the e-mail established are lost.

The second linguistic strategy is to purposely use general words. What is a "dealer communication analysis program"? Frankly, the prospective customer wouldn't know what it is, and that's the idea. We spoke about general words and their interpretation (see chapter 32). In this instance, the e-mail is building credibility, momentum, and rapport. The original e-mail was self-centered and closed with "For a free evaluation of our robust solutions." In the revised version we are purposely using a general word structure (dealer communication analysis program) because we want the customer to interpret these terms in the way that is most important to the customer and relevant to his problems and aspirations.

One final point, while this example is of an e-mail, this message structure applies to letters as well.

Sales Call Strategy: Forget about repeating your standard product pitch in your introductory communications and think about the benefactions you offer. Put yourself in the customer's position and theorize on the psychological, political, operational, and strategic value you and your solutions provide. Control your destiny! Don't send e-mails that are mini-infomercials that give away the power of responding solely to the customer. Study the message structure above as if your livelihood and career depend upon it. Fight the urge to explain too much. Instead, structure the e-mail so the customer finds it enticing and awaits your follow-up action with anticipation.

67. Credibility Message of the 1, 2, 3, Rest, Repeat Campaign

The purpose of the first message of the 1, 2, 3, Rest, Repeat Campaign is to establish credibility and develop some level of recognition with the customer you are trying to reach. In the example below, Michael Corleone, a salesperson for Acme Advertising, is trying to reach Vincent Vega, the chief marketing officer of ABC Technology Company, a multibillion-dollar technology giant. Pay particular attention to the tone of the e-mail. It's not too personal. Since the two men have never met, the message is intentionally more formal. However, Michael doesn't want to be overly formal with his use of language and the salutation or the recipient will discount the letter as a sales pitch.

To: Vincent Vega, CMO@ABC Technology Company
From: Michael Corleone@Acme Advertising

Subject: Vincent, Marketing Campaign Meeting Request

Hello Vincent,

Acme Advertising has developed marketing campaigns for many leading technology companies including:

Apple	IBM	NEC
Cisco	Intel	Oracle
EMC	McAfee	SAP
Hewlett-Packard	Microsoft	Symantec

Our clients have cost-effectively improved their brand recognition while increasing new sales opportunities.

"Acme Advertising's direct response marketing campaign increased our lead generation activities nearly threefold."
—Jack Sparrow, CMO, Oracle Corporation

"Acme's 'One World, One System' commercial series has improved our name recognition across all our key market segments."
—James T. Davis, CMO, Hewlett-Packard Corporation

"We were thrilled to win the prestigious Zippy Award for best print advertisement in a technical magazine."
—David Bowman, CMO, Intel Corporation

I'd be delighted to meet with you and share some thoughts and ideas we have for ABC Technology Company.

I look forward to hearing from you,

Michael Corleone
Michael.corleone@acme.com
(123) 456-7890

The subject line is the cowcatcher, solely intended to encourage Vincent to open the e-mail. His name is part of the subject, so the inference is that the message is from a real person asking for a meeting, not from an automated spambot. As he opens the e-mail, the first thing his eyes will focus on is the list of recognizable company names. This is due to the e-mail's "heat map" (see chapter 84).

This is the hook that makes him go back and read the entire message. Notice how this e-mail avoids making outrageous claims like "Acme is the world's leading advertising firm." Rather, it is completely factual: these are our clients, and this is what they have to say about us. Nor does the e-mail go into a detailed explanation of what Acme Advertising does.

The subject line and first sentence use the term "marketing campaign." To a CMO like Vincent, the term can mean a wide variety of things: advertising campaigns, lead-generation programs, online marketing, customer research, competitive research, brand development, and so on. Intentionally, the e-mail does not point out what it's referring to. This is an example of a broadcast-unicast messaging technique. It's intended to let the recipient derive his own personal meaning from an ambiguous term. His internal dialogue believes the message is intended solely for him.

While researching the business, Michael found out that ABC Technology's sales are down from last year. Therefore, he theorizes that the sales department is haranguing marketing about needing more qualified leads. If this is the case, Vincent might interpret the e-mail from the standpoint of lead generation, and Michael has a higher likelihood of securing a meeting. The first customer quote reinforces this interpretation. This is an example of a background suggestion.

The list of companies provided in this e-mail is extremely important. Examples of customers that are successfully using a company's products and services are the most important metaphors a salesperson can use. The personal connection between a customer example and its relevancy to the prospect's experiences will determine to what extent the salesperson's claims are accepted. Therefore, the pertinence of the examples chosen is critical. Presenting a company that closely mirrors the prospect's business environment will make the salesperson's statements more powerful. Presenting a company that the prospect doesn't recognize will have less impact. In reality, it may actually hinder the argument because the prospect might think the product is not pervasive or popular.

Specific customer quotes were selected for this e-mail. Since Michael has never met Vincent, he really doesn't know what's on the CMO's mind. He doesn't know if he thinks his job is in jeopardy or he's next in line to become the president of the company. So Michael wants quotes that will connect to the different benefactions. The first customer quote focuses upon pain avoidance. Based upon Michael's past experience working with CMOs, he knows that lead generation is always a source of pain. The second quote can relate to multiple benefactions. Maybe Vincent feels inferior to his peers at the other companies listed in the e-mail. He might hire Acme so he can be part of the group. This is self-preservation. Or since he's worked with his current ad agency for seven straight years, he might feel it's time for a refreshing change. This is mental and emotional well-being. The third quote is based upon self-gratification. What CMO wouldn't want to win a prestigious Zippy Award and prominently display the trophy in his office?

The final sentence is an example of the imagination persuasion technique, which entails directing the recipient to form mental images, concepts, situations, and sensations. Michael wants to share some thoughts and ideas his company has for Vincent. Upon reading the sentence, Vincent will probably start to wonder what these ideas are. Michael is guiding Vincent's internal dialogue to become curious.

Sales Call Strategy: The credibility message you send to a prospective customer is a critical communication event. Creating a message that earns you an initial meeting is both an art and a science. Over the past year alone, I have reviewed hundreds of credibility messages for my clients, and more than three quarters of them actually do more harm than good. Now it is time to conduct a very important exercise. I would like you to close this book and review the standard introduction e-mail or letter you send to customers. Put yourself in their position. How would you respond to it?

68. Tactical-Offer Message of the 1, 2, 3, Rest, Repeat Campaign

Assuming the customer didn't respond to your first e-mail, you send him a second, tactical-offer e-mail. In the example below, Luke Skywalker, a salesperson for XYZ Technologies, is trying to secure a meeting with Norman Bates, chief information officer at Wonderful Telecommunications.

> To: Norman Bates, CIO@Wonderful Telecommunications
> From: Luke Skywalker@XYZ Technologies
> Subject: Norman, Recession Strategies for CIOs
>
> Norman,
>
> During today's tough times, IT organizations are required to maintain round-the-clock uptime with smaller budgets and fewer resources than ever. Below, you will find links to articles that address this critical issue.

7 CIO Strategies to Maintain Application Availability with Fewer Resources

Gartner Group Study of the Recession's Impact on Long-Term IT Planning

How to Reduce Operational IT Costs by Outsourcing

When and Where Outsourcing Makes Sense

XYZ Technologies has helped hundreds of CIOs maximize their IT budgets through application outsourcing.

"We were surprised by the cost savings. It has been 20 percent more than we expected."
—Charles Foster Kane, CIO, AT&T

"We started small by outsourcing non-mission-critical applications three years ago. Today, 70 percent of our applications are outsourced."
—Forrest Gump, CIO, Johnson & Johnson

"We've achieved our primary goal of reducing costs while maintaining our service levels. Now we've freed up valuable resources to work on critical new business projects."
—Stanley Kowalski, CIO, General Electric

Norman, please let me know if you are interested in our complimentary outsourcing cost-savings analysis. The complimentary study takes approximately two days to complete and will provide you with a detailed savings assessment, key risk factors, and completion timelines. I will follow up with you next week to answer any questions you may have about our analysis program.

Luke Skywalker
Luke.skywalker@xyz.com
(123) 456-7890

Based upon Luke's research and experience, he knows that one of the main challenges CIOs face during tough economic times is providing high levels of service with less money and fewer resources. "Norman, Recession Strategies for CIOs" is a topical cowcatcher. It's quite different from "Norman, Meeting Request." The subject line also indicates that the e-mail is not from a salesperson asking for a meeting but from an important source of independent information that could potentially help the CIO.

Obviously, Luke wants to secure a meeting so that he can begin the cost-savings study. However, any forward progress in starting a relationship with the CIO should be considered positive. For instance, if Norman clicks on a link to one of the articles, this is a positive step and the e-mail was a success.

This e-mail has three major parts. The first part is the offer. This fulfills the e-mail's requirement that it provide independent information. Four links are provided to articles that most CIOs would find relevant and interesting. Although they may have been written by XYZ Technologies, they are informational as opposed to vendor centric promotional collateral. (It's important to note that e-mails with attached documents are more likely to be caught by spam filters.) The articles are the e-mail's hook.

The second part is composed of customer metaphors, stories from customers confirming the salesperson's solution or company. Since most CIOs are extremely risk averse, all of the quotes are intended to make Norman feel more comfortable that outsourcing is mainstream. Included are quotes from CIOs of another telecommunications company and traditionally conservative companies General Electric and Johnson & Johnson.

These customer quotes are also examples of the simulation persuasion technique. Simulation is structuring language to provoke a particular emotional or physical response. For example, salespeople want the customer to simulate the benefits and feelings of owning their products during a sales cycle. Car salespeople are experts at using simulation. The test drive is a way to get the buyer to simulate the fantasy of owning the car. They want the test driver to enjoy the smoothness of the ride, experience the "new car" aroma, and feel the power of the acceleration. They know that a person who successfully simulates ownership during the test drive is a good prospect for a sale.

The same principle applies to the CIO. If Luke can get Norman to envision being a happy customer while reading the e-mail, he is well on the road to securing a meeting. Simulation exercises the senses, engages the personality, and occupies the internal dialogue. Luke wants Norman to ask himself, "Why aren't we outsourcing?"

The third part of the e-mail is the tactic to get the initial meeting. This is the call to action. The e-mail in chapter 66 titled "How Toyota Maintains Critical Dealer Relationships" was a tactical e-mail based upon telling customer stories and offering a free dealer communication analysis. In the above e-mail, Luke is asking Norman to participate in a cost-savings analysis project. A tactical e-mail needs to have a much stronger closing statement than a credibility e-mail because you are specifically asking the executive to take action to fulfill one of his fantasies. Therefore, an operator is added that explains what the analysis entails.

Sales Call Strategy: All sales involve selling a fantasy. The fantasy is that the product you are selling is going to make the customer's life easier, make the customer more powerful, save money, or enable the customer to make more money. The feature set of your product validates the fantasy elements of your story. To gain the initial sales call, communicate how you can turn your customer's fantasy into a reality when your product is purchased. The structure of the tactical-offer message is to promote all of the customer's fantasies.

69. Final Message of the 1, 2, 3, Rest, Repeat Campaign

At this point, you may have attempted to contact the customer twice without success. You can either send another credibility message, a follow-up tactical offer message, or the "final" message of the campaign. In the example below, Willy Loman, a salesperson for Interstar Networks, is trying to reach John Blutarsky, the chief technology officer of Freedom Financial Investments. Through his research, Willy knows that Freedom Financial Investments is using his archrival's product, Schlomo Networks. Please note that it is more important to pay attention to the more aggressive tone and structure of the language in this example than to understand the technical terms being used.

To: John Blutarsky, CTO@Freedom Financial Investments
From: Willy Loman@Interstar Networks
Subject: John, Schlomo Networks Performance Comparison

John,

I've sent you e-mails to explain Interstar Networks' advantage over Schlomo Networks. We offer superior performance because our architecture is based upon virtual processes. This is more efficient than Schlomo Networks' architecture, which uses a single-machine address. While the single-machine address solution redundantly broadcasts all messages, our solution sends specific information packets to the applicable computer. This results in up to 75 percent less network traffic.

For example, ABC Company recently switched from Schlomo Networks and improved its network performance by over 60 percent. I would be delighted to set up a conference call for you to talk with John Smith, ABC's CTO. Please expect my call to schedule a meeting time.

Willy Loman
Willy.Loman@Interstarnetworks.com
(123) 456-7890

A good rule of thumb is to always assume the salesperson you are competing against is as friendly, professional, and knowledgeable as you are. Like yourself, he is trying to win over the customer with his product knowledge, business acumen, and personal charm. To the customer, the claims you both make will sound identical.

The above e-mail shows several examples of how operators can be used. Operators are required to take the generic claims and translate them into proof points the customer understands and believes (see chapter 32). For example, in the e-mail to the CTO, the general word "performance" is being operated on by the descriptor "architecture is based upon virtual processes." The term "more efficient than" is being operated on by the phrase "uses a single-machine address." The salesperson then details the differentiation between the two architectures, which is less traffic and faster performance.

To further validate his argument, Willy offers a specific customer example to illustrate his claims. Equally important, to have his claim accepted as the truth, he offers to introduce the prospect to the existing customer. In other words, he says, "Don't take only my word on this; talk to my customers!"

Successful communication and comprehension are linked together, hand in hand. Successfully reaching new customers requires that your message be understood and acted upon. Most importantly, it requires a concerted and concentrated campaign that is conducted within a psychologically compelling linguistic framework such as the 1, 2, 3, Rest, Repeat Campaign.

Sales Call Strategy: The last in the series of messages of the 1, 2, 3, Rest, Repeat Campaign is called the "final message." After sending this message you will not contact the customer for weeks or even months in some cases. Therefore, you need to structure the final message more aggressively than the credibility and tactical messages. The final message should have a harder close than the credibility and tactical messages. Add text that includes foreground suggestions rather than background suggestions (see chapter 56) and always grant yourself permission to call the prospect.

70. Comprehension and Your Communication Level

All communication consists of one of three types of messages—recreational, instructional, and frustrational. A recreational message is socially enjoyable communication. Examples include talking to a friend, listening to music, and reading a novel. This type of communication has the highest level of comprehension where the meaning, nature, and importance of the words are personally understood. At a minimum, 90 percent of the words are known and recognized.

Instructional messages are based on teaching, telling, or passing along knowledge. Instructional messages include directions, commands, advice, and even questions. When customers ask you questions, they are actually instructing you to give them the specific information they need. Instructional messages are sent during briefings, training sessions, chalk talks, and sales calls. However, they typically have a slightly lower level of comprehension than recreational communication—around 80 percent.

Frustrational messages include any type of communication that is either not understood or is considered objectionable by the recipient. Let's say you and I are having a conversation and I say that a colleague of ours is a "loquacious prevaricator." Our level of rapport would drop if you did not know that these words meant "talkative liar."

Frustrational messages include offending or disagreeable messages. For example, a command given by someone who does not have greater expertise or authority over the recipient is a frustrational message. The inclination is not to follow it. Frustrational messages have the lowest level of comprehension, under 50 percent.

These three types of messages are interspersed throughout conversations, letters, and e-mails. For example, I may be talking to my wife on the phone about her day (recreational message) and she might ask me to stop by the store to pick up some groceries (instructional message). When she tells me to pick up some flipsides I become frustrated because I have no idea what they are.

In addition, comprehension requires that the message be conveyed at the recipient's communication level, not too far below or above the level of the words in his or her lexical dictionary.

Here's an exercise to determine your communication level. Gather at least ten different samples of your writing. These could be proposals, letters, reports, or e-mails. Cut and paste them into one Microsoft Word document. Assuming you are using Windows 7, under the Review tab, click on Spelling & Grammar and click on Options in the pop-up box. Select Proofing in the new window and then enable the "Show readability statistics" box. Now spell-check the entire document, and you will see your Flesch-Kincaid grade level index. (For additional step-by-step instructions, enter "readability" in the Word Help search—instructions vary by release.) The result is a number that corresponds to the grade level at which you communicate. For example, a score of 9.0 would indicate that the text is understandable by an average student in ninth grade.

I typically write at a Flesch-Kindcaid grade level score around 12. That is my natural communication level. It's also an appropriate communication level for my target audience. The majority of sales books that target business-to-consumer salespeople, who sell products like cars, are written at the sixth- to eighth-grade levels. Since my target market is senior salespeople who typically have a university degree, a level of 12 is appropriate.

Sales Call Strategy: What is your communication level? What is the communication level of the customers you sell to? If they have advanced degrees in computer science, engineering, or finance, are you communicating at their level? One way to find out is to perform Flesch-Kincaid grade level scoring on all the communications they have sent you and those you can find on the Internet. Whether in person or via e-mail, you must make sure you are communicating at their level. If you use a level that is too low, you will not be respected and will never be in a position to establish dominance. Conversely, if it's too high you may be misunderstood.

71. How Strangers Meet

Meeting new people is stressful. If you watch strangers meet at a party, you'll notice that they are on guard. We typically don't have to worry that someone is physically threatening; we have to worry if they are a psychological threat. Therefore, we try to ascertain whether a stranger is in a dominant, equal, or submissive position in comparison to our position. Next, we try to find out what we have in common by discovering intersecting activities. Finally, we try to classify the relationship into a familiar pattern so we can decide how we should behave and whether we should invest more time with the person. The sequence is shown in figure 71.1.

Figure 71.1 The process of meeting a stranger

The instinctual comparison of dominance tends to occur quickly when people meet. Just as packs of animals instinctively establish a hierarchy so that the group can function more efficiently, people are naturally inclined to seek structure in group environments. Therefore, they create mental pecking orders to understand their place in complex social settings such as parties and sales calls.

But what makes someone dominant? Dominance can be the result of a diverse set of attributes. When two people talk at a party, one person may be better looking, more intelligent, funnier, wealthier, or better respected or have a quality that the other person lacks, such as kindness, generosity, humility, aggressiveness, assertiveness, or selfishness. Even a trait that is perceived as negative by society can make someone dominant. For example, how do you act when you see a tattooed, leather-clad motorcyclist in the rearview mirror when you are driving?

When meeting someone new, people experience varying amounts and types of stress depending on whether they perceive themselves to be dominant, equal, or submissive. A person who feels inferior to someone else is under much more stress than a person who feels dominant. The stress manifests itself in different ways. How differently would you feel about meeting Bill Gates versus meeting the counterperson who serves you coffee? Most likely, you would be far more nervous when meeting one of the richest men in the world. However, if you have a secret crush on the counterperson, your behavior would be quite different than if you had little interest. You would be in the submissive position because you'd want to be liked.

While some dominant people will surround themselves with submissive people, most dominants want to associate with people whom they perceive as equals. Equals converse with relative ease. This is a critical point. One of your most important goals when meeting with a customer is establishing yourself as an equal. That's one of the main reasons why you need to speak the technical specification language, the business operations language, and the confidential language described in chapters 37, 38, and 40.

You may have noticed at parties that people naturally coalesce into small groups of equals. These groups are segregated from each other by an attribute. It might be age, attractiveness, where they live, what they do for a living, or even the nature of their personalities. These people are equals because they share an intersecting activity.

The natural course of party conversations is for the strangers to try to find out what they have in common. Through intersecting activities, people display their personal interests, character, and temperament and express their value systems. Intersecting activities create shared bonds and reduce the level of stress involved in meeting someone new. Intersecting activities play an equally important role in sales calls. Regardless of whether the salesperson or the customer initiated the meeting, the first intersecting activity is the sales call itself. It is the first point in common between the salesperson and the customer.

The strategy is to use the first intersecting activity (the sales call) to find *personal* intersecting activities. By doing so, you develop rapport and begin the process of building a personal friendship. In essence, you try to relieve the stress caused by the typical dominant-submissive meeting between a customer and a vendor by turning it into a conversation between equals.

The intersecting activities salespeople talk about can be quite diverse—the local professional sports team, cars, movies, or any hobby. Usually, these first conversations are on "safe" topics, with little risk that someone's revelations will create controversy, because the goal is to reduce stress, not create more of it. In sales calls, dominance is always initially on the customer's side since he has the ultimate say over whether any relationship will be created. However, this dominance is based upon the situation, not personal attributes. In a different social setting, the salesperson might be truly dominant because he is more charismatic, athletic, witty, and so on.

Once the strangers establish who is dominant and they have searched for what they have in common, then each person tries to characterize the relationship by placing it into one of the categories of familial relationships he or she is familiar with, such as a relationship with a father figure, big sister, best friend, or son.

Sales Call Strategy: Customers are personally evaluating you during the first few minutes of a sales call and making an initial judgment about whether they like you or not. They'll spend the remainder of the call validating whether their preliminary decision was correct. Think about how you can use the process of how strangers meet to your advantage. What intersecting activities do you like to talk about with customers, and how would they classify their relationships with you?

72. The Better Person Syndrome

At the root of true dominance is the "Better Person Syndrome," which is based on the theory that people will naturally gravitate toward people they feel are better than themselves in some way. In this respect, the Better Person Syndrome helps explain the old saying that opposites attract. For example, my wife has many qualities that I admire. She is far more patient and kind than I'll ever be. I am attracted to these qualities.

The theory also applies to sales. When customers are choosing between two similar products, they will not always buy the better product. Rather, their tendency is to buy from the salesperson they believe is the better person. So while one salesperson may have a slightly better product and be more proficient in explaining its features and functionality, in the end the customer will buy from the person who has the personal attributes the customer most admires. (Obviously, if one product is light years ahead of another, then the Better Person Syndrome is neutralized.)

Some customers will gravitate to a friendly and responsive salesperson. They admire and respect these qualities. Others might enjoy being around an aristocratic salesperson in cufflinks and a monogrammed dress shirt. Perhaps these customers behave and dress in a similar way and have some deep-seated desire to be like him. Because people admire different qualities in other people, every sales call is unique.

Your dominance in any setting is dependent upon the submissiveness of the person you are talking with. It is not a measure of how easily you overpower the person. Rather, it depends on the traits that the other person respects, admires, or does not possess. For example, a customer may be submissive to a salesperson's industry expertise, technical aptitude, or product knowledge. Many people become submissive when they perceive a salesperson to be better looking, more charismatic, or more enthusiastic than they are. For instance, I know several vice presidents of sales who will hire a good looking salesperson with average sales skills over a great salesperson who is not so attractive.

Most customers tend to gravitate to salespeople who are similar to themselves. They want to be surrounded by competent, successful people. However, opposites attract as well. For example, very meticulous, no-nonsense customers sometimes bond with lackadaisical, carefree salespeople who are their exact opposites. These customers seem to be hypnotized into a submissive position. One of the best salespeople I ever knew was the most unorganized, lackadaisical, smart-mouthed goof-off I ever met. However, a certain cross section of executives absolutely adored him because he always said exactly what was on his mind in the most politically incorrect way. Surprisingly, the executives he bonded with were usually straight-laced, button-down CFOs and CIOs. I think they found his uniqueness intoxicating compared to the personalities of the staff members they had to deal with daily.

Now it's time to do a quick exercise to help you discover what makes you dominant in customer meetings. The list below includes just a few of the wide range of dominant traits that people respond to submissively. As you read the list, think about when you used one of these attributes to put yourself in a dominant position over your main contact (who was probably a midmanagement or lower-level person) at a recent account you won. Recall not only the account but the specific person who responded to you submissively and followed your lead.

Athleticism	Humor	Product knowledge
Attractiveness	Hyperactivity	Professionalism
Business knowledge	Industry expertise	Sales acumen
Charisma	Integrity	Sense of humor
Cleverness	Lackadaisicalness	Seriousness
Compassion	Negotiation skills	Straightforwardness
Curiosity	Open-mindedness	Technical aptitude
Eloquence	Optimism	Thoroughness
Empathy	Organization	Thoughtfulness
Enthusiasm	Passion	Tolerance
Friendliness	Persistence	Trustworthiness
Honesty	Pessimism	Wholesomeness

Now repeat the same exercise while thinking of the seniormost executive you met with at the same account. Were you able to establish dominance? If so, was there a difference in your dominance and the attribute you used when compared to your meetings with the lower-level person? Remember, even a trait that is typically associated with weakness can be used to establish dominance.

You probably have used a wide range of attributes, depending upon the customers you have met with. That's a fundamental trait of Heavy Hitters. They behave in a way that makes them dominant, even if that means they must behave submissively. For example, empathetically listening to a customer describe his problems is submissive behavior, but it will enable you to establish a dominant position with him later. Only by knowing his goals, objectives, frustrations, and fantasies will you be able to explain how you can address them with your solution. In reality, you will be in a dominant position because you will control his happiness. Now all you have to do is use the right linguistic strategy to convince him of it.

Sales Call Strategy: A salesperson's goal is to gain dominance over a submissive customer. While dominance is commonly associated with brute force, this is not the case in sales. It's simply how people judge others. People are continually sensing whether their position is superior to yours, relatively equal, or inferior in some way. In turn, this impacts what they say during the conversation and how they behave. Relaxed dominant people are free to speak and do as they like. Anxious submissive people speak guardedly and are forced into restricted behavior.

Obviously, a salesperson who can employ a wider range of dominant traits can sell to a wider range of customers. Knowing which trait to draw upon is determined by your sales intuition. For instance, in one account you might display an optimistic attitude in order to instill optimism when the evaluators are nervous and scared. You might say to them, "I've worked with many other customers with the identical problem. They have been able to solve the problem within a couple of months of implementing our solution with far fewer resources than you have to dedicate to this project."

In this example, the salesperson has become a dominant source of hope to someone in pain. In another account you might display outward skepticism and say, "I am not sure you have the wherewithal to implement our solution," forcing the customer to explain why he believes he can implement the solution successfully. In both circumstances you have established dominance.

73. Classifying Relationships

We all have many different types of personal relationships. We have friends, family, coworkers, and neighbors. When we meet someone new at a party, we decide if we like the person and whether he or she might become a friend or is more likely to remain a distant acquaintance.

This classification also happens on sales calls. However, each customer may have an entirely different perception of your character. For example, you may be characterized as a friend by one customer and an acquaintance by another. You could be a little brother to an older customer or a big brother to a younger one. You could be thought of as a father, lover, uncle, cousin, or even an enemy.

Let's do another exercise. Take a moment and think of the last three accounts you won. Write down the characterization that best describes your relationship with your main contact at each account. Most likely, your relationship can be described in close family terms. Here are some possible characterizations:

Acquaintance	Employee	Lover
Aunt	Father figure	Mentor
Best friend	Friend	Mother figure
Big brother	Girlfriend	Nephew
Big sister	Godparent	Neighbor
Boss	Grandchild	Niece
Boyfriend	Grandfather	Son
Buddy	Grandmother	Soul mate
Childhood friend	Husband	Stepchild
Cousin	In-law	Stepparent
Coworker	Little brother	Stranger
Daughter	Little sister	Uncle
Deadbeat	Loser	Wife

Now try the same exercise for the last three accounts you lost. You'll probably find quite a difference in the way you characterize the relationships.

When I ask salespeople what role they take in sales calls, the majority say, "Consultant." Unfortunately, every salesperson competing for a deal is trying to be a consultant. You need to establish a stronger relationship. Some may consider this advice counterintuitive and risky. However, as part of your planning for a meeting, I recommend that you actually identify the familial relationship you wish to achieve with that person ahead of time.

Depending upon your background, you may want to be the trusted father figure, the up-and-coming son, or the soul mate the customer is searching for. Whatever it is, don't be solely a consultant. It is human nature for all customers to categorize you into a familial or friendship relationship. Knowing whether you are a customer's submissive little brother or a dominant mother figure and when to act like a buddy or be a mentor plays an important role in the sales call. When customers treat you like they would a loved one, that's a great sign that you will win the deal. Conversely, you are in big trouble if everyone in the account treats you like the weird uncle.

Sales Call Strategy: While it's perfectly normal to act conservatively in accounts where you are far ahead of the competition, playing it safe when you're behind is a mistake. You must take chances when you meet with customers in accounts where you think you are losing. A primary objective should be to establish a stronger personal relationship (as a son, father figure, wife, etc.) that supersedes the relationship the customer has with the salesperson of the leading vendor. Besides, since you have nothing to lose, why water down your own unique selling style and your effervescent personality?

74. Listening, Silence, and Selling Past the Close

All salespeople know they should listen intently when a customer talks. But did you know there are actually two types of listening? Active listening is intently paying attention to what the customer is saying. You are focused on understanding the meaning of his words and his purpose for saying them. Passive listening is surface-level listening where you quickly pass judgment on the speaker's thoughts. Consequently, you are mentally fixated on your response while the person is talking. What type of listener are you on sales calls?

Silence is one of the most important linguistic structures you can use on sales calls. Silence can actually help you establish dominance because it forces the other person to have to speak. You have conducted a perfect sales call when the customer has been persuaded to buy even though you listened far more than you spoke.

A vice president of sales told me the following story that illustrates the importance of silence. His company had invested nearly half a million dollars trying to persuade one of the world's largest auto manufacturers to use its services. After more than a year of persistent work, his company had finally earned the right to meet with the bully with the juice, the executive vice president, who was also one of the most powerful people in the entire company.

Only three people attended this all-important meeting: the salesperson, the vice president of sales, and the bully with the juice. They were sitting casually around a table and the salesperson was about three-quarters of the way through his PowerPoint presentation when the bully with the juice reached over, closed the laptop, and asked for advice on how they should get started with the project. The surprised salesperson stopped momentarily, opened the laptop, and said that he had a few more slides to present.

I think every sales manager has witnessed defeat snatched from the jaws of victory. You have the deal won and someone on your team (salesperson, technical engineer, or high-ranking executive) inadvertently talks the customer out of doing business. Sometimes it is best to hold your tongue and let your silence speak on your behalf.

Sales Call Strategy: Why do salespeople feel compelled to talk all the time when sometimes silence is golden? In comparison to what the customer has to say, your words are really unimportant. Remember, listen more than you talk and don't sell past the close!

75. Customer Decision Making

Customers dread making decisions because every decision activates fear, uncertainty, doubt, and stress. Today's customers dread the number and similarity of options they must evaluate. While they have more choices than ever, competing products share the same basic features, functions, and benefits. If no single vendor stands out above the others, customers tend to base their final decision on their emotions and esoteric intangibles instead of widely known facts.

Customers also dread having to verify the information presented by vendors. While salespeople believe all buyers are liars, customers believe everyone in sales tells tall tales. Salespeople will exaggerate, describing a product's benefits as greater than they really are and talking about larger-than-life results their product cannot deliver. Customers know it's their responsibility to discount such claims and validate that the facts are as they have been represented. They are the watchdogs of their pocketbooks and organizations, and this is a tremendous responsibility.

People who have been traumatized by a stressful event will suffer from posttraumatic stress disorder. They may have recurring nightmares, continually replay the event in their minds, or suffer from depression. Conversely, customers can suffer from "pretraumatic stress syndrome," whereby the stress of making a selection traumatizes decision makers. This is fundamentally why sales calls are stressful to the customer.

Customers dread uncertainty. They anticipate they will have problems with every purchase. They fear the worst. For example, a customer selecting a contractor for a long-awaited building project fears it will run over budget and behind schedule. Customers selecting a complex computer system fear they will face technical difficulties and the system will be hard to use. A customer implementing new manufacturing machinery fears unforeseen production-line problems. All these customers fear that when all is said and done, they will be no better off than they were before they made the purchase.

Finally, customers dread the pain of selecting between vendors. Recent research of brain scans suggests that the anticipation of pain is equal to the actual pain itself. Customers often engage in long, protracted selection processes even though they have already made up their minds about which product they will buy. Although they would not admit it, they are only searching for the minimal information necessary to further validate their initial choice.

One vendor almost always has an unfair advantage going into the formal evaluation process because the final decision is made very early in the sales cycle. Dethroning the chosen vendor is an extremely tough task, and all the other vendors jump through the customer's sales process hoops for nothing. Because the customer is motivated to shorten the wait and end the pain of making a selection as quickly as possible, he informally makes a decision early, even though it may not be formally announced until months later. This enables the customer to bond with the favored person during sales calls and keep all the other salespeople they meet with at an arm's distance personally.

Certain conditions exacerbate this situation—for example, one vendor is the clear market leader or the competing products are nearly identical. Under these circumstances, customers face little risk of choosing the wrong product so they can quickly settle on a favorite. Obviously, if customers have used one of the products, they know what to expect. The old cliché "Better the devil you know than the devil you don't" describes what they tend to do. Figure 75.1 illustrates factors that influence when customers are likely to make their decision.

Decision likely to be made before the selection process begins	Decision likely to be made during the selection process
The market has a dominant leader. Competing products are similar. The customer has previous product familiarity. *The customer is motivated to eliminate dread.*	The market has several significant players. Competing products have tangible differences. The customer has no previous product familiarity. *The customer seeks to shorten the period of dread.*

Figure 75.1 The impact of dread on customer decision making

Customers are stressed out. They don't know whom or what to believe. They are under immense peer pressure, and they are torn between doing the right thing for the greater good of the company and acting in their best personal interest. This inner turmoil manifests itself during the selection process, which customers dread. To make matters worse, the vendors increase the pressure by injecting claims of their superiority and accusations about their competitors' inferiority.

Sales Call Strategy: Always assume the customer has a favored vendor and a favorite salesperson. For your top accounts that you are currently working on, replay the last sales call you had with the customer in your mind. Now honestly ask yourself if they treated you like the favorite or just an also-ran. Then update your forecast accordingly.

76. No Decision: Fear, Uncertainty, and Doubt

Customers will go to great lengths to reduce the stress of buying. They might list their needs in documents that are hundreds of pages in length. They might hire consultants to verify that they are making the right decisions. And they'll conduct lengthy evaluations to test prospective products, talk to existing users of the products, and complete pilot testing to ensure the products work as advertised—all in an effort to eliminate their fears, reduce their uncertainties, and satisfy their doubts.

However, customers are never 100 percent sure they are purchasing the right product. Regardless of their confident demeanor, on the inside they are experiencing fear, uncertainty, and doubt. In fact, fear, uncertainty, and doubt are at the core of every sales cycle. They play a key role in determining the winner of the deal. Fear, uncertainty, and doubt create stress. Therefore, all salespeople need to understand this lowest common denominator of human decision making—they need to understand the nature of stress.

From a psychological perspective, stress causes people to act out of the norm. It shortens attention spans, increases aggression, escalates mental exhaustion, and encourages poor decision making. Therefore, it's important to understand the four main sources of customer stress: informational stress, peer-pressure stress, executive-level stress, and corporate-citizenship stress.

Informational Stress: Is the Information Being Presented Truthful?

We live in very skeptical times in which information presented by experts and authorities is continually challenged and constantly debunked. Our society is naturally skeptical of the motives of and information from our government, politicians, sports heroes, religious leaders, and business leaders because in recent years, leaders in all these areas have engaged in misinformation, unethical behavior, and the abuse of power.

Not only do we question information, but we expect it to be a half-truth at best. However, the "question authority" mantra is even more extreme when applied to salespeople. It is actually "question everything; believe nothing!" In addition to being subject to the general cynicism of our society, most customers have had negative experiences with salespeople. Their doubts and suspicions about the integrity of the sales profession have been proven true.

Whereas our court system is based upon the presumption of innocence until proven guilty, to customers, salespeople are guilty until proven innocent. Therefore, customers are always in the stressful position of separating fact from fiction. Meanwhile, even the most ethical salesperson carries the stressful burden of proving he's not a crook during sales calls.

Peer-Pressure Stress: How Do My Colleagues Perceive Me?

Peer pressure is a powerful influencer of group dynamics. From an organizational point of view, three types of peer-pressure occur in organizations: upper-level pressure from managers and executives, horizontal peer pressure from those who function at the same organizational level, and lower-level pressure from employees who are constantly evaluating management's actions.

Managers create performance pressure because they continually assess subordinates by how well they perform their jobs and run their departments. They are the judging eyes of the company. Peers create competitive pressure because all are striving to progress in their careers and move upward in the organization. Subordinates create validation pressure. They are continually seeking proof of their manager's ability because the power of their department and the progress of their careers are tied to the business and political acumen of their leader. In essence, they want to know if they have hitched their wagon to the right horse.

Executive-Level Stress: What Pressure Is Company Leadership Under?

C-level executives are extremely worried about what the members of the board of directors think of them (upper-level pressure). They also are continually thinking about how the other members of the senior leadership team feel about them (horizontal peer pressure). And of course, they want their employees to respect them as well (lower-level pressure). Whether from above, below, or the same level in an organization, coworkers are continually evaluating the behavior, success, and failures of those tasked with the decision-making process. Obviously, this exerts pressure on customers to make the right decision and not to make a decision if there isn't a clear-cut winner.

Corporate-Citizenship Stress: Is It in the Best Interest of the Company?

While customers inherently want to do what's in the best interest of the company and to be good corporate citizens, the fundamental dynamic of corporate-employee loyalty has changed. Business is a "survival of the fittest" world where employment is never guaranteed and loyalty goes unrewarded. Therefore, customers feel continual pressure to put their individual needs before the company's.

Achieving the company's goals sometimes contradicts the selfish wants and desires of senior leaders. Other times, it contradicts the desires of colleagues, subordinates, and superiors, causing more and more stress. With so many different types of stress, it's no wonder that customers often delay or can't make a decision. Figure 76.1 illustrates the probability of no decision being made.

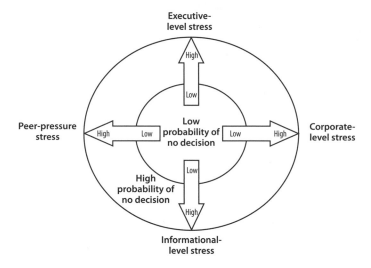

Figure 76.1 Probability no decision will be made

One persuasion technique that can be used to combat no decision is the metaphor. Metaphors are stories, parables, and analogies that communicate ideas by using examples that people can relate to and identify with. Metaphors enable complex concepts and theories to be explained in an understandable, interesting, and persuasive manner. Using metaphors is a nonthreatening way to make the skeptical, stressed-out customer more receptive to moving forward with the purchase.

Metaphors are more than simple anecdotes or interesting tales. They connect the presenter's message to the recipient's personal experience and collective knowledge. They quickly communicate complex ideas to the conscious mind. More importantly, metaphors are language structures with multiple layers of interpretation. While they talk to the conscious mind, they also communicate with the subconscious mind. Therefore, they are valuable tools that can be used to change a person's habits, disposition, and beliefs and relieve fear, uncertainty, and doubt.

We can use three different types of metaphors to overcome no decision; educational, personal, and action based. Educational metaphors are analogies that help explain new concepts using common terms or everyday situations. When you walk the customer through your product presentation or make a drawing of your product's architecture to show the customer how it operates, you're using an educational metaphor. Explaining how your product works in detail helps customers understand and minimize the implementation risks. The story you tell about how one of your customers is successfully using your product is an example of a personal metaphor. Knowing that many other companies are successfully using your product helps puts the customer's mind at ease. Action-based metaphors use physical movement to communicate additional meaning and highlight important concepts. For example, a product demonstration is actually an action-based metaphor that shows customers how easily they can use your product. Site visits and reference calls with existing customers are action-based metaphors intended to make prospective customers comfortable making the decision to move forward.

Sales Call Strategy: The real enemy isn't your archrivals; it's no decision. Achieving the company's goals sometimes contradicts the selfish wants and desires of decision makers. Other times, it contradicts the desires of colleagues, subordinates, and superiors, causing more and more stress. With so many different types of stress, it's no wonder that customers dread making decisions—so they frequently won't make one. Use metaphors as a weapon to fight the dreaded no decision. Metaphors connect with both the conscious and subconscious minds to help relieve the stress of decision making.

77. The Subconscious Decision Maker

To understand the impact of the subconscious mind on decision making, let's study Bob, a college-educated professional with a doctorate in computer science. Successful in his career, he has become an executive of a Fortune 500 company. Bob is a smart businessman who employs sound business practices and possesses the acumen to get to the top of the corporate ladder.

Let's say Bob is facing two very important decisions. The first decision involves making a multimillion-dollar purchase to upgrade some equipment of the division he runs. The second decision involves proposing marriage to Maggie, his girlfriend of nine months. Bob approaches each of these decisions in a very different way.

For the business decision, he first conducts an in-depth study of the inefficiencies of his current infrastructure. Next, he presents his findings with an internal rate-of-return study for replacing the old equipment with state-of-the-art machinery to the senior management team of the parent company. Then he performs a detailed analysis of the various equipment vendors and makes a final selection.

Getting married is one of life's most important decisions. Bob has fallen in love with Maggie. He feels good being with her, thinks about her often, and looks forward to their time together. She has the qualities he admires, and when compared to girlfriends of the past, she is the best. Bob decides he will ask her to marry him.

However, as he moves forward in his decision-making process, an unexpected change in Bob's thought process occurs. The subconscious mind, the self-regulating system designed to prevent us from making unwise choices, is on vigilant watch. It drives Bob to perform a "gut-check" of the rational, logical information regarding the equipment purchase. Beyond the facts and figures, does the decision feel right? He second-guesses himself and asks whether the move will help or hurt his career.

Conversely, the emotional high associated with the idea of marriage is tempered by reality. He now evaluates Maggie's little habits that he once thought were cute with a more rational eye. He studies other aspects of their relationship with equal intensity. Figure 77.1 illustrates the changing nature of the decision-making process.

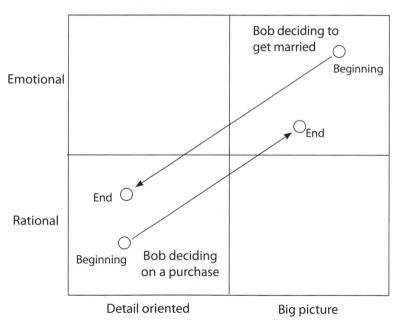

Figure 77.1 The changing nature of decision making

We've all worked on accounts where, after studying every aspect of your and your competitor's products, customers went into analysis paralysis. They had so much information that they couldn't make a decision. On the opposite end of the spectrum are customers who change their minds on a moment-by-moment basis: you might be winning one moment and losing the next. Overwhelmed with information, their conscious mind vacillates from one extreme to the other.

At this point, the subconscious mind takes an active role in decision making. One of its main responsibilities is protection. Much like a guardian angel, it's on the lookout for perilous situations and possible circumstances that might endanger the person physically and mentally. To perform this task, it assumes a third-person observation role and acts as a separate entity, even though it resides deep inside the individual. It guides a decision maker from the emotional to the logical and vice versa.

Sales Call Strategy: Anticipate the impact of the subconscious mind during the sales cycle and take it into account during sales calls. The customer with whom you had a "red hot" initial sales call will suddenly turn cold and fail to respond to your follow-up calls. The prospect who has established an elaborate selection process will ultimately be influenced by emotions. Knowing this ahead of time, you can plan to use different types of words that correspond to a logical, emotional, and psychological appeal in interactions with your customers.

78. Measuring Sales Call Rapport

Customers will have one of five different reactions to everything you say during a sales call. They will either reject your statements and ideas outright, ignore what you say, acknowledge they've heard you, accept what you say but do nothing, or internalize your recommendations and take action. The reaction you receive is influenced by the level of rapport you have established with the prospective customer.

Similarly, sales calls can be classified by the level of rapport. Combative sales calls are antagonistic interactions with nonexistent rapport. Most likely, this type of situation occurs because the customer has a preexisting bias against your solution or an incompatibility exists between you or your company and the customer. Contentious sales calls may begin congenially but are characterized by controversy or topical disputes that lead to ill feelings by the end of the call. Unemotional sales calls lack outward displays of affection, and even though the call may last an hour, the customer remains aloof and unsympathetically distant. Friendly sales calls are situations where the customer is generally receptive, cooperative, and open to your ideas. In synergistic sales calls, the customer shows genuine excitement, is receptive to your advice and recommendations, and jointly plans the future steps of the sales process with you.

Customers can experience many different types of receptive states with salespeople, ranging from fear and hate to love and trust. For example, combative and synergistic sales calls are at the extreme ends of the scale of receptive states. Experiencing a synergistic sales call is dependent upon establishing four different receptive states of rapport:

- *Personal receptive state.* The first priority is to build a personal receptive state with each individual. To accomplish this, perform a pattern interruption (see chapter 43), search for intersecting activities you might have in common (see chapter 36), and speak the customer's unique languages (see chapters 34).

- *Technical receptive state.* Take great care to build a technical receptive state through understanding the customer's problem. Execute a series of premeditated vignettes (see chapter 30) to qualify the customer's technical fit to the solution you offer. These vignettes should also provide the logical arguments that your solution can solve the customer's technical problem.

- *Business receptive state.* As you demonstrate that your primary interest is in the customer's success, you begin to build a business receptive state. At this point, the customer starts to consider you more than a vendor. You have proven your value as a business partner (see chapter 54) who has the expertise to solve the customer's problem.

- *Political receptive state.* You enjoy a political advantage over the competition when the customer believes that only your solution will help him fulfill his fantasies (see chapter 4) and achieve his personal benefactions (see chapter 2).

Complete rapport exists when these four receptive states are established. For example, synergistic sales calls are typically based upon complete rapport whereas friendly sales calls only may have a personal or technical receptive state established.

Sales Call Strategy: Preplan how you will create a personal receptive state at the beginning of the sales call. As the sales call progresses, continuously monitor the level of rapport of each attendee and ask yourself if you are creating the four different receptive states: personal, technical, business, and political. These receptive states provide the positive environment that will enable your recommendations to be accepted and acted upon. After the call, analyze if you achieved each of the receptive states. Finally, be sure to prepare your colleagues who will join you on the sales call by helping them understand what type of sales call to expect (combative, contentious, unemotional, friendly, or synergistic) and their role in your strategy to achieve complete rapport.

79. The Persuasive Elevator Pitch

Even senior salespeople find the next exercise to be very challenging. What makes it difficult is that you already think you can do it easily. The exercise requires you to time yourself because it must be completed in no more than forty-five seconds. Ideally, you want to be in a private place where you can say your answer aloud.

I would like you to pretend that you are in an elevator at one of your industry's trade shows. You are heading down to the lobby when the doors open on the thirtieth floor. You instantly recognize the executive who walks in and quickly glance at his name badge to confirm he is the CEO of the most important account you would like to start working with. You have never met him before nor have you been able to generate any interest from his organization. You have forty-five seconds to introduce yourself, explain what your company does in a way the CEO would find interesting and applicable, and motivate him to take the action you suggest. Ready? Go!

So, how did you do? You are to be commended for completing this exercise. Even the most successful salespeople find this pressure-packed exercise difficult. At sales meetings, I will ask salespeople to perform this exercise with me in front of their peers. Many times they become flustered or quit halfway through and they ask me if they can start over again. My answer is always no because you have only one chance to make a great first impression. Here are the six most common mistakes salespeople make with their elevator pitch:

- *They use truisms.* They believe their company's own marketing pitch, which makes claims that are not considered entirely true by the listener. As a result, they instantly lose credibility.
- *They describe themselves using buzzwords.* They repeat industry buzzwords or, worse yet, use technical buzzwords that are known only within their company.
- *They use fillers.* They make too much small talk or ask frivolous questions that reduce their stature and make them even more submissive to the customer.
- *They demean themselves or the listener.* Their statements turn them into mere salespeople, not business problem solvers. They unintentionally demean the listener by asking impertinent questions or assuming the listener knows exactly what they are talking about.
- *They present an unreasonable close.* They don't take into account that they are talking to a senior company leader and use a close that is unrealistic or demands too much of the customer.
- *They are incongruent.* Their tone, pitch, and tempo of speech don't match. They speak too fast and their quivering tone broadcasts that they're nervous and submissive.

Here's an example of a poor elevator pitch. The problems are identified in brackets. Luke Skywalker, a salesperson for XYZ Technologies, is attending a trade show and happens to be in the elevator with Norman Bates, chief information officer at Wonderful Telecommunications.

Hello, Norman. How are you today [filler]? Do you have a moment to talk [filler]? My name is Luke Skywalker and I work for [demeans salesperson] XYZ Technologies. Have you heard of XYZ Technologies [demeans listener]? Umm . . . [filler] Well, we are the leading provider [truism] of business transformational outsourcing [industry buzzword]. We have a unique extended-hybrid implementation methodology [technical buzzword]. Do you have time for me to buy you a cup of coffee and hear more about it [unreasonable close]?

A successful elevator pitch will incorporate the following linguistic structures:

- *Softeners.* A softener eases listeners into the next thought or is used to set expectations. When you say, "I'm sorry to bother you," you are using the preapologizing softener technique.
- *Facts.* A fact is the undisputed truth. Facts are recognized instantaneously.
- *Logic.* Logic is inferred by the listener to be true. Two main types of logic are used in sales situations: linear and geometric. The formula for linear logic is A plus B equals C, meaning when A and B are true statements, then the C statement or idea is also true. For example, "Our solution is 10 percent faster" and "we are 25 percent cheaper"; therefore, "we are the better solution." The formula for geometric logic is if X is true, and X equals Y, then any statement that is true for X also applies to Y. For example, "We are helping Allstate Insurance reduce costs 10 percent" and "You are an insurance company like Allstate Insurance"; therefore, "We can help you reduce your costs 10 percent."
- *Metaphors.* In chapter 76 we discussed the three different types of metaphors: educational, personal, and action based. The purpose of each of these metaphors is to tell, teach, and enlighten the listener, with the ultimate goal of changing his or her opinion or behavior. While educational metaphors appeal to the conscious intellect, personal and action-based metaphors can be tailored to the subconscious mind. Also, all

three types can be connected, interwoven, and mixed together in any combination.

- *Suggestions.* Foreground suggestions are direct and explicit ("*Consumer Reports* gave our product the highest rating"). Background suggestions are indirect and their meaning is inferred ("One of their customers recently switched to our product").

- *Fallback position.* Every customer conversation is actually a negotiation between verbal dominance and submissive silence. Instead of giving ultimatums that force the customer to accept or reject your close, provide options from which customers can select. Always have alternate suggestions prepared in advance. (See chapter 56.)

- *Silence.* Silence is an important and useful linguistic structure. It indicates you are listening and waiting for a response. Silence can actually be used to gain dominance during conversations.

Here's an elevator pitch that incorporates these linguistic structures:

Norman, hi, I'm Luke Skywalker with XYZ Technologies [fact]. It's a pleasure to meet you [softener]. I'm not sure if you are familiar with us [softener], but we work with AT&T [fact]. They've had to reduce their IT costs during these tough times [geometric logic]. I'm here because James Bond, the CIO of AT&T, is presenting a case study on how he cut his IT costs by 20 percent using our outsourcing solution [metaphor, background suggestion]. There'll be CIOs from some of our other customers, including General Electric and Johnson & Johnson, speaking as well [fact, background suggestion]. The session is tomorrow at 1:00 p.m. if you can make it [foreground suggestion, softener]. [Pause—silence, waiting for response.] That's too bad [softener]. I'd be delighted to send you his presentation [fallback position, foreground suggestion]. Great. Just to confirm your e-mail address, that's Norman.bates@wonderful.com. Is there anyone else I should send it to [fallback position]? [Pause—silence]. Okay, that's Ferris Bueller, your vice president of infrastructure. Thanks, Norman. You'll be hearing from me shortly.

The most important linguistic structure used in this elevator pitch are the metaphors. Ideally, a metaphor will cause the mind to immediately recognize the importance of the information, accept the message, and follow the suggestion. The proof of a metaphor's success is evidenced by a change in the verbal and physical language the listener emits. This could range from an enthusiastic verbal response to a subtle readjustment of the body from a closed posture to an open posture (see chapter 28).

Sales Call Strategy: Your words are your most important competitive weapons. In this regard, your ability to deliver a compelling elevator pitch is your biggest and most reliable armament.

There are many sales situations where you have only a minute or two to conduct an entire sales call. For example, you could be walking down the customer's hallway and bump into the president or meeting with a lower-level contact when the vice president drops in. You must be able to deliver a compelling and memorable message during this pressure-packed time-sensitive encounter.

Write down your elevator pitch and analyze its structure for the use of buzzwords, fillers, and truisms. Use language structures such as softeners, metaphors, and suggestions to improve its persuasiveness. If you understand how listeners process language, you can help them decipher meaning. This ensures that your message will be successfully received and the action you suggest will be followed. Finally, be sure to practice your pitch aloud so your delivery is congruent. Remember, a sales call can happen anywhere and at any time. Always have a prepared elevator pitch.

80. Renewal, Persuasion, and Creation Sales Calls

Sales cycles can be classified as transactional or enterprise deals. In transactional deals, the salesperson has only one or two interactions with a potential customer, whereas enterprise deals involve many customer interactions. For example, retail sales are typically transactional deals and business-to-business sales are usually enterprise deals.

The three basic types of enterprise deals are renewal, persuasion, and creation deals. Renewal deals involve selling more products and services to existing customers or trying to close a multiyear contract that is coming up for renewal. Persuasion deals are extremely competitive customer evaluations that usually involve the customer creating an RFP or similar document. In these deals you are usually competing against your archrivals. Finally, in creation deals you target and penetrate a new account, trying to get the customer to use your products for the first time with the hope that the customer will make a much larger purchase in the future. Figure 80.1 shows the three different enterprise sales cycles.

Each of these enterprise sales cycles requires a different sales call strategy. In renewal deals the goal is to execute a "sales virus" strategy where the salesperson is continually spreading out to meet everyone within the customer's organization across all departments and at all levels.

Persuasion sales calls are quite different because they are based solely on the transmission and receipt of information. In essence, they are a series of response-based sales calls where the customer is comparing your answers to his questions against those from your competitors. Therefore, all the salespeople involved in the deal are continually saying to the customer, "We are the best because . . . "

The persuasion sales cycle has two critical sales calls. The first is the vendor interview. This is one of the few chances you'll have to develop relationships and uncover the political structure of the account. Asking questions is an excellent way to demonstrate your knowledge. Questions are actually metaphors that show your expertise and the competency of your company.

The most important moment is the vendor presentation. Why? Because this is one of the few moments during the entire sales cycle when senior executives (the bully with the juice and the emperor) are present. In most cases, it is your only opportunity to win them over. Therefore, your presentation has to be persuasive, to differentiate you from the competition, and to be flawlessly executed.

Creation sales calls are just the opposite. They are hypothesis sales based upon establishing trust where the salesperson says to the customer, "We can help you do X better. Let us come in and prove it!" The salesperson's goal is to win a "beachhead deal" and get the customer to start using his company's product or to start a small project to validate the solution. The hope is that this project will successfully culminate with a big purchase.

The creation sales cycle is primarily based upon establishing trust. Unlike the persuasion sales cycle, which is based upon persuasive words, the creation sales cycle is based upon completing actions that create trust, building respect, and forming alliances with employees who will promote the solution within their organization.

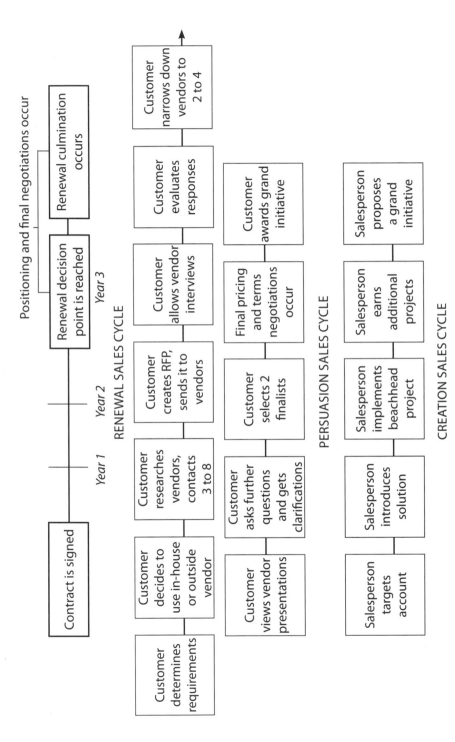

Figure 80.1 Renewal, persuasion, and creation enterprise sales cycles

Sales Call Strategy: The type of sales cycle you are working will determine how you disseminate information during sales calls. In renewal sales calls, do not become "single-threaded," where you are tied to a single customer contact. Instead, adopt the sales virus strategy and use the sales call to establish as many relationships as possible. Persuasions sales calls require you to win the argument that your product is better than the competition's. Creation sales calls are based upon establishing trust and recruiting individuals who will promote your cause within their companies. Therefore, you must adapt your selling style and what you say and do to fit these vastly different sales cycles.

81. Turning Points and Buzz Kills

Every type of sales cycle (renewal, creation, or persuasion) has a critical moment, or "turning point," where it is won or lost. In some cases, the turning point is easy to spot. For example, a salesperson may be presenting his solution and encounters a deal-breaking objection that he is unable to overcome. Even though the customer remains cordial for the rest of the meeting, a turning point has occurred and the deal is lost. In most cases, the turning point occurs when the salesperson isn't present. It's in casual hallway conversations or internal e-mails that selection team members share opinions that influence vendors' futures. The only outward sign that a turning point has occurred is the perceptible change in deal momentum as evidenced in figure 81.1.

You probably noticed the term "buzz kill" on the graph. This represents the person, business reason, political issue, or technical obstacle that causes momentum to turn downward. Ninety-nine out of one hundred times you will not recover from a buzz kill. However, some companies won't let salespeople stop working deals. You may even be familiar with the following drill, which I call the "walk of shame." All the various sales managers meet with the rep and theorize about all the possible ways to win. Then they mandate that the selling continue even though the salesperson knows working on a deal past a buzz kill is a waste of time.

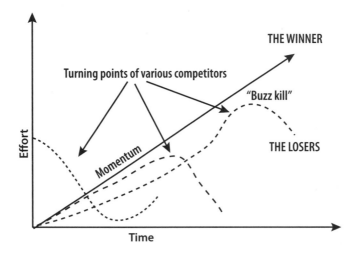

Figure 81.1 Turning points of various competitors

Sometimes salespeople will decide on their own to continue the walk of shame. Since they have invested so much time, energy, and emotion into the deal, they find it impossible to let it go. This is particularly true for salespeople who have neglected to build up a pipeline of future business opportunities.

Time takes on an additional dimension of meaning during the sales cycle. Usually, we think of time as a continuum. We spend most of our mental energy thinking about the immediate tasks before us. We typically don't consider time to be a finite resource. There's always tomorrow, next week, next month, or next year. During the sales process, time is not just minutes and days; it is actually a measure of deal momentum. Therefore, increasing momentum in a deal represents good or positive time, and backward momentum is bad or negative time. Heavy Hitters keep the negative time they spend on deals to a minimum.

Time is a salesperson's enemy because time is finite. On average, there are thirty days in a month and ninety days in a quarter. Time is the governor that determines how many deals can be worked and where effort should be focused. The relentless march of time creates artificial deadlines by which deals must be won. Time is a precious resource that must be conserved, respected, and above all, used to your advantage.

Sales Call Strategy: Your most valuable asset is your time. First, in order to protect your time you must be able to recognize when a buzz kill occurs during sales calls. Second, if you are unsure why you are losing momentum during sales calls, bring along your manager or someone else and ask that person to help you identify buzz kill moments. Finally, write down the buzz kill moments of five deals you recently lost and prepare a counteractive strategy for each so history doesn't repeat itself again in the future.

82. Structuring the Sales Presentation

After evaluating hundreds of corporate sales presentations, I can honestly say that they all are basically the same. You could take slides from one company's presentation and insert them in another's and no one would notice. They are all fact-based infomercials with no discernable differences.

It's not enough to say that to stand out you have to be different. Rather, you need a more sophisticated, indirect approach that differentiates your solution in the minds of customers. You can't *tell* customers you're unique, different, and one of a kind. You must *demonstrate* it to them, starting with the psychological and linguistic framework of the corporate presentation.

Traditional corporate sales presentations are typically organized into six sections: my company, my products, how they work, their benefits, our customers, and a call to action. Your presentation should be divided into four sections. It should start with a pattern interruption, move on to customer metaphors, be followed by explanations, and close with suggestions. This way of presenting is distinctly different from the presentations of your competitors. Let's examine each section of the presentation in detail.

Section 1—The Pattern Interruption

The first goal of your presentation should be to perform a pattern interruption to break the customer's mode of thinking that you are like other salespeople and to stand out from the competition. The pattern interruption starts the process of building rapport, engages the audience, and provokes open-mindedness. Your pattern interruption will consist of an attention-grabbing cowcatcher (see chapter 43).

Unfortunately, the first few slides of most corporate presentations have little panache. The obligatory introduction states some facts about the company's financial position, how long it has been in business, and its office locations. (The worst actually show pictures of the company's buildings as if this were something astounding.)

Section 2—Customer Metaphors

One of the biggest problems that most salespeople have on sales calls is that they are too eager to tell the customer about their products. The same is true for a corporate presentation, and when this happens, the presentation does not build a storyline that piques interest. Instead of launching into slides about the product line and technical aspects of the products, the second section of the corporate presentation should focus on customers.

Following the cowcatcher, you need a hook. Now that the listeners' interest is piqued, you need to hook them on why they should use your product. Your best hook is to tell them stories about your customers. Most corporate presentations include an obligatory slide that shows twenty or so logos of the major companies that use the salesperson's products. That's not what I am referring to here. The second section should include six to eight slides of how specific customers are using the products, the operational results that have been improved, and the financial impact on the bottom line. In addition, it should include a quote from a customer whose name and title the audience can identify with psychologically. For example, include a quote from a customer's CFO when presenting to a financial department. Finally, this section should have some eye-catching graphics that tie the whole story together. These could be pictures of your product at work, the person who provided the quote, or an example of the end result.

As we discussed in chapter 48, the pertinence of the customer examples is very important. Presenting examples from companies that closely mirror the prospect's business objectives will make the statements more powerful. Presenting examples from companies that the prospects don't recognize will have less impact.

Section 3—Explanations

The third section of the presentation is based upon an intellectual and logical appeal to the customer's conscious mind. Here the goal is to continue to build credibility by methodically explaining background information and facts behind the customer metaphor slides.

For example, let's say you are selling manufacturing-shop-floor equipment and one of your customer metaphor slides is about how General Electric saved $20 million in the first year of using your product. In this section you would drill down through the critical features of your product that streamlined operations. You could explain in detail how these features work technically and how they compare to other methods of accomplishing the same tasks.

The explanations section is typically the largest of the presentation. Keep in mind that iPods, television, and the Internet have changed people's attention spans and the way they want information presented to them. The best presentations deliver information in small chunks. No single slide should take more than two minutes to cover. If it lasts longer than that, you may lose the audience's attention. Therefore, if a slide takes four minutes to explain, split it into two slides to keep the presentation moving.

Since most salespeople are well versed in the logic of selling, it doesn't make sense to reiterate here what you already know. Instead, let's emphasize some steps you can take to make an intellectual appeal more compelling:

- Provide independent confirmation of your facts wherever possible.
- Provide quotes from authorities (customers, analysts, and the press).
- Quantify beneficial claims with specific numbers.
- Use real-world examples, which are more powerful than hypothetical statements.
- Arrange your arguments from strongest to weakest.
- Keep it simple. Remember Occam's razor: the simpler explanation is always preferred.
- Be prepared for contradictory facts from other vendors and have factual responses ready.

- Quantify results from adverse consequences (for example, loss of revenue due to equipment downtime).
- Present the extremes and worst-case scenarios to make the other options to solve the problem look worse than they really are.
- Use alliterations—repetition of the same letter or sound of adjacent words—so that concepts are more easily remembered (for example, "durability, dependability, and adaptability").
- Include mnemonics where initial letters of words spell out a tangible word (for example, ACRONYM equals "a clever reword nudges your memory").
- Use the rule of three: whenever you make a claim, support it with three different facts.
- Create your own euphemisms that reflect the importance of your product or a particular feature. For example, a rubber band could be called a "multipurpose business instrument."
- Understand that it is all right to draw big conclusions from small statistics. Sometimes the biggest points can be made from the smallest samples.
- Brighten up the facts with interesting graphics that represent them pictorially.
- Become a storyteller, not a human dictionary. Use metaphors to explain concepts. Instead of saying, "A poll showed customers prefer us three to one," say, "Harris Poll surveyed four thousand buyers from across the country and found that three thousand, or 75 percent, thought our solution was far superior."

Logical arguments alone, no matter how well you present them, will not change skeptics into believers. Finessing customers to change their opinions requires an appeal to their human nature.

Section 4—Suggestions

The typical close to a corporate presentation is a one-slide summary of the major topics that were covered. The salesperson basically says, "I hope we passed the audition." A better way to end a presentation is with a very specific action item that is based upon the goal you wanted the presentation to accomplish.

For example, if the goal of the presentation was to make the customer's short list, an appropriate close would be to explain the seven reasons why you believe you should be on the short list. If you are further along in the sales cycle and your goal was to close the deal, walking the customer through the implementation process or explaining your pricing methodology is an appropriate close.

These action items should be worded in the form of foreground and background suggestions. Examples of foreground suggestions include "I spoke to my contacts at General Electric yesterday and told them I was presenting to you today. They extended an invitation to come to their operation for a site visit" and "All of the analyst firms strongly encourage that customers benchmark all the products they are considering."

Background suggestions are indirect. Showing your pricing model is a background suggestion to negotiate price. If earlier in your presentation you described how the customers at General Electric made their decision, what products they evaluated, and why they selected your solution, walking the customer through their implementation process is a background suggestion to make the customer think about implementation. Another example of a background suggestion is "The regional vice president for Arch-rival Software just joined our company because he was tired of dealing with continual product support problems." This background suggestion triggers a more profound emotional reaction as the customers will want you to tell them why.

Two very important slides that should be included in your presentation are called the "strategy slide" and the "money slide." The strategy slide clearly defines the business problem that needs to be solved (or the opportunity that can be created), the cause of the problem (or reason for the opportunity), the goal realized when the problem is solved (or when the opportunity is realized), and all the possible options that could be utilized to solve the problem or achieve the opportunity. The strategy slide is based upon defining the first four boxes of figure 54.1: problem, cause, goal, and possible options.

The strategy slide is not vendor specific. Rather, it presents the customer's situation from an unbiased third-party point of view. You know you have created the perfect strategy slide when the customer asks for a copy of it so that he can post it on his office wall. Conversely, the money slide shows how your specific solution solves the problem from the strategic, operational, and, most importantly, financial perspectives. This slide summarizes the strategic value of your solution including all costs, ROI, and payback assumptions. It also shows the operational value of your solution that results from its unique features and functions. This slide summarizes why the customer should select your solution over all the others.

The strategy slide and the money slide can be used at the very beginning of your presentation as the pattern interruption. Or they can be placed at the end and incorporated into a background or foreground suggestion. In reality, your entire presentation boils down to these two slides. Do you understand the customer's problem and have you developed the credibility to recommend a solution? Have you demonstrated that you can solve the problem better than the competition?

Sales Call Strategy: In over one thousand win-loss interviews, the sales presentation was the most frequently cited turning point during the entire sales cycle. It's the moment when you either gain momentum on your way to winning or lose momentum that you will never recover. Usually, this is one of the few moments during the sales cycle when the bully with the juice and the emperor are present and may be your only opportunity to win them over. Therefore, structure your presentation into sections (pattern interruption, customer metaphors, explanations, and suggestions) for greater impact. Be sure to include a strategy slide and a money slide.

83. Pause-to-Check Method

Even though empathy is a core human emotion, not everyone is equally empathetic. Empathy is now thought to be a genetic trait determined by your DNA makeup. An estimated 15 percent of the U.S. population are "empaths," people born with the trait of high sensitivity.[1] If you are not a natural empath, use the "pause-to-check" method to improve your listening sensitivity. After every few minutes during a sales call or customer presentation, pause for a moment and check with your audience. Specifically, check for nuances in their facial expressions and how they are holding their bodies. Do you think they are more or less engaged? Why? It's okay to stop and say, "Are you still with me?" or "I hope I didn't confuse anyone."

Sales Call Strategy: When presenting to groups, use the pause-to-check method to ensure that everyone is engaged and following along with you. Many people will not voice their objections during group meetings because of peer pressure. Therefore, it is important to read each audience member and elicit the thoughts from those with whom you are losing rapport. You do not want them to leave the meeting with negative impressions that can poison the entire group when you aren't around. You want their objections out in the open so you can immediately address them in front of the entire room.

84. Creating Better PowerPoint Slides

Let's finish the discussion about presentations we started in chapter 82 by considering the look and feel of your slides. What colors are used in your corporate presentations? I like to use two basic color schemes in my slides, red and blue. Red signifies change, aids memorization, and subconsciously tells people to slow down and pay attention—like a stop sign. Blue encourages creativity, and people associate it with explorative feelings and a sense of wonder—like the sky.

How well your presentation is received will vary depending on whether it was created by a Visual, Auditory, or Kinesthetic and who is in the audience. Slide after slide after slide of bullet points will torment Visuals. A sterile look and feel turns off Kinesthetics. Don't show Auditories too many graphs and pictures because they need something to read. Ideally, you want your slides to match the word catalog makeup of your audience. I'd recommend you assume a general audience is composed of 40 percent Visuals, 40 percent Auditories, and 20 percent Kinesthetics.

The typical sales presentation is made to a group of people, many of whom you have never met before, who probably have different word catalog wirings. In this situation, another strategy is to present all of your ideas and thoughts in neutral wording without any reference to word catalogs. Neutral wording enables listeners to apply the catalog of their choice to gain meaning. Here are some examples of word catalog usage (the first phrase in each pair) and the corresponding neutral wording usage (the second phrase):

- Instead of "I see what you mean," use "I agree with you."
- Instead of "I hear you," use "I understand."
- Instead of "Looks good," use "I think it will work."

The direction in which your audience reads influences how they receive information, and the layout of your slides should reflect this. English, for example is written left to right. A "heat map" is a representation of where the eyes look first and gravitate toward next when initially viewing a website page, PowerPoint slide, letter, or e-mail. Areas are colored according to the instinctual tendency to look at them from hot (high) to cold (low). Figure 84.1 shows an example of a heat map for a PowerPoint slide.

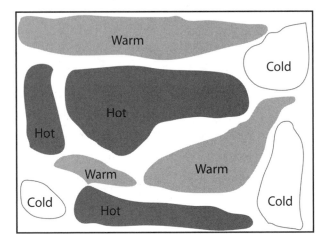

Figure 84.1 Sample heat map for a PowerPoint Slide

As you can see, the eyes tended to look at the left-hand side first. They also focused on certain areas more than others, and the right side of the slide attracted very little attention. When the eyes see an object, whether a picture or PowerPoint slide, they don't initially fixate on a single location. Instead, they look at various points of the object and send the corresponding electrical nerve impulses to the back of the brain that is responsible for vision. Your eyes really don't "see" anything; it's your brain that interprets the impulses into something recognizable.

Sales Call Strategy: When you take into account word catalogs, your sales presentation will connect much better with your audience and be more influential with their subconscious minds. Provide Auditories slides they can read to themselves, engage Visuals with eye-catching graphics, and give examples that cause Kinesthetics to emote. You can use neutral wording when you don't have any idea of the audience's word catalogs. Finally, be conscious of the heat maps of the PowerPoint slides, letters, and e-mails you create.

85. How Customers Use Coping Mechanisms

We naturally assume that customers will react in one of two ways to our pitch: they'll like it or they won't. However, customer behavior is far more complex. Customers use sophisticated coping mechanisms when facing the stressful situation of selecting between salespeople and their solutions. Coping mechanisms are psychological and behavioral strategies people use to manage stress and threatening situations. Here's a list of the common buyer coping mechanisms you can expect to encounter on sales calls:

- *Attack.* Some customers categorize all salespeople as unethical evildoers and therefore attack you as being part of the group. Do not take this attack personally. These buyers are not excited about making a purchase decision. Generalizing all salespeople into a single group helps them handle the ordeal of buying.

- *Avoidance.* Certain customers will seek to avoid the people and situations that cause distress. They'll keep the conversation solely at the surface level and won't answer tough questions. Confronting customers who use this coping mechanism causes them to avoid stressful people and situations all the more.

- *Business-level conversation.* Some customers instinctively try to keep the conversation at a business level with the nonfavored salespeople. They do this to protect themselves because they don't want to let anyone down. This is one of the more prevalent coping mechanisms buyers use to deal with salespeople.

- *Compensation.* Customers sometimes make up for a weakness in one area by overemphasizing another. For example, a business-oriented senior executive who can't follow the technical conversation of subordinates with a salesperson may blurt out, "I'm in charge of the selection."

- *Intellectualization.* Some customers will avoid showing any emotion and focus instead on facts and logic. However, even the most analytical and unemotional customers have a sentimental favorite that they want to win.

- *Passive-aggressiveness.* Some customers project a friendly superficial presence but are secretly plotting against you. This is one of the worst predicaments for any salesperson to be in.

- *Rationalization.* Certain customers use logical reasons in an illogical way to publicly validate their emotional favorite. For example, they'll say they can't use your product because it doesn't support international monetary conversions, even though they don't conduct any international business.

- *Reaction formation.* Some customers take a polar opposite position to everything you say. They simply don't want to buy from you.

- *Trivialization.* Some customers trivialize a favored vendor's major deficiency while maximizing the minor shortcomings of the other vendors. This is another sure sign that they are against you.

Finally, sometimes what customers say about you really applies to them. They'll say your price is too high when, in reality, they couldn't have afforded it in the first place. They will say your solution is technically inferior when they don't have the wherewithal to implement it. In other words, the most significant and prevalent customer coping mechanism is lying.

Sales Call Strategy: The customer has developed a pattern of behavior for dealing with salespeople after hundreds of interactions. Since it is usually based upon negative experiences, the first goal of every sales call should be to perform a pattern interruption. You want to dissociate yourself from all the other salespeople and their previous negative sales calls. One way to accomplish this is by "detaching" and doing something completely different or totally unexpected.

Detaching can be an effective tool in sales situations where you want to change behaviors quickly. For example, when you greet someone, you will typically cheerfully say, "How are you doing?" The automatic response is "Fine" or "Okay." It is the expected and anticipated response attached to that particular question. Let's pretend you respond, "My dog just died." This answer is completely opposite from the expected response. Immediately, the person who asked the question would be detached from being cheerful and become somber or apologetic.

Perform detaching when customers resort to their favorite coping mechanism during your sales call. For example, when a customer attacks you by saying "Your price is too high!" you might say, "I could rationalize all the reasons why we charge what we do, but those would be 'rational lies.' Tell me how we can find the middle ground to make this business happen."

86. Using a Sign-In Sheet

Many salespeople really don't know who attends their sales presentations. Even though introductions are typically made before a meeting starts, full names, exact titles, and complete contact information are rarely collected. Sometimes introductions are made so quickly or the audience is so large that it's impossible to write down or remember all the information. You can't count on attendees to bring business cards either. Sometimes the best you can do is remember their first names. Also, people will come in late to the presentation and leave early. It's not practical to stop and ask them who they are and what they do.

One way to keep track of attendees is to create a presentation sign-in sheet. The sheet should have the following columns: name, title, phone number, and e-mail address. A final column should say, "Add to e-mail list (Y/N)?" Pass around the sign-in sheet at the beginning and end of the presentation or whenever someone enters the room. In addition, whether people write *Y* or *N* in the final column provides an interesting piece of information about where they stand.

Sales Call Strategy: Keep a couple of sign-in sheets with you at all times so you can correctly identify meeting attendees when you want to contact them later.

87. Conquering Nervousness

Sales is a profession based upon pressure: pressure from sales management to make your quota, pressure from competitors who are trying to defeat you, pressure you place on yourself to be number one, and pressure to perform well on every sales call. Pressure upon the salesperson during sales calls has a profound impact. It creates an emergency situation that triggers the body's fight-or-flight system.

Here are a few of the physiological changes that happen to a salesperson who is making a stressful sales call or conducting the critical presentation he hopes will land him a big deal:

- The eyebrows instinctively rise and the eyes widen. The iris muscles of the eye contract, causing the pupils to dilate. These actions enhance vision so that maximum visual information about the perceived threats can be sent to the brain.

- The brain's cortex interprets the visual information it is receiving and transmits messages to the brain's hypothalamus. The hypothalamus activates the adrenal gland, which instantaneously releases adrenaline into the bloodstream. The hormone adrenaline activates the body's emergency response systems.

- The heart pumps at up to twice its normal rate. Breathing quickens so that the lungs can supply more oxygen to the blood. Oxygen-rich blood is sent to the brain for clearer thinking and to muscles for quick reactions. The stomach stops digestion so that blood can be diverted elsewhere in the body. The liver releases sugar reserves for a quick boost of energy, and the bladder sends a message that it wants to be emptied so the body can flee faster.

- On the outside of the body, perspiration forms as sweat glands are activated to reduce the body heat caused by the increased flow of blood. The mouth widens so that air can be taken in faster than through the nose. The face loses color and appears ashen as blood is diverted for more important uses.

The increase in bodily activity corresponds to the escalation of mental activity as well. Your internal dialogue speeds up, jumps from subject to subject, and second-guesses itself. "Are they with me?" "What should I say next?" This tension and fear are exposed in some salespeople's speech. They talk too fast, repeat themselves, stutter, or under extreme stress completely forget what they were going to say.

Sales Call Strategy: You must project a calm, cool, collected presence to customers at all times. To do otherwise would increase customers' stress levels. Nervousness and agitation may be misinterpreted and convince customers that you have something to hide. Verbal faux pas may be thought of as incompetence. Think about your last visit to the dentist. What would your reaction have been if the dentist had seemed nervous, agitated, or flustered before he or she started to work on your mouth? You would have been scared and had a very stressful appointment.

88. Anchoring Yourself to Success

I still get nervous when I meet with important executives or before I have to give a big presentation. In my opinion, nervousness is not only normal but positive because it drives you to better prepare yourself beforehand. However, once a meeting starts, you want your nervousness to stop. The tool I use to calm my nerves is a psychological anchor. Anchoring is the process of associating a premeditated feeling to an object.

Now it's time to do one of the most interesting exercises of the entire book. Think of the best day of your business career. Have a very specific day in your mind. Stop and think about it. Remember how great you felt. Perhaps it was a day you received an award or were promoted. Whatever it is, try to relive the feelings, hear the sounds, and recreate a picture of it in your mind. While holding these thoughts, take your right hand and gently pinch the back of your left hand and hold it while you think of the memory until the back of your pinched hand starts to tingle, usually around thirty seconds. You have now created a psychological anchor.

Would you be nervous speaking in front of one thousand salespeople? Well, I am. That's why I use anchors all the time. Now go ahead and pinch the back of your hand again. Did you feel the tingle again and a reassuring sensation? If not, repeat the entire process very slowly with single-minded concentration. Stop reading and concentrate on your memory.

There's no reason to be nervous when you meet with important customers. Regardless of how many people surround someone and how much fortune, fame, and power you think a person has, everyone is lonely in his or her own way. Loneliness isn't only about being alone. It is about feeling disconnected, isolated, alienated, unwanted, inadequate, self-conscious, unloved, and scared. Keep this idea in mind. The next customer you meet needs a friend.

Sales Call Strategy: The most important words you speak are the words you say to yourself. When we talk to ourselves internally, it's usually in the context of our shortcomings. Personally, I am more likely to tell myself that I am a failure at something than that I am great at something else. However, the congruence you emanate to anyone you speak with is based upon a positive perception of yourself, and anchors can help establish this mind-set.

Now it is time for another exercise that takes just a few seconds. Read the following statement slowly out loud, pause, and then repeat it again twice: "I am a success." Perhaps the only person who remains to be convinced that you are a success is you.

89. How to Cope with Losing

When we're closing a deal, life's great! When we're on the losing side of a deal, we're miserable and we sometimes feel like our entire world has fallen apart. Losing is a subject that most salespeople don't like to talk about.

First, the only way to act after you receive the painful news is graciously and professionally. Although you might fantasize about annihilating the decision maker's reputation and career, you must fight the urge for confrontation. I speak from experience on this. On more than one occasion I have thrown a verbal temper tantrum when I lost an important deal. Frankly, it didn't make me feel any better; it only made me feel worse.

By exiting on good terms, there's always a one-in-a-hundred chance that the customer may call you back later when your competitor fails. But the real reason for maintaining your composure is your own mental health. Think of it in these terms: You've invested a great deal of energy into something you wanted badly and were counting on. In spite of your best efforts, you have been told that you weren't good enough. You have just been through a traumatic experience. The first step in dealing with any personal crisis is acknowledging it. By doing so, you will be able to get back to selling sooner. To help you get back into the winning frame of mind as soon as possible, here are four recommendations:

- *Commiserate with colleagues.* You will start to feel better by talking with fellow salespeople who have been in your position. Instead of repressing your pain and doubts, sharing your experience and venting your frustrations will help get you back on your feet. Catharsis enables you to let go of your negative thoughts and feelings. In addition, researchers have found that repeatedly uttering a swear word actually reduces physical pain![1]

- *Take a break.* After a big loss, we often think it's best to buckle up our feelings and put our nose right back on the grindstone. However, no matter how we act on the outside, we're often depressed, tired, and full of self-pity. Unfortunately, this message will be sent subconsciously to customers. As a sales manager, I learned the best way to rejuvenate the team was a "mental health" day. Typically, it was the first business day after the close of a quarter. Regardless of whether you had a good or a bad quarter, you were invited to disappear. As a result, everyone came back refreshed and ready to get back to a winning frame of mind.

- *Reanchor success.* We introduced the concepts of anchors in chapter 88. An anchor is the premeditated association of a specific feeling to an object. After a particularly tough loss, you may have forgotten what it feels like to win. In this situation, go visit some "friendlies." These are customers who have purchased from you, like you, and appreciate your company. By doing so, you reanchor your mind to success.

- *Keep perspective.* I remember being on the road and receiving the bad news that I had lost a important deal to my archrival. On the plane flight from New York back home to California, I sat staring out the window. My mind was filled with destructive thoughts and other self-defeating prophecies. About halfway across the country I made a sudden realization. Not a single person in all the cities we passed over cared.

Sales Call Strategy: After you have missed your number, your first reaction is to think the sun has finally set on your career and your hot streak is over. However, you need to remind yourself that there's always next month, next quarter, and next year.

As salespeople, our world is structured on a value system that is intimately tied to the production of a single revenue number. This number is how the rest of our world measures our contribution, and it is also how we tend to judge our own worth.

However, you will never be truly happy or satisfied if you measure your self-worth solely by the revenue you generate. You know you are not a good person because you make your number, just as you are not a bad person if you don't. Life is about being with your family and friends and, most importantly, having a relationship with your creator. These relationships are a true reflection of your life's significance.

90. You Are a Walking, Talking Metaphor

Your most important metaphor is you. You are a walking, talking metaphor. The way you dress, present yourself, and represent your product provides important symbolism to the customer. Your customer has standards and certain expectations about the way you will act, look, and speak. These standards vary greatly among customers, companies, industries, and places. Selling drilling equipment in Texas is different from selling computer chips in Silicon Valley or hotel supplies in Hawaii. Each requires a salesperson to use a different presence and demeanor to build credibility and gain rapport.

Presence and demeanor will greatly influence the customer's decision. For example, would you hire a personal trainer who was extremely out of shape? An interior designer who dressed sloppily or out of style? Would you visit a dentist who had terrible teeth and who used dilapidated equipment? Physical presence projects an important message to the customer.

Therefore, it makes sense to dress like your customers and express yourself in a manner they are comfortable with. The way you dress should show that your first concern is the customer's success, not your own self-interests. While we want to communicate success, we don't want the customer thinking he's being overcharged. That's why I frown on elaborate adornments and expensive jewelry such as cufflinks and watches. Leave them at home unless the customer is wearing them too. Remember, a salesperson's dress and demeanor and how he treats the customer serve as a metaphor for their future relationship.

Sales Call Strategy: All salespeople are friendly, helpful, and attentive during the sales cycle because they know the customer is constantly evaluating them. It's after the sale is made and the commission paid when true service begins. A salesperson's humility is in fact a metaphor for service and selflessness. An ostentatious salesperson who is full of bravado will alienate far more customers than he wins over. The customer doesn't expect to see him once the deal closes. Meanwhile, the unpretentious salesperson naturally builds rapport. People expect he'll stay around after the deal closes.

If you scored high in dominance in the personality test in chapter 57, you should carefully select what you wear based upon the customer you're meeting with. You do not want your physical presence to cause you to be perceived as arrogant. On the other hand, no one wants to associate with a vagabond who looks like he slept in his clothes. Find a point between the two extremes, where the clothes you wear communicate your professionalism without alienating the customer.

Finally, people naturally want to be around positive people. Conversely, salespeople who constantly criticize the competition are less likely to win over customers. Think about yourself for a moment: do you like to be around people who are negative and demeaning?

91. Persuasion Techniques

Being able to turn a negative into a positive is a fundamental part of selling. In sales, you are frequently placed in uncomfortable situations where rapport is nonexistent. Under these circumstances, your job is to create an environment that makes the customer receptive to your message. To do so, include the following persuasion techniques so you can communicate with the customer's conscious and subconscious minds:

- *Belief system.* Over the years, your belief system has been formed based on observation, experience, and faith. It may include a spiritual belief in the afterlife, a scientific belief in the big bang theory, or a hope in the Chicago Cubs winning the World Series. The unique aspect of such philosophical frameworks is that all people consider their own belief systems correct. Presenting a message that is in alignment with the customer's belief system adds credibility to your message. His degree of skepticism is lowered since the message is concealed within the Trojan horse of an existing belief system. For example, chapter 5 is based upon the common belief system among salespeople that all buyers are liars.

- *Broadcast-unicast.* The broadcast-unicast technique enables all listeners to derive their own personal meaning from what you have said. Each listener's internal dialogue (see chapter 8) believes the story is intended solely for him or her. Use customer success stories (see chapter 48) in group presentations and general words (see chapter 32) to employ the broadcast-unicast technique. Refer to chapter 67 for another example.

- *Humor.* At some level, people agree with you either consciously or subconsciously when they laugh with you. Humor helps build rapport and lower the defenses between buyers and sellers. Remember, everyone is somewhat nervous during a sales call, and humor lightens the mood and helps everyone relax. Self-effacing humor, where salespeople poke fun at themselves, is particularly effective. Observational humor about common experiences such as children, traffic, or taxes is a safe area too.

- *Imagination:* The imagination technique is based upon guiding the listener's internal dialogue to become preoccupied with a pervasive image, sensation, or idea. For example, telling you that chapter 42 is my favorite of this entire book may cause you to wonder what it is about. Refer to chapter 67 and the conversation about snakes in the introduction for examples of the imagination technique.

- *Mirroring.* To build rapport, mirror the customer's posture and breathing, and maintain the same tone, tempo, and patterns of his speech (see chapters 20 and 29).

- *Simulation.* Simulation is structuring language to provoke a particular response before actually experiencing a situation, product, or process. Refer to chapter 68 for an example of the simulation technique.

- *Split brain.* The split-brain technique involves making the customer carry on a factual conversation with the "logical" side of the brain while carrying on another stimulating discussion with the "emotional" side of the brain. Use metaphors (see chapter 49) to employ the split-brain technique.
- *Suggestions.* Here's an example of how suggestions (see chapter 56) can be used to guide the listener's actions. You probably have never noticed it, but you breathe in a certain way, and as you breathe, you can feel your chest rising and falling. There's also a certain sensation in your nose when you breathe and you are able to feel the temperature of the air. As you become more aware of your breathing, it's harder to concentrate on other details. Reading this description about breathing may have caused you to notice and change your breathing pattern.

Whether they realize it or not, all salespeople are natural hypnotists who structure language during the course of normal conversation that disarms customers' conscious defenses. Like a therapeutic hypnotist who wants to solve clients problems, a salesperson guides clients through the process of selecting the correct solution. Both professionals use the power of words to implant posthypnotic suggestions to create profound changes in attitudes and actions.

Sales Call Strategy: In every customer conversation, both conscious and subconscious communication is being transmitted, assessed, and cataloged. And each layer of the human communication model (see chapter 6) is capable of sending observable (conscious) and unobservable (subconscious) messages simultaneously. Although each listener can receive only a finite amount of information at any one time, very little of the information that is transmitted across all layers is lost. What isn't consciously received is processed subconsciously. Instead of barraging the customer's conscious mind solely with logical arguments, facts, and figures, use these persuasion techniques to talk directly to the subconscious mind to accomplish real change.

92. Survival, Success, and Significance

Whom would you rather sell to? A person who has been working in a company for sixteen years or someone who has been there for only six months? The answer depends on what stage the person is at in his or her career and the type of product you sell. Everyone is in one of three career stages: survival, success, or significance. In survival mode, people are struggling to exist. Their career or job is in jeopardy or under an imminent threat. Successful people are competent at their jobs and secure in their positions, while significant people want to make their mark on the company and have an impact on the organization.

Over the course of my career, I have naturally gravitated toward selling to significant people. Why? Because they are personally motivated to get something done, and the products I sold required a major shift in the way the company conducted business. Since significant people are the movers and shakers of their companies, they are the individuals who are naturally interested in innovation. In fact, the type of person I most enjoy selling to is a senior executive who has been with his company for only a short time. I know that this person is on a mission to make a name for himself.

My second favorite group to sell to is people in survival mode. I like to work with people who must do something or perish. However, if I were selling office products, I would probably want to deal with successful people in successful companies—people who are competent at their jobs and will be there later when it is time to reorder.

The concept of survival, success, and significance also applies to companies. In this regard, I would rather sell to successful and significant companies. However, since companies in survival mode are extremely motivated, I'll still go after their business—but more cautiously. Therefore, I proactively prospect for successful and significant companies and react to requests from companies in survival mode. What's your strategy?

Sales Call Strategy: Whenever you attend a meeting, always try to classify the stages of the participants' careers and their company. Doing so will help you understand the participants' motivations and frame your solution to match the stages they're in.

93. Improving Curiosity

The phrase "Curiosity kills" simply does not apply to sales calls. In fact, the situation is quite the opposite. Your curiosity can actually save you! I have met many Heavy Hitter salespeople through the years, and one of the main characteristics they have all shared was natural inquisitiveness. They always seemed to be asking themselves why to satisfy their insatiable desire to know.

Like people in general, salespeople have different levels of inquisitiveness. However, the majority have a healthy curiosity. They have grown accustomed to asking questions since it is ingrained into the sales process. They are also adept at answering questions because of their experiences with both customers and managers.

Sometimes salespeople must exhibit the ultimate form of curiosity: obsession. They'll become obsessed with one deal or a goal to the point where it is always on their minds and nothing else in life seems to matter.

I have three very good friends with vastly different selling styles who are equally successful salespeople. Jeffrey has extreme dominance and transparency instincts. He's a verbal warrior who'll say exactly what's on his mind. However, he's not reckless about his words. Rather, he uses them with precision to tunnel to the core of the customer's psyche and reveal the hidden biases and silent objections that are always in the back of someone's mind.

Pete has a completely different style. He naturally evokes a high degree of empathy from his customers. He also knows that this ability is one of his strengths so he's very transparent about it. His modus operandi is to continually ask customers for help and constantly seek their reassurance about the deal. As a customer recites the reasons why the deal will happen, Pete triangulates with other helpers in the account. The technique has an interesting impact on customers as well. By continually repeating why the deal will happen, they convince themselves to buy!

John is an extremely curious person by nature. He reminds me of a plane-crash investigator because he continually analyzes small pieces of information in order to construct the entire puzzle. He is driven to know how things work and is not comfortable until all the i's are dotted and the t's are crossed. He's also an extremely independent person who is eager to share his theories about why the plane crashed in the first place. He places himself in the customers' shoes and knows when and why they will buy.

All three of these salespeople are incredibly successful, and that's the point. Your individual style is based upon your personal mixture of these instincts, and someone can be successful with any combination.

Sales Call Strategy: Curiosity is frequently described as a person's "hunger for knowledge." Your natural level of curiosity correlates to whether you have an active and passive presence during sales calls. If you have an active presence, you desire to close the gap between the information you know and the information you want to know.

Curiosity and language are intimately connected. In fact, it is believed that one of the main areas of the brain responsible for language is also closely connected to a person's curiosity.

Here are four steps you can take to become more curious during sales calls. First, don't take anything the customer says for granted. Instead, ask follow-up questions that contradict your assumptions. Second, don't accept what the customer says at face value. Ask him to explain why he believes what he said. Third, slow down the sales call. Don't be in such a hurry and live in the moment. Actually enjoy the company of your customer and ask yourself what you can learn from him. Finally, curiosity requires you to pay attention to what the customer is saying using active listening (see chapter 74).

94. Sales Call Segmentation and Decision-Making Roles

Many companies segment their vendors by value and whether or not they are considered to be strategic to the organization, a key partner who is important, or a tactical supplier who is replaceable. Companies also classify their existing customers by the amount of money they spend, profitability, or the products they buy. Unfortunately, very few companies today perform any type of segmentation of the sales calls their sales force makes. As a result, valuable win-loss-related information isn't captured and sales force effectiveness is lost.

Not all sales calls are the same because the dynamics of how companies make decisions and the people involved are quite different. However, sales calls can be divided into segments based upon the decision maker's attributes and their different roles within the organization. Linguistic segmentation will help you better understand where you win and why you lose. Equally important, it is intended to provide the linguistic blueprint to build the sales call. It is based upon the psychographic classification of sales call participants based upon their opinions, motivations, beliefs, perception of power, and attitudes toward their company.

Whenever a company makes a purchase decision that involves groups of people, self-interests, politics, and group dynamics will influence the final decision. Individuals will jockey for position to ensure their favorite vendor is selected, align themselves with more powerful coworkers for political gain, or stay out of the fray and refuse to take part in the decision.

Tension, drama, and conflict are normal parts of group dynamics because typically any decision on what to do is not unanimous. Selection team members always feel an underlying tension because they are never 100 percent certain they are picking the right solution. Drama builds as the salespeople make their arguments and provide conflicting information to refute their competitors' claims. Interpersonal conflict between group members, as evidenced by disparaging remarks and criticisms, occurs whenever there is intense competition for a highly sought-after prize.

Beyond their formal titles and their positions on organization charts, people take on specific roles when they are part of a selection committee. Some assume roles they believe will enable them to take control of the group and steer the decision toward their preference. Others adopt new behavioral roles to deal with the tension, drama, and conflict. You may not have realized it, but even your presence as a salesperson influences how customers act.

Selection committee members, ranging from the CEO to the lowest-level evaluator, will adopt four different group decision-making roles during sales calls and sales presentations. These roles are based upon information, character, authority, and company:

- *Information roles.* Information roles are based on the type of information people believe they should gather and the unique way in which they process and transmit information.
- *Character roles.* Character roles are based on the way people feel they should behave when they are part of a decision-making group.
- *Authority roles.* Authority roles are based on people's degree of command and their ability to dominate the group.
- *Company roles.* Company roles are based on the political power people wield and their personal disposition toward their company.

Figure 94.1 summarizes the four different categories of roles that prospects adopt during sales calls and presentations.

Information roles	Character roles	Authority roles	Company roles
Anal analytical	Class clown	Bureaucrat	Hired gun
Gullible	Dreamer	Dictator	Fifth columnist
Intellectual	Hothead	Empty suit	Intern
Slacker	Maven	Old pro	Politician
Summary seeker	People pleaser	Proctor	Pollyanna
	Schadenfreuder	Pundit	Revolutionary
	Straight shooter	Soldier	Vigilante

Figure 94.1 The four group decision-making roles

In chapters 95 through 98, we'll introduce each of these psychographic roles and explain how they specifically apply to sales calls and presentations.

Sales Call Strategy: While it makes sense to determine the role of every person during sales calls, it is crucial to understand the roles of the key decision makers. Ideally, you want to anticipate their behavior beforehand so you can use the right demeanor, create the right messages, and then deliver those messages in the way that they will be best received and understood.

In addition, you probably aren't going to attend all your sales calls alone. You might bring along your sales manager, vice president of sales, product marketing manager, professional services director, and even your CEO. Therefore, you need a common terminology to describe the customer to others. Segmenting sales calls by these roles will help you communicate your sales call strategy to colleagues and prepare them for the type of customer they are going to meet.

95. Information Roles

Everyone involved in the sales call and selection process has the responsibility to assess vendor information for accuracy and provide an opinion as to which solution is best. However, evaluators assume this duty with different levels of due diligence, ranging from focusing on minutiae to being big-picture oriented. Here are the most common information roles that evaluators assume.

Anal Analytical

Anal analyticals are full of doubt and have the highest levels of skepticism. They verify every statement made by a salesperson, and they want to validate every piece of information. Therefore, anal analyticals immerse themselves in features, functions, and specifications. They take their role as information gatherer very seriously and do not want to be embarrassed by missed details.

Customers with advanced degrees in the sciences (computers, mathematics, engineering, etc.) are more likely to be anal analyticals. This should not be a surprise since they've had years of systematic education followed by a business career that was heavily focused on scientific methods and data analysis.

When meeting with a anal analytical, do not go on the call without someone on your side who has commensurate technical or industry knowledge. You have only one chance to make a great first impression, and being unable to satisfy the customer's analytical mind will be the death knell of the meeting.

However, your overriding objective should not be to let technology talk or deep discussions about minutiae dominate the entire meeting. Rather, you must keep the meeting on track and drive the agenda to reach your desired outcome for the call. Never let your own technical team hijack the meeting and take control. They should know in advance that they are there under your direction.

Gullible

You will meet some gullible customers who unquestioningly accept your information at face value because they are not well versed in working with salespeople or buying products. It might be early in their career, or they might be new to the management role or the company. Gullibles don't know what questions to ask or how to make a major procurement within their own company. If this is the case, you must adopt a different familial role with them than when working with an anal analytical. You need to mentor them through the process like a father explaining to his adult son how to fill out his tax forms or an older brother explaining to his younger sibling the criteria that should be used when selecting a college.

While gullibles are rare, they have the propensity to be found in certain departments. For example, the vice president of human resources, chief talent officer, or chief learning officer are wired quite differently than the CFO, CEO, and CIO. They're usually not as adept at dealing with salespeople. Since they don't wield much organizational power, they often don't know how to make large purchases happen. Therefore, if the seniormost leader in the deal is a gullible, there is a higher likelihood that no purchase will ever be made.

Intellectual

When it comes to details, an intellectual is the opposite of an anal analytical. Intellectuals are more interested in the theoretical and philosophical aspects of products. Intellectuals approach the gathering of information in a cerebral, professorial way. They are open to learning and seek personal enlightenment. For example, an anal analytical might want a side-by-side checklist comparison of a product's features, whereas an intellectual would be more interested in the product's underlying architecture and why it was made in the first place.

Be forewarned about intellectuals. You're going to think a meeting with them went great because the topic of conversation was at the 30,000-foot level. Usually, meetings with intellectuals end on a positive note and with everyone involved feeling good. That's the style of intellectuals. They're not typically going to confront you and devalue your solution in person. For them, every meeting is a learning experience.

Later, intellectuals will let their department members sift through the details. You should anticipate that this team will find technical objections and a variety of other reasons why your solution won't work for them. Therefore, you must continually be selling at all levels of the organization if you suspect the C-level executive is an intellectual. Solely executing a top-down sales strategy will most likely fail.

Slacker

Slacker customers will conduct a low level of due diligence and a cursory verification of the information that is presented to them. Slackers don't know, don't care, or will mistakenly ignore important information. In addition, they will deny that they know anything when asked tough questions by salespeople.

Slackers are typically found in very large companies with immense bureaucracies where one department has no clue what another is doing. While slackers are rare, you might run into one in federal, state, and local government accounts or monolithic industries such as automobile and insurance.

The single most important question to ask yourself when you meet a slacker is, Does this decision maker have the wherewithal to make a purchase? Nine times out of ten the answer will be no.

Summary Seeker

A summary seeker is a curious person who is more concerned with the big picture than small details. Summary seekers quickly grasp complex subjects and tend to make snap decisions about the relevance of information. They are typically more trusting than anal analyticals but less patient than intellectuals. Heavy Hitter salespeople love to sell to summary seekers.

It's not surprising that the majority of C-level executives are summary seekers because they are extremely busy. The nature of running a department or company means they have to manage down to employees, out to customers, and up to even more important executives and the board. Therefore, they don't have the time or mental bandwidth to process tons of detailed information. That's why important facts, risk assessments, value judgments, and the rewards of moving forward with the purchase should be summarized and presented to them in a succinct manner that is easily understood.

Sales Call Strategy: Identifying information roles helps you understand whether to present a high-level summary to a summary seeker or be prepared to dive into the details with an anal analytical. If the latter is the case, you know that you must bring along your colleagues who have a commensurate industry background and technical expertise.

The type of information gatherers you call on vary by industry. Anal analyticals are more common in the semiconductor business because of the technical nature of designing and manufacturing computer chips. There are far more summary seekers in the advertising industry, and this makes sense because people tend to make quick decisions on ads based upon first impressions. Over time, your goal should be to develop the specific breakdown of information role types for customers you call on for the industry you're in. For example, you should know that on 55 percent of your sales calls are with anal analyticals, 25 percent with summary seekers, and 20 percent with intellectuals.

96. Character Roles

Just as people change their behavior whenever they are in groups, evaluators adopt new character traits depending upon which of their colleagues are participating with them on the sales call. They will behave quite differently in front of fellow employees than when they are alone with you. Here are the most common character roles that evaluators assume.

Class Clown

Class-clown customers thrive on being the center of attention and always seem to have a smart remark or joke handy. While a psychiatrist might say the class clown's disruptions are driven by thoughts of inadequacy, this character role serves an important selection-process function: the class clown's silliness releases the evaluation team's pent-up stress.

Be careful when you meet with class clowns. Since they are so friendly and jovial, it is easy to be lulled into a false sense of security and take their word at face value. Moreover, when evaluators become class clowns, they are attempting to remove themselves from the stressful position of being the final selector and dissociate themselves from the decision.

Dreamer

Whether they have a momentary daydream about a vacation to a tropical destination or a fantasy about marriage that has been fostered since childhood, people love to dream about the future. Some dreamers are fixated on one goal, while others long for just about everything. During sales calls and the selection process, dreamers tend to fall in love quickly with a particular salesperson or the solution they believe will help them realize their fantasy soonest. However, they are impulsive buyers who suffer from immense mood swings, which can cause them to second-guess their initial selection and frequently change their minds.

As opposed to the class clown, dreamers are salespeople's dreams come true. Their main motivation is usually based upon satisfying their ego, and that's a powerful purchase driver. In a perfect world you want your dreamer to also be a powerful customer—someone who can make the grand initiative happen because he is the bully with the juice or the emperor (see chapter 53). However, you should be extremely skeptical of dreamers because they will talk the big talk but in reality are frequently duds (see chapter 53).

Hothead

Based upon a survey of 9,282 adults, the National Institute of Mental Health estimates that 5 to 7 percent of the population suffers from intermittent explosive disorder, which is characterized by raging outbursts that are way out of proportion to the situation.[1] While these destructive temper tantrums are most commonly associated with road rage, customers have fits of rage as well. If these figures are correct, one out of every twenty customers you encounter is a hothead.

You definitely know when you meet with a hothead. Sometimes hotheads explode during the sales call and publicly berate their own employees and colleagues. Worse is when they are combative and condescending to you. Hotheads don't like to meet with salespeople, so they verbally abuse them in front of their staffs! The best way to handle this intentional act of humiliation is to maintain your composure as best you can and not take the attack personally. Remember, you are dealing with a person who suffers from a mental disorder. Many company founders happen to be hotheads. They are used to barking orders and getting their way through domination.

Maven

The goal of maven customers is to use the selection process to demonstrate their knowledge and intelligence to others. They're smart and they know it. Quite often, mavens are fascinated by electronic gadgets and own the latest technologies. They may adorn their bodies with these precious objects in an expression of prowess. They typically won't listen to the opinions of others or accept personal criticism because they already know exactly what's best. Therefore, you won't win arguments with mavens. Selling to them requires an indirect psychological sales strategy as they will not be swayed by any vendor's logic or reason.

Rather, you must sell to a maven's ego. At every opportunity elicit his feedback, not so much for its own merits but so your maven can hear himself talk about your solution. Bring the specialists within your company to your meeting—technical gurus, product managers, and various members of the executive staff. Invite them to participate on customer advisory boards or provide feedback on internal product specification reviews. If you treat the maven with the respect he deserves, you'll find out he isn't such a tough person to sell to after all.

People Pleaser

Some evaluators feel compelled to befriend everybody, including all the salespeople from the various companies who are calling on the account. People pleasers dislike confrontation and feel very uncomfortable knowing that someone is at odds with them. Therefore, the information they provide must always be discounted because it is being given for the sole purpose of pleasing the questioner and may not be the actual truth. People pleasers will be amenable to any decision because they always go along with the group.

Personally, I cannot stand people pleasers. I want to know where I stand in an account. I want to know the answer to the most important question in all of sales: "Will I win the deal?"

Tell me the truth as soon as possible so I don't waste my precious time. I don't want prospective customers to tell me what they think I want to hear. I want the truth, and so should you.

Schadenfreuder

Some people take delight in the failure and misfortune of others. This delight is called "schadenfreude." While a hothead wears his emotions on his sleeve and might explode in rage, a schadenfreuder plots quietly behind the scenes against you. While a hothead is searching for the best solution and actually plans on buying something, quite often the schadenfreuder never intended to buy from you in the first place. It is all a game to him and he delights in tormenting salespeople. The most extreme schadenfreuders are misanthropes—they hate people.

Schadenfreuders are truly evil, and at the end of your encounter you will have psychological scars to prove it. Sometimes they present just enough optimistic information to keep you engaged when they really have no intention of buying your product. They'll entice you with claims of big purchases that are just off in the horizon. I remember attending a meeting with one of my salespeople who called on a schadenfreuder CTO. At one point the CTO asked the junior salesperson how he was going to spend all the commission he was going to make off the sale. It was an obnoxious trick question and I wanted to punch him in the nose. You must exercise self-respect and walk away from the schadenfreuder's account.

Straight Shooter

Straight shooters have a strong sense of honor and integrity. They are not alarmists but usually even-keeled evaluators who will listen to what each salesperson has to say. Heavy Hitters love selling to straight shooters. Straight shooters are sincerely interested in finding the best solution for the people who will implement and use it. They work together with their colleagues toward a common goal and vision. They are open-minded, they listen to others' opinions, and they take pride that they are part of the team.

The best way to sell to a straight shooter is to become one yourself. While an aggressive, high-energy strategy might be appropriate in certain sales situations, mirroring the straight shooter's behavior is an equally effective strategy. Every communication with him should be structured and well documented. Don't fudge on the truth; give definitive truthful answers to his questions. Consciously slow down your speech, breathing, and mannerisms from your normal hyperactive pace.

The straight shooter's orientation is long-term, and you will probably not be able to accelerate the selection process. The evaluation process will be well thought out and lengthy. The winner will be the last vendor standing, the one who exhibited the attributes necessary to satisfy the straight shooter. In essence, the sales cycle is a miniature dry run of the long-term relationship.

Sales Call Strategy: Knowing the character roles informs you how to act in their presence. You adopt a "tell it like it is" demeanor with a straight shooter, carefully select your words with a hothead, and foster the fantasies of dreamers. You should not believe the schadenfreuder's claim that there is a big deal to be won, and you should expect the people pleaser to give your competition the same compliments that were given to you. Mavens and class clowns narcissistically believe themselves to be uniquely special, so treat them as the center of attention.

97. Authority Roles

People's authority does not always correlate to how long they have worked for their company or have been employed in their profession. In reality, selection committee members adopt authority roles in order to influence their colleagues and the decision outcome. Here are the most common authority roles that evaluators assume.

Bureaucrat

Bureaucrats are focused on selection processes and procedures. However, they will use the selection processes for their selfish gain or to exercise their political power. Many bureaucrats are consumed with maintaining the status quo. Most frequently, the best way to prevent change is to stop the purchase process entirely, so that is what bureaucrat customers often try to do.

A sales call with a bureaucrat can be extremely frustrating for two reasons. First, he will use a variety of psychological coping mechanisms (see chapter 85) to dominate you. He knows that salespeople tend to lack patience and attention to detail and don't like forms and paperwork. He'll purposely exploit these weaknesses to protect himself and his company.

The second reason has to do with how the bureaucrat behaves during the meeting with you. The meeting with the bureaucrat may have been arranged by an underling (midlevel or low-level person) who enthusiastically supports you and your solution. Because he has been championing your cause internally, you are optimistic about your chances of winning the business. However, when you meet the bureaucrat, you quickly realize that a purchase will never happen or that the bureaucrat has other ideas about whom the company should do business with. After months of time and effort, all the hopes you had to win the account are gone. This is why you must meet with C-level decision makers early in the sales cycle.

Dictator

Dictator customers are focused on decreeing the company's direction. Whereas a class clown uses humor to keep himself in the spotlight, dictators use unrelenting power to maintain their prominence. These domineering taskmasters are usually interested only in immediate results, what your solution has to offer here and now.

Even if an evaluation team has been assembled under the guise of making an impartial selection, the dictator rules its members through oppression, intimidation, or fear. Most dictators are narcissists (preoccupied admirers of themselves). However, they are typically very polished executives. They don't necessarily broadcast their power or goose-step around the office like a fascist ruler, but they rule their obedient masses with the same ruthlessness. When you shake the hand of a dictator, you are always shaking the hand of the bully with the juice (see chapter 53).

Empty Suit

Empty-suit customers protect themselves by hiding behind inflated job titles that are not justified by their experience, knowledge, or ability to lead. While empty suits may be charming and gregarious individuals, they have misconceptions about their own strengths and how the organization views them.

A customer who is an empty suit will typically make a great impression on the first sales call. However, each subsequent meeting becomes more frustrating. Because empty suits are mainly preoccupied with keeping their jobs, they are extremely hesitant to move a purchase forward or to ruffle the feathers of others within the organization.

Old Pro

Old pro customers are case-hardened evaluators who have years of experience working with vendors. They are experts at managing the selection process, they know what to expect from the vendors, and they command respect.

You don't exaggerate to an old pro because he'll call you on it every time. Even though the old pro's demeanor may be gruff and cantankerous, deep inside is an individual who seeks friendships. Heavy Hitters love to sell to old pros. The key is finding an intersecting activity you have in common and selling yourself to them by establishing a trusting familial relationship (see chapter 73).

Proctor

In the academic world, proctors oversee the administration of tests to ensure that none of the students cheat. The business world has proctors whose sole purpose, so it seems, is to ensure that the selection process is followed to the letter.

Whereas a bureaucrat is motivated to stop the purchase decision, a proctor seems more concerned about following the rules of the selection process than the actual selection itself. For example, a purchasing manager who is a proctor will punish vendors who violate the selection process. This obviously creates a challenge because your goal is to implement a strategy that changes the selection process to your benefit. Therefore, you must either be in the account first and attempt to set the rules with the proctor or develop rapport with another higher-level executive, an old pro for instance, so that he can override the proctor.

Pundit

Every group has a pundit—a person who feels compelled to continually parade his or her opinions. On selection committees, these constant critics are the equivalent of a backseat driver. They assail other committee members, find fault with the direction they are taking, and attack vendors with a barrage of criticism.

Pundits will authoritatively pass judgment on you and your solution in your presence to throw you off track. They'll say things right in front of you like "That will never work for us" or "Your competition is better." These assaults are pundits' self-defense mechanism for avoiding a relationship with you (because they favor another competitor) or dissociating themselves from their decision-making responsibilities. Never forget, one of a customer's most prized possessions is his or her opinion.

Soldier

Corporate soldiers are paid to perform their jobs without question. Soldier customers have the lowest level of power and will dutifully follow orders passed down the chain of command. The soldier's mantra is "Ours is not to question why; ours is but to do or die."

When the CEO tells the CFO what company to do business with, the CFO becomes a soldier C-level executive who has just received his marching orders. This is why you should always sell at the highest possible level in every account because you want to meet the person issuing the orders, not executing them.

Sales Call Strategy: Recognizing the authority roles will provide insight into sales calls during the decision-making process. Is the customer a dictator who will bully the selection committee? Is he a proctor who is more concerned about the rules of the selection than the selection itself? Is he an empty suit who lacks the where-withal to make any decision at all? Customers' words and actions during sales calls will reveal who they are and what action you should take next.

98. Company Roles

People's titles tell only part of the story about their role within a company. In the business world, selection-committee members take on additional company roles beyond their position on the organization chart. These roles show their true political power and their personal disposition toward their company. Here are the most common company roles that evaluators assume.

Hired Gun

Hired guns are corporate expatriates. They are not emotionally invested in their jobs or completely committed to the company they work for. They tend to select products they believe will help them get their next job. The motto of a hired gun is "There is no such thing as a bad product if it helps you get your next job."

Hired guns are market-share sensitive. They like to do business with gorillas, the dominant players in the market. Therefore, if you sell for a chimp-sized company, you are in an extremely dangerous position when the bully with the juice (see chapter 53) is a hired gun.

Fifth Columnist

Fifth columnists are rebels who are dissatisfied with their personal predicament inside the company. The term "fifth column" originated during the Spanish Civil War and refers to a group of people who clandestinely plan to undermine a larger group. In the business world, fifth columnists feel cheated by their company in some way. They might believe they are not receiving the recognition and respect they deserve.

Frequently, fifth columnists are out to prove themselves better than someone else at their company or to prove that their department is the best in the company. They'll purchase products not only to further their cause but to undermine the success, power, and authority of others inside the company. During the sales cycle, they will frequently identify with and relate to a salesperson more than to their own coworkers. It is actually best to meet with a fifth columnist alone so that he will share his secret plans with you.

Intern

Interns either will delegate their evaluation responsibilities to others or are the junior members of the selection team so they can't contribute to the selection process. They may be new to the company or profession or lack experience in selecting products.

Sometimes, a high-ranking executive is classified as an intern because he doesn't care to be involved with the procurement process. The project is not important enough to warrant his time and attention. Since the intern doesn't have industry domain expertise or technical aptitude, the bulk of the evaluation work falls on the shoulders of others who are experienced with company operations or low-level personnel who have deep technical knowledge. These people become the bullies with the juice in the account while the executive intern is the emperor (see chapter 53). Interns like this typically become involved very late in the sales cycle, after the preliminary recommendation had been made for their review.

Politician

Politicians in a company are smooth schemers who opportunistically maneuver to hold onto or gain power within the organization. They speak with carefully selected words and try to display a professional demeanor at all times. It's not surprising that most higher-level executives are politicians because it requires political acumen to make it to the top.

Politicians are the influential statesmen of companies. They are experienced in dealing with company issues, know how to make things happen, and get their way in the process. They're more polished than interns. They hold their cards close to their chest and won't broadcast their intentions until you have proven that it is in their political interest to do so.

Pollyanna

Pollyannas believe the company they work for is the best, whether it is or not. Usually, they absolutely love their jobs and find good in everyone and everything. Typically, these overly optimistic customers are hard workers and may have spent their entire careers at a single company.

Pollyannas have a tendency to ignore ugly facts and underestimate the complexity of the solutions they purchase. They are genuinely excited about the upcoming purchase, and Heavy Hitters are grateful for their naiveté. Obviously, it makes sense for salespeople to mirror their excitement and enthusiasm.

Revolutionary

Revolutionaries are out to create upheaval in their organization. They are agents of change who seek to remake the company's culture, its mind-set, or the way it does business.

As opposed to fifth columnists, revolutionaries have sincere motives and want the company to succeed. For example, they might be trying to change a technology-driven company to a customer-focused one, to reinvigorate company morale, or to enter new markets. They seek solutions that will help them accomplish their revolution. Whenever a new executive joins a company, he becomes a revolutionary who seeks to consolidate his power by creating grand initiatives. That's why you should always keep track of executives on the move and be the first salesperson to meet with them in their new job.

Vigilante

Company vigilantes are extremely pessimistic people who want to protect their company from the claims of vendors. Usually they are eternal naysayers, out to prove that none of the vendors' proposed solutions will work for their company. Vigilantes see their right to voice their opinion as a sacred trust. They take the decision-making process very seriously and vote for the product they believe adds the most value to the company's day-to-day operations and long-term strategy.

Vigilantes are skeptical and do not trust salespeople. They'll make every vendor respond to immense RFPs and complete laborious spreadsheets—each product feature and operation has to be fully documented to prove it exists. They'll require meticulous hands-on evaluations of each product and painstakingly documented findings. They won't buy until they are completely satisfied, and when they meet with salespeople, they are cross-examiners as opposed to collaborators like C-level fifth columnists.

Sales Call Strategy: Identify company roles so you can understand how each customer perceives himself within the organization. A hired gun wants to be reassured that selecting you will selfishly help his career while a revolutionary wants to know that you are equally committed to the cause he is fighting for. Don't be misled by the Pollyana's optimism or discouraged by the vigilante's pessimism. Expect the intern and fifth columnist to quickly open up to you and complain about their personal situation while a politician will not confide in you until he feels it's safe.

99. Applying Sales Call Segmentation

During sales calls and the selection process as a whole, the role each team member adopts (see chapters 95–98) will depend on the roles other members of the decision process occupy. For example, there typically can be only one dictator, maven, and class clown at a time. Selection team members have to assume other roles once these roles are taken. Conversely, a team can have multiple pundits, schadenfreuders, and anal analyticals. People assuming these roles actually encourage other selection team members to join them.

The roles people take on during the sales cycle determine how you will communicate with them. Most interestingly, these roles can vary from purchase to purchase. For example, a CIO who has a vested interest in the Internet provider his company uses to run its business might be an anal analytical during the selection process. Conversely, he's a slacker when it comes to the purchase of toner cartridges because he doesn't care.

Perhaps the most important aspect of customer role-playing to remember is that customers do not play the same role with each vendor. For example, an evaluator might present himself as a schadenfreuder and vigilante to you while being a straight shooter and politician with your competitor. Under these circumstances, you will not win this deal. Therefore, you must evaluate not only how selection-team members are relating to you but, equally important, theorize how they are relating to your competitors.

How do you communicate with a person you have never met before? How do you best present your story, and what demeanor should you use to persuade him to speak in confidence with you? These roles help us understand evaluators' dispositions and motivations and the granularity of the information you should present. Why should you segment sales calls by the different customer decision-making roles? Because it will help you strategize, plan, and execute your sales call. Figure 99.1 summarizes the purpose of determining each role category.

Information role	Helps determine how you will present information and who should attend the customer sales call
Character role	Prepares your colleagues for the unique group dynamics of the customer's meeting
Authority role	Provides insight into the customer's decision-making process
Company role	Explains the customer's ulterior motives, how he perceives himself, and his power within the company

Figure 99.1 Purpose of determining customer decision-making roles

Some group decision-making combinations are dangerous and unpredictable. Be extremely cautious when meeting customers who are hothead dictators, schadenfreuder bureaucrats, pundit fifth columnists, and proctor vigilantes. One bad move during sales calls with these customers and the account is lost. Conversely, slacker class clowns, gullible people pleasers, empty-suit Pollyannas, and soldier interns are extremely bad combinations for another reason. The likelihood that these customers can make a major purchase happen is infinitesimal.

For the purposes of applying group decision-making roles, let's pretend we are part of the sales team working on the Acme account, a Fortune 1000 company that is making a million-dollar purchase of state-of-the-art business software to replace its existing antiquated mainframe software. The Acme decision-making team is composed of Bob Adams, chief information officer; Nancy Smith, director of information technology; Mitch Jackson, project leader; and Mortimer Jones, vice president of purchasing. They are evaluating different enterprise software solutions.

Since the initiative to replace the mainframe software was championed by Bob, we surmise he is the emperor. Therefore, our sales strategy must include sales calls with Bob. This is also a persuasion sales cycle type (see chapter 80) because it has a well-defined selection process and has issued an RFP, and we know we are competing against our two archrivals. We know there is a 30 percent chance the team already has a favored vendor who will win the deal. Therefore, we need to determine if biases exist and build relationships at all levels as soon as possible in order to develop a coach (see chapter 59).

Next, we make our assessment and segment the sales call by customer decision-making roles of the Acme evaluators as represented in figure 99.2.

	Information role	*Character role*	*Authority role*	*Company role*
Bob Adams CIO	Summary seeker	Straight shooter	Old pro	Politician
Nancy Smith IT Director	Intellectual	Maven	Soldier	Pollyanna
Mitch Jackson Project Leader	Anal analytical	Maven	Pundit	Hired gun
Mortimer Jones VP of Purchasing	Anal analytical	Hothead	Bureaucrat	Vigilante

Figure 99.2 Acme's decision-making roles

Bob's a seasoned executive with the business skills and political acumen to lead the organization. Nancy has worked for Bob for seven years and is a maven who understands the details of the daily operations of the department. She's an optimistic soldier who marches to Bob's orders. Mitch is an accomplished technical expert. He's a cocky pundit who has little loyalty to the company. Mortimer is a hard-to-get-along-with numbers guy.

We theorize and prioritize the kinds of stress each person is under (see chapter 76). Bob is mainly under corporate citizenship stress. He's worried about cutting costs during tough economic times. Nancy is under pressure from Bob. Bob has mandated that she cut her budget by 30 percent this year. She's worried about how Bob perceives her. Mitch is an anal analytical who wants to understand every technical detail, so he makes sure they are selecting the product with the best functionality. He suffers from informational stress. Mortimer is consumed with corporate citizenship stress. He's an anal analytical who wants all aspects of the business relationship documented in the contract. He believes he is the company's fiscal watchdog.

All of the evaluators have different motivations based upon their company roles. As a result, their perceptions of our solution's strategic, operational, political, and psychological value (see chapter 39) will be different. Here are the different values we provide Bob:

- Our strategic value is that we are the most cost-effective solution the team is considering.
- Our operational value has many aspects: we automate a number of functions that employees currently do by hand, our system is faster so they will be able to process orders faster, and the software has more functionality so user satisfaction will increase.
- From a political standpoint, our state-of-the-art graphical user interface will help improve the image of the IT department within the company.

- From a psychological standpoint, Bob's been worried about the old system for years, ever fearful that it will crash at critical times of the month and year. Our system will bring him much-needed peace of mind.

We will have to speak a variety of different languages during the sales calls with each decision maker. We'll talk visually to Bob, kinesthetically to Nancy, and auditorily to Mitch and Mortimer (see chapters 14–26). We'll talk about technical specifications (see chapter 37) with Mitch and provide higher business operations level information (see chapter 38) to Bob. We'll even mirror the way Bob speaks—his tone, tempo, speaking patterns (see chapter 20)—to ensure our sales call is successful.

In order to establish personal relationships, we want to talk about the intersecting activities we share with the evaluators (see chapter 36). We collect personal information about the evaluators through research, casual conversations, and quick examinations of the pictures, objects, and mementos in their offices. Bob's biography on the company website says he is an avid golfer, Nancy has three children (all girls), Mitch likes sailing, and Mortimer wears a wedding ring, so he must be married.

Sales Call Strategy: Sales linguistic segmentation enables you to theorize about the people you will be meeting so you can plan your sales call accordingly. Your goal is to mirror the customers' group decision-making roles. "Mirroring" is a psychological term for the conscious act of changing your behavior to match your surroundings. In chapter 20, we discussed how to build rapport by mirroring the tone, tempo, and speaking patterns of Auditories, Visuals, and Kinesthetics.

You should also adapt your selling style to match the segmentation based upon a customer's group decision-making roles. Prepare yourself with facts and specifications in anticipation of meeting the anal analytical. Massage the maven's ego during the call. Tell it like it is and don't fudge the truth when meeting with an old pro. Support the revolutionary's goal to become the organization's change agent.

100. Building Your Sales Intuition

How often have you attended a sales call with a colleague who had a different opinion of the success of the meeting? Most likely, the difference in reading the meeting resulted because one person collected more data than the other and had more experiences to compare it against. The difference in opinions resulted from a difference between the strengths of sales intuition.

Sales intuition is the ability to correctly read and anticipate a customer's actions. The five components of sales intuition are recognizing all the elements of a sales call, decoding the meaning, storing the experience, retrieving and comparing information, and finally, verbalizing the results, as shown in figure 100.1.

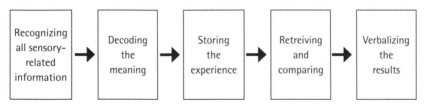

Figure 100.1 Components of intuition

The first component of sales intuition is recognizing all the verbal and nonverbal communication during a sales call. It is being aware of phonetic, content, purpose, word catalog, and physical layers of the human communication model (see fig. 6.1). After the information is distinguished, it must be decoded and interpreted for its meaning. Proper decoding requires correctly ascertaining the meaning people are actually trying to communicate by the words they select, the order of the words, and the way the words are said. Decoding also requires determining the congruency of people's communication. It's not only making sure the speaker's and listener's dictionaries are the same but also checking if the speaker's verbal and nonverbal communications are in agreement.

Next, the experience is stored in the mind. The mind's ability to store information is sophisticated and attributes of sales calls are stored as objects. The objects are pictures, sounds, feelings, or actions that represent experiences. In addition, each object has the potential to be a key by which the mind can search, retrieve, and compare past experiences. Figure 100.2 shows how sales calls would be stored in memory.

Attributes—pictures/sounds/feelings/action

Sales Call #1	Data	Data	Experience	Data
Sales Call #2	Data	Experience	Data	Data
	Key	Key	Key	Key

Figure 100.2 Sales calls stored in memory

The mind then retrieves and compares previous experiences based upon similar situations. Let's pretend a salesperson is on a new sales call and recognizes the person he is meeting with is a Visual. By recalling past sales calls with Visuals, he is able to access the other attributes from these sales calls, which enables him to determine the best course of action for the meeting. Figure 100.3 shows how two different previous sales calls with customers who were Visuals were accessed in his memory. You will notice that the sales call with the summary seeker (see chapter 95) was successful.

Assuming the salesperson was meeting with a summary seeker, he would draw upon this specific memory in order to repeat his behavior.

Attributes—pictures/sounds/feelings/action

Sales Call #1	Joe Smith	Visual primary	Sales call successful	Summary seeker
Sales Call #2	Jane Doe	Rejected trial close	Visual primary	Anal analytical
	Key	Key	Key	Key

Figure 100.3 Two sales calls and their attributes

Sales intuition is the process of comparing a series of past experiences against current circumstances. You can think of intuition as a highly developed model for making decisions and a powerful heuristic engine that is constantly learning from the past. In other words, you are constantly learning from every decision you make and continually incorporating these new reference points as part of your decision-making process. When you invoke your intuition, you're accessing previous complete experiences in order to gather the widest range of information. Once your conscious and subconscious minds have retrieved all the information about a current deal, it can be compared to previous sales cycles you have worked on. This results in the best possible decisions being made.

The final component in sales intuition is verbalizing the results. Typically, the verbalization is a conversation between your sales intuition and internal dialogue. For example, when you are face to face with the customer, your sales intuition is busy processing and comparing information. It is constantly interacting with your internal dialogue, which tells you what to say to the customer next. The process is similar when you are asked to present your strategy to win an account by your sales manager. Both of these situations require concentration to access your sales intuition. But here's the most important point: if you cannot verbalize your account strategy, you don't have one. You're not using your intuition to plan ahead. Instead, you are making it up as you go along and are winging it by the seat of your pants.

Never forget, you have developed sophisticated ways of cataloging the enormous amount of data you see, touch, and hear daily. And you are able to process and interpret this information into objects in order to catalog their relevant meaning. You can congregate haphazard information and derive meaning from seemingly nonsensical data as in this following example.

> It denos't mtater waht oredr the ltteers in a wrod are, the olny iprmoatnt tihng is taht the frist and lsat ltteer be at the rghit pclae. The rset can be a total mses and you can sitll raed it wouthit nay porbelm. Tihs is bcuseae the huamn mnid deos not raed ervey lteter by istlef but the wrod as a wlohe.

All salespeople store their conscious experiences. However, Heavy Hitters are able to see a wider spectrum of data, have a keener sense of the situation they're in, and are more in tune with the customer. They have a more fully developed awareness of verbal and nonverbal information. In addition, they have more effective methodologies to store and retrieve all the visible and invisible layers of the human communication model. Since their intuition is far superior to that of average salespeople, they have a greater proficiency to win business.

Sales Call Strategy: You continually learn through the ongoing accumulation and consolidation of information from sales calls and your interactions with customers. One of the purposes of this book is to help you build your sales intuition by providing a more comprehensive way of cataloging your sales calls. Moreover, the strength of your sales intuition is directly related to the quantity and quality of the attributes you are able to commit to memory. This requires you have to have a detailed methodology by which you segment your customer interactions.

How can you improve your sales intuition? Every subject on the sales call preparation checklist in the following chapter can be used an attribute to catalog your sales calls with more detail. For example, describing a CIO as the bully with the juice and emperor.

101. Sales Call Preparation Checklist

The diligence with which you prepare yourself and your colleagues for a sales call will directly influence the success of your meeting. However, it's an imperfect world and you will never have 100 percent of the information you would like to have about the customer you will be meeting with. In this case, you need to theorize about the missing pieces of information based upon your past meetings with customers and summon your sales intuition. Use the following checklist to help you prepare for your next meeting. [Source chapters are referenced in brackets.]

What is the customer's ultimate fantasy? [4]

What is our goal and my personal outcome for the meeting? [35]

Do I expect a combative, contentious, unemotional, friendly or synergistic sales call? [78]

What problem is the customer trying to solve, worded in the business operations language? [38]

What is the cause of the customer's problem and our solution to solve the problem, worded in the business operations language? [54]

What is our value to the customer? [39]

Strategic value:

Operational value:

Political value:

Psychological value:

What benefactions are behind his motives? [2]

Pain avoidance:

Well-being:

Self-preservation:

Self-gratification:

What elevator pitch will I use? [79]

What customer stories will I use to explain our value? [48–49]

Is this a renewal, persuasion, or creation sales call? [80]

Who is my coach, and is he a frenemy, well-wisher, weak spy, strong spy, or guide? [59]

Who are the bully with the juice and the emperor, and what are my relationships with these people? [53]

Is the customer a Visual, Auditory, or Kinesthetic? [14–17]

How will I adapt to the customer's word catalog wiring? [20]

What is the customer's source of stress, and how does our solution defuse it? [75–76]

What familial role do I plan to assume during the call? [73]

What intersecting activities do we share with the customer? [72]

Is the customer in survival, success, or significance mode? [92]

Is the customer a domain expert or business expert? [26]

Where do I plan to sit at the meeting? [28]

What pattern interruption and cowcatcher will I employ at the opening stage of the meeting? [43]

What offensive and defensive call statements will I use? [46–47]

What persuasion techniques will I use? [91]

What is the customer's Flesch-Kincaid communication level? [70]

How will I convey congruence? [33]

How will I establish dominance? [30, 57, 72]

How will I structure our PowerPoint presentation? [82]

    Pattern interruption:

    Key customer metaphors:

    Differentiating explanations:

    Closing background and foreground suggestions:

    Strategy slide:

    Money slide:

    Learning style: [21]

List the top ten questions I would like to ask the customer and triangulate on (what, how, why, when, who). [44]

List five leading questions I plan to ask. [45]

List the top five questions I should prepare for. [50–51]

Has the customer spoken the confidential language with me in the past and what did he confide? [55]

What turning-point and buzz-kill moments should I prepare for? [81]

How will I counteract inertia and no decision? [76]

What is the customer's informational decision-making role? [95]

What is the customer's character decision-making role? [96]

What is the customer's authority decision-making role? [97]

What is the customer's company decision-making role? [98]

What are our primary closing strategy and fallback positions? [56]

If I'm nervous, what anchors do I plan to use? [88]

Sales Call Strategy: Unfortunately, we have been trained to think of customers and ourselves as rational decision makers who use logic and reason exclusively. When you sell based solely upon logic, you are destined to be outsold. The successful influencer is the salesperson who understands and appeals to the emotional, political, conscious, and subconscious decision maker. When you take the time to think about all the items on the checklist, you are thinking logically about the psychological reasons the customer buys—something your competition is incapable of doing or won't take the time to think about. You can download the sales call preparation checklist at http://www.heavyhitterwisdom.com/checklist.

Epilogue: Final Advice

Researchers have made an amazing discovery about how the use of language changes behavior. People who speak two languages unconsciously change their personality when they switch languages. From their study, the researchers found evidence of "frame shifting," the change in a person's self-perception and underlying behavior depending upon the language the person used. For example, test subjects were more assertive when they spoke Spanish versus English.[1]

The concept of frame shifting is extremely relevant to you. Think about it for a moment. Your job is to build rapport with a wide variety of people across different companies. You have to communicate with lower-level operations people, midlevel managers, and most importantly, C-level executives. In order to do so, you need to change your demeanor and speak different languages depending upon the person you are meeting with. You wouldn't think of talking to and treating a CFO as you would a shop floor foreman. Intuitively, you already know you must frame shift your behavior and language to match the customer's in order to build rapport.

The salesperson's most important competitive weapon is his mouth, and the winner is the salesperson who uses words that reduce the customer's doubt, ease his fears, and foster his fantasy. That's why it is critical that salespeople learn sales linguistics, the study of how the customer's mind uses and interprets language. With a sense of urgency, you must master these techniques before your enemies learn how to speak more persuasively.

And now I would like to have a word with your subconscious mind. Your genetics may explain your predispositions in life, such as your height and the color of your eyes, but they certainly don't decide your ability to learn something new. Understanding and using these new language strategies will make you not only a better salesperson but a better person. Now, it's up to you to make the decision to start using them.

Finally, the words you say to yourself are the most important words you use all day. Do you continually question yourself or give yourself positive reinforcements throughout the day? Do you tell yourself, "It's just a job," or are you excited about what you do for a living? Your internal mantra, whether good or bad, will be conveyed to customers. Is it negative and hurtful or reaffirming and helpful? What do you really say to yourself about who you are, and how would you describe the importance of the life you have lived so far? In the end, nothing else really matters.

Notes

Chapter 1

1. First Steps, "Brain Development," http://www.firststeps.us /parents_braindevelopment.shtml (accessed July 13, 2011).

2. Speech Therapy Information and Resources, "Vocabulary," http://www.speech-therapy-information-and-resources .com/vocabulary.html (accessed July 13, 2011).

3. Kevin Lee, "Strategies to Improve Vocabulary," http://www .ehow.com/info_7868824_strategies-improve-vocabulary .html (accessed July 6, 2010).

Chapter 7

1. Carole Martin, "Nonverbal Message Speaks Louder Than Words," *Repertoire 11*, no. 9 (2003), http://www .repertoiremag.com/Article.asp?Id=1667 (accessed July 13, 2011).

Chapter 22

1. Soichi Nagao, "Discovering the Source of Long-Term Motor Memory," Phsyorg.com, November 15, 2010, http:// www.physorg.com/news/2010-11-source-long-term-motor -memory.html.

2. Melinda Wenner, "Moving Your Eyes Improves Memory, Study Suggests," *LiveScience*, January 11, 2008, http://www .livescience.com/1473-moving-eyes-improves-memory -study-suggests.html.

3. Sara Godarzi, "Where We Store What We See," *LiveScience*, August 29, 2006, hhttp://www.livescience.com/7110-store .html (accessed May 17, 2011).

4. Jim Phelps, M.D, "Mood," PsychEducation.org, http://www.psycheducation.org/emotion/brain%20pix.htm (accessed May 3, 2011).

5. Michele Solis, "Imaging Study Ties Brain Connection to Sociability," Simons Foundation Autism Research Initiative, September 15, 2009, https://sfari.org/news/-/asset_publisher/6Tog/content/imaging-study-ties-brain-connection-to-sociability?redirect=/news (accessed May 2, 2011).

Chapter 49

1. Dave Sharpe, "Effective Communication," Montana State University, circ.1291, May 1991, http://www.msuextension.org/communitydevelopment/pubs/c1291.pdf.

Chapter 51

1. Robert Roy Britt , "Lies Take Longer Than Truths," *Live Science*, January 25, 2009, http://www.livescience.com/technology/090125-lie-detector.html.

Chapter 83

1. Jim Hallowes and Amy Hallowes, "Being Highly Sensitive," About.com, http://healing.about.com/od/empathic/a/HSP_hallowes.htm (accessed September 3, 2005).

Chapter 89

1. Megan Gibson, "WTF? Study Shows Swearing Reduces Pain," Times NewsFeed, http://newsfeed.time.com/2011/04/18/wtf-study-shows-swearing-reduces-pain/ (accessed April 20, 2011).

Chapter 96

1. Lindsey Tanner, "Study Says Millions Have 'Rage' Disorder," *Yahoo! News*, June 6, 2006, http://news.yahoo.com/s/ap/20060605/ap_on_sc/road_rage_disease.

Epilogue

1. Reuters, "Switching Languages Can Also Switch Personality: Study," June 24, 2008, http://www.reuters.com/article/lifestyleMolt/idUSSP4652020080624.

Index

About the Author

Steve W. Martin is the foremost expert on sales linguistics, the study of how salespeople and customers use language during the complex decision-making process. He began his career programming computers. Through working with computers, he became acutely aware of the preciseness and structure of language. In addition, programming is built upon models—verbal descriptions and visual representations of how systems work and processes flow. Models enable repeatable and predictable experiences.

Early in his career, he was also introduced to the concepts of neurolinguistics (the science of how the human brain constructs and interprets language). When he transitioned his career into sales, he realized that he could build models to create successful relationships based upon customers' language and thought processes. Without any sales experience to speak of, he was the number one salesperson in his company for the following four years.

Steve went on to be a top sales producer for a billion-dollar software company and was promoted into management to imprint his selling model on other salespeople within the organization. As vice president of sales, Steve successfully trained his salespeople on the sales strategies and communication skills that are necessary to close large accounts.

Steve is the author of the critically acclaimed Heavy Hitter series of books for senior salespeople. His books have been featured in *Forbes*, the *Wall Street Journal*, and *Selling Power* magazine. They are recommended reading by the Harvard Business School, *Customer Relationship Management* and *Sales and Marketing Management*.

A highly sought-after speaker and sales trainer, Steve is both entertaining and provocative. He has presented to hundreds of organizations. His clients include Acxiom, Akamai, Allstate Insurance, AT&T, DHL, EMC, Experian, Ferring Pharmaceuticals, IBM, McAfee, NEC, Oracle, PayPal, Philips, Prudential, Staples, Telus, and UTI Worldwide Logistics. When not working with his clients, Steve teaches sales strategy at the University of Southern California, Marshall MBA program. Please visit http://www. heavyhitterwisdom.com for further information.